Cisco Networking Academy Program

CCNP 1: Advanced Routing Lab Companion

Second Edition

Cisco Systems, Inc.
Cisco Networking Academy Program

Cisco Press
800 East 96th Street
Indianapolis, IN 46240 USA

Cisco Networking Academy Program
CCNP 1: Advanced Routing Lab Companion
Second Edition

Cisco Systems, Inc.

Cisco Networking Academy Program

Published by:
Cisco Press
800 East 96th Street
Indianapolis, Indiana 46240 USA

Printed in the United States of America   1 2 3 4 5 6 7 8 9 0
First Printing   May 2004
ISBN: 1-58713-134-X

Warning and Disclaimer

This book is designed to provide information based on content from the Cisco Networking Academy Program *CCNP 1: Advanced Routing* course. Every effort has been made to make this book as complete and as accurate as possible, but no warranty or fitness is implied.

The information is provided on an "as is" basis. The author, Cisco Press, and Cisco Systems, Inc., shall have neither liability nor responsibility to any person or entity with respect to any loss or damages arising from the information contained in this book or from the use of the programs that may accompany it.

The opinions expressed in this book belong to the author and are not necessarily those of Cisco Systems, Inc.

This book is part of the Cisco Networking Academy® Program series from Cisco Press. The products in this series support and complement the Cisco Networking Academy Program curriculum. If you are using this book outside the Networking Academy program, you are not preparing with a Cisco trained and authorized Networking Academy provider. For information on the Cisco Networking Academy Program or to locate a Networking Academy, please visit http://www.cisco.com/edu.

Trademark Acknowledgments

All terms mentioned in this book that are known to be trademarks or service marks have been appropriately capitalized. Cisco Press or Cisco Systems, Inc., cannot attest to the accuracy of this information. Use of a term in this book should not be regarded as affecting the validity of any trademark or service mark.

Corporate and Government Sales

Cisco Press offers excellent discounts on this book when ordered in quantity for bulk purchases or special sales. For more information please contact:
U.S. Corporate and Government Sales 1-800-382-3419 corpsales@pearsontechgroup.com
For sales outside the U.S. please contact: International Sales international@pearsoned.com

Feedback Information

At Cisco Press, our goal is to create in-depth technical books of the highest quality and value. Each book is crafted with care and precision, undergoing rigorous development that involves the unique expertise of members of the professional technical community.

Readers' feedback is a natural continuation of this process. If you have any comments regarding how we could improve the quality of this book, or otherwise alter it to better suit your needs, you can contact us at networkingacademy@ciscopress.com. Please be sure to include the book title and ISBN in your message.

We greatly appreciate your assistance.

Publisher	John Wait
Editor-in-Chief	John Kane
Executive Editor	Mary Beth Ray
Cisco Systems Representative	Anthony Wolfenden
Cisco Press Program Manager	Nannette M. Noble
Production Manager	Patrick Kanouse
Development Editor	Andrew Cupp
Project Editor	San Dee Phillips
Technical Editors	K Kirkendall, Jim Lorenz
Copy Editor	Karen A. Gill
Composition	Sheri Cain

CISCO SYSTEMS

Corporate Headquarters
Cisco Systems, Inc.
170 West Tasman Drive
San Jose, CA 95134-1706
USA
www.cisco.com
Tel: 408 526-4000
      800 553-NETS (6387)
Fax: 408 526-4100

European Headquarters
Cisco Systems International BV
Haarlerbergpark
Haarlerbergweg 13-19
1101 CH Amsterdam
The Netherlands
www-europe.cisco.com
Tel: 31 0 20 357 1000
Fax: 31 0 20 357 1100

Americas Headquarters
Cisco Systems, Inc.
170 West Tasman Drive
San Jose, CA 95134-1706
USA
www.cisco.com
Tel: 408 526-7660
Fax: 408 527-0883

Asia Pacific Headquarters
Cisco Systems, Inc.
Capital Tower
168 Robinson Road
#22-01 to #29-01
Singapore 068912
www.cisco.com
Tel: +65 6317 7777
Fax: +65 6317 7799

Cisco Systems has more than 200 offices in the following countries and regions. Addresses, phone numbers, and fax numbers are listed on the
Cisco.com Web site at www.cisco.com/go/offices.

Argentina • Australia • Austria • Belgium • Brazil • Bulgaria • Canada • Chile • China PRC • Colombia • Costa Rica • Croatia • Czech Republic
Denmark • Dubai, UAE • Finland • France • Germany • Greece • Hong Kong SAR • Hungary • India • Indonesia • Ireland • Israel • Italy
Japan • Korea • Luxembourg • Malaysia • Mexico • The Netherlands • New Zealand • Norway • Peru • Philippines • Poland • Portugal
Puerto Rico • Romania • Russia • Saudi Arabia • Scotland • Singapore • Slovakia • Slovenia • South Africa • Spain • Sweden
Switzerland • Taiwan • Thailand • Turkey • Ukraine • United Kingdom • United States • Venezuela • Vietnam • Zimbabwe

About the Technical Editors

K Kirkendall is an instructor at Boise State University in Boise, Idaho. He has been a teacher for the Cisco Networking Academy Program for six years and teaches CCNA, CCNP, Fundamentals of Voice and Data Cabling, IT Essentials I, IT Essentials II, Fundamentals of UNIX, and Fundamentals of Web Design. K has the following industry certifications: CCNP, CCDA, CCAI, MCP, CNA, A+, Network+, and Server+. He also works for the Networking Academy assessment group. K has a great wife, five great children, and two grandchildren.

Jim Lorenz is an instructor and curriculum developer for the Cisco Networking Academy Program. He has more than 20 years of experience in information systems and has held various IT positions in Fortune 500 companies, including Honeywell and Motorola. Jim has developed and taught computer and networking courses for both public and private institutions for more than 15 years. He is coauthor of the Cisco Networking Academy Program Fundamentals of UNIX course, contributing author for the *CCNA Lab Companion* manuals, and technical editor for the *CCNA Companion Guides*. Jim is a Cisco Certified Academy Instructor (CCAI) for CCNA and CCNP courses. He has a bachelor's degree in computer information systems and is currently working on his master's degree in information networking and telecommunications. Jim and his wife Mary have two daughters, Jessica and Natasha.

Table of Contents

Foreword

Throughout the world, the Internet has brought tremendous new opportunities for individuals and their employers. Companies and other organizations are seeing dramatic increases in productivity by investing in robust networking capabilities. Some studies have shown measurable productivity improvements in entire economies. The promise of enhanced efficiency, profitability, and improved standard of living is real and growing.

Such productivity gains are not achieved by simply purchasing networking equipment. Skilled professionals need to plan, design, install, deploy, configure, operate, maintain, and troubleshoot today's networks. Network managers must ensure that they have planned for network security and for continued operation. They need to design for the required performance level in their organization. They must implement new capabilities as the demands of their organization—and its reliance on the network—expands.

To meet the many educational needs of the internetworking community, Cisco Systems established the Cisco Networking Academy Program. The Networking Academy is a comprehensive learning program that provides students with the Internet technology skills that are essential in a global economy. The Networking Academy integrates face-to-face teaching, web-based content, online assessment, student performance tracking, hands-on labs, instructor training and support, and preparation for industry-standard certifications.

The Networking Academy continually raises the bar on blended learning and educational processes. All instructors are Cisco Certified Academy Instructors (CCAIs). The Internet-based assessment and instructor support systems are some of the most extensive and validated systems ever developed, including a 24/7 customer service system for Networking Academy instructors and students. Through community feedback and electronic assessment, the Networking Academy adapts the curriculum to improve outcomes and student achievement. The Cisco Global Learning Network infrastructure designed for the Networking Academy delivers a rich, interactive, and personalized curriculum to students worldwide. The Internet has the power to change the way people work, live, play, and learn, and the Cisco Networking Academy Program is in the forefront of this transformation.

This Cisco Press title is one of a series of best-selling companion titles for the Cisco Networking Academy Program. Designed by Cisco Worldwide Education and Cisco Press, these books provide integrated support for the online learning content that is made available to Networking Academies all over the world. These Cisco Press books are the only authorized books for the Networking Academy by Cisco Systems. They provide print and CD-ROM materials that ensure the greatest possible learning experience for Networking Academy students.

I hope you are successful as you embark on your learning path with Cisco Systems and the Internet. I also hope that you will choose to continue your learning after you complete the Networking Academy curriculum. In addition to its Cisco Networking Academy Program titles, Cisco Press publishes an extensive list of networking technology and certification publications that provide a wide range of resources. Cisco Systems has also established a network of professional training companies—the Cisco Learning Partners—who provide a full range of

Cisco training courses. They offer training in many formats, including e-learning, self-paced, and instructor-led classes. Their instructors are Cisco certified, and Cisco creates their materials. When you are ready, please visit the Learning & Events area on Cisco.com to learn about all the educational support that Cisco and its partners have to offer.

Thank you for choosing this book and the Cisco Networking Academy Program.

Kevin Warner
Senior Director, Marketing
Worldwide Education
Cisco Systems, Inc.

Introduction

Cisco Networking Academy Program CCNP 1: Advanced Routing Lab Companion, Second Edition, supplements your classroom and laboratory experience with version 3 of the CCNP 1 course in the Cisco Networking Academy Program. Furthermore, the Lab Companion is designed as a complementary text to the *Cisco Networking Academy Program CCNP 1: Advanced Routing Companion Guide*, Second Edition, which provides focused coverage of the topics that you will need to understand to successfully complete the labs.

The CCNP 1 course trains you on topics pertaining to the Building Scalable Cisco Internetworks exam (642-801 BSCI), which is a qualifying exam for the Cisco Certified Network Professional (CCNP) certification. This Lab Companion consists of all the labs in the current Cisco Networking Academy Program, with some additional information. Most of the labs are hands-on and require access to a Cisco router or lab simulator.

Audience of This Book

This book is written for anyone who wants to learn about advanced Cisco routing technologies, although the target audience focuses on students in the CCNP 1 course as part of the Cisco Networking Academy Program in a high school, community college, or four-year university.

How This Book Is Organized

Table I-1 outlines all the labs in this book, the corresponding target indicator (TI) in the online curriculum, and the time it should take to do the lab.

Table I-1: Master Lab Overview

Lab TI	Title	Estimated Time (Minutes)
1.4.1	Introductory Lab 1—Getting Started and Building Start.txt	30
1.4.2	Introductory Lab 2—Capturing HyperTerminal and Telnet Sessions	30
1.4.3	Introductory Lab 3—Access Control List Basics and Extended Ping	45
1.4.4	Implementing Quality of Service with Priority Queuing	30
1.5.1	Equal-Cost Load Balancing with RIP	45

Lab TI	Title	Estimated Time (Minutes)
1.5.2	Unequal-Cost Load Balancing with IGRP	45
2.10.1	Configuring VLSM and IP Unnumbered	45
2.10.2a	VLSM 1	15
2.10.2b	VLSM 2	15
2.10.2c	VLSM 3	15
2.10.2d	VLSM 4	15
2.10.3	Using DHCP and IP Helper Addresses	45
2.10.4a	Network Address Translation—Static NAT and Dynamic NAT	45
2.10.4b	Network Address Translation—Port Address Translation and Port Forwarding	45
3.6.1	Migrating from RIP to EIGRP	45
3.6.2	Configuring IGRP	45
3.6.3	Configuring Default Routing with RIP and IGRP	45
3.6.4	Configuring Floating Static Routes	45
4.4.1	Routing Between RIP v1 and RIP v2	45
4.4.2	RIP v2 MD5 Authentication	20
5.7.1	Configuring EIGRP	30
5.7.2	Configuring EIGRP Fault Tolerance	30
5.7.3	Configuring EIGRP Summarization	25
5.8.1	EIGRP Challenge Lab	25
6.9.1	Configuring OSPF	40
6.9.2a	Examining the DR/BDR Election Process	30

Lab TI	Title	Estimated Time (Minutes)
6.9.2b	Configuring Point-to-Multipoint OSPF Over Frame Relay	45
6.9.3	Configuring Multiarea OSPF	60
6.9.4	Configuring a Stub Area and a Totally Stubby Area	45
6.9.5	Configuring an NSSA	45
6.9.6	Configuring Virtual Links	30
6.10.1	OSPF Challenge Lab	60
7.7.1	Configuring Basic Integrated IS-IS	90
7.7.2	Configuring Multiarea Integrated IS-IS	60
7.7.3	Configuring IS-IS Over Frame Relay	50
8.5.1	Configuring Distribute Lists and Passive Interfaces	45
8.5.2a	Configuring Route Maps	50
8.5.2b	NAT—Dynamic Translation with Multiple Pools Using Route Maps	45
8.5.3	Redistributing RIP and OSPF with Distribution Lists	45
8.6.1	Route Optimization Challenge Lab	60
9.11.1	Configuring BGP with Default Routing	50
9.11.2	Configuring BGP with NAT	60
9.11.3	Using the AS_PATH Attribute	30
9.11.4a	Configuring IBGP and EBGP Sessions, Local Preference, and MED	90
9.11.4b	BGP Route Reflectors and Route Filters	30
9.11.4c	The BGP COMMUNITIES Attribute	20
9.11.4d	BGP Peer Groups	20
9.12.1	BGP Challenge Lab	90

This Book's Features

Many of this book's features help facilitate your understanding of the networking and routing topics covered in the labs:

- **Objective**—Identifies the goal or goals that are to be accomplished in the lab.

- **Equipment requirements**—Provides a list of the equipment to be used to run the lab.

- **Scenario**—Allows you to relate the lab exercise to real-world environments.

- **Questions**—As appropriate, labs include questions that are designed to elicit particular points of understanding. These questions help to verify your comprehension of the technology that is being implemented.

The conventions that are used to present command syntax in this book are the same conventions that are used in the *Cisco IOS Command Reference*:

- **Bold** indicates commands and keywords that are entered literally as shown. In examples (not syntax), bold indicates user input (such as a show command).

- *Italic* indicates arguments for which you supply values.

- Braces ({ }) indicate a required element.

- Square brackets ([ ]) indicate an optional element.

- Vertical bars (|) separate alternative, mutually exclusive elements.

- Braces and vertical bars within square brackets (such as [x {y | z}]) indicate a required choice within an optional element. You do not need to enter what is in the brackets, but if you do, you have some required choices in the braces.

Chapter 1

Overview of Scalable Internetworks

Lab 1.4.1: Introductory Lab 1—Getting Started and Building Start.txt

Estimated Time: 30 Minutes

Objective

This lab introduces new CCNP lab equipment and certain IOS features. This introductory activity also describes how to use a simple text editor to create all or part of a router configuration and apply that configuration to a router.

Equipment Requirements

The following equipment is required for this exercise:

- A single router, preferably a 2600 series, and a workstation running a Windows operating system

- One 3 1/2-inch floppy disk with label

Preliminary Information

Modular Interfaces

Cisco routers can come with a variety of interface configurations. Some models have only fixed interfaces. This means that users cannot change or replace the interfaces. Other models have one or more modular interfaces. This allows the user to add, remove, or replace interfaces as needed.

Fixed interface identification, such as Serial 0, S0, and Ethernet 0, E0, might already be familiar. Modular routers use notation such as Serial 0/0 or S0/1, where the first number refers to the module and the second number refers to the interface. Both notations use 0 as their starting reference, so S0/1 indicates that there is another serial interface S0/0.

FastEthernet

Many routers today are equipped with FastEthernet interfaces. FastEthernet has 10/100 Mbps autosensing. FastEthernet 0/0 or Fa0/0 notation must be used on routers that have FastEthernet interfaces.

The ip subnet-zero Command

The **ip subnet-zero** command is enabled by default in IOS 12. This command allows IP addresses to be assigned in the first subnet, called subnet 0. Because subnet 0 uses only binary zeros in the subnet field, its subnet address can potentially be confused with the major network address. With the advent of classless IP, the use of subnet 0 has become more common. The labs in this manual assume that addresses can be assigned to the router interfaces using subnet 0. If any routers are used that have an IOS earlier than 12.0, the global configuration command **ip subnet-zero** must be added to the router configuration.

The no shutdown Command

Interfaces are shut down by default. Remember to type a **no shutdown** command in interface configuration mode when the interface is ready to be brought up. The command **no shutdown** will not appear in the output of the **show running-config** command.

Passwords

The **login** command is applied to virtual terminals by default. This means that for the router to accept Telnet connections, a password must be configured. Otherwise, the router will not allow a Telnet connection, replying with the error message "password required, but none set". An enable secret password must also be configured on the remote router to enter privileged mode after a Telnet session has been established. If the remote router does not have an enable secret password, the router replies with the error message "% No password set", and only User mode commands are available.

Step 1

Take a few moments to examine the router. Become familiar with any serial, BRI (ISDN), PRI (ISDN), and DSU/CSU interfaces on the router. Look closely at any connectors or cables that are not familiar.

Step 2

Establish a HyperTerminal session to the router. Enter privileged EXEC mode.

Step 3

To clear the configuration, issue the **erase startup-config** command.

Confirm the objective when prompted. The result should look something like this:

```
Router#erase startup-config
Erasing the nvram filesystem will remove all files! Continue? [confirm]
[OK]
Erase of nvram: complete
Router#
```

When the prompt returns, issue the **reload** command.

Answer **no** if asked to save changes and confirm the reload when prompted.

```
System configuration has been modified. Save? [yes/no]: no
Proceed with reload? [confirm]
```

After the router finishes the boot process, choose not to enter the system configuration dialog. Also, choose not to use the AutoInstall facility by pressing **Enter** to accept the default choice, which should be yes, as shown:

```
--- System Configuration Dialog ---
Would you like to enter the initial configuration dialog? [yes/no]: no
Would you like to terminate autoinstall? [yes]:
Press RETURN to get started!
```

Step 4

In privileged mode, issue the **show run** command.

Note the following default configurations while scrolling through the running configuration:

- The version number of the IOS.

- The **ip subnet-zero** command, which allows the use of subnet 0.

- Each available interface and its name.

  Note: Each interface has the **shutdown** command applied to its configuration.

- The **ip http server** command, which allows a web browser to access the router. Some routers and IOS versions disable this feature by default using the **no ip http server** command.

- No passwords are set for CON, AUX, and VTY sessions, as shown here:

Note: The **transport input none** command is not applicable in IOS 12.2.

```
line con 0
transport input none
line aux 0
line vty 0 4
```

Using Copy and Paste with Notepad

In the next steps, use the copy and paste feature to edit router configurations. You need to create a text file that you can paste into the routers and use as a starting point for the initial router configuration. Specifically, you must build a login configuration that you can use with every lab included in this manual.

Step 5

If necessary, issue the **show run** command again so that **line con** and **line vty** are showing on the screen:

```
line con 0
transport input none
line aux 0
line vty 0 4
!
end
```

Select the text as shown in this step, and choose **Copy** from the HyperTerminal Edit menu.

Next, open Notepad. You typically can find Notepad on the Start menu under Programs, Accessories. After Notepad opens, select **Paste** from the Notepad Edit menu.

Edit the lines in Notepad to look like the following lines. The one space indent is optional:

```
enable secret class
line con 0
 transport input none
 password cisco
 login
line aux 0
 password cisco
 login
line vty 0 4
 password cisco
 login
```

This configuration sets the enable secret to "class" and requires a login and password for all console, AUX port, and virtual terminal connections. The AUX port is usually a modem. The password for these connections is set to "cisco".

Note: You can set each of the passwords to something else if so desired.

Step 6

Save the open file in Notepad to a floppy disk as **start.txt**.

Select all the lines in the Notepad document and choose **Edit** > **Copy**.

Step 7

Use the Windows taskbar to return to the HyperTerminal session, and enter global configuration mode.

From the HyperTerminal Edit menu, choose **Paste to Host**.

Issue the **show run** command to see if the configuration looks correct.

As a shortcut, you can now paste the contents of the start.txt file to any router before getting started with a lab.

Other Useful Commands

To enhance the start.txt file, consider adding one of the following commands:

- **ip subnet-zero** ensures that an older IOS allows IP addresses from subnet 0.

- **ip http server** allows access to the router using a web browser. Although this configuration might not be desirable on a production router, it does enable an HTTP server for testing purposes in the lab.

- **no ip domain-lookup** prevents the router from attempting to query a DNS when a word is input that is not recognized as a command or a host table entry. This saves time when you make a typo or misspell a command.

- **logging synchronous** in the **line con 0** configuration returns to a fresh line when the input is interrupted by a console logging message.

- **configure terminal (config t)** can be used in a file so that you do not have to type a command before pasting the contents of the file to the router.

Step 8

Use the Windows taskbar to return to Notepad and edit the lines so that they read as shown:

```
config t
!
enable secret class
ip subnet-zero
ip http server
no ip domain-lookup
line con 0
 logging synchronous
 password cisco
 login
 transport input none
line aux 0
password cisco
 login
line vty 0 4
password cisco
 login
!
end
copy run start
```

Save the file to the floppy disk so that the work is not lost.

Select and copy all the lines, and return to the HyperTerminal session.

Because the **config t** command was included in the script, entering global configuration mode before pasting is no longer necessary.

If necessary, return to privileged EXEC mode. From the Edit menu, select **Paste to Host**.

After the paste is complete, confirm the copy operation.

Use **show run** to see if the configuration looks correct.

Using Notepad to Assist in Editing

Understanding how to use Notepad can reduce typing and typos during editing sessions. Another major benefit is that you can do an entire router configuration in Notepad when at home or at the office and then paste it to the router console when access is available. The next steps look at a simple editing example.

Step 9

Configure the router with the following commands:

```
Router#config t
Router(config)#router rip
Router(config-router)#network 192.168.1.0
Router(config-router)#network 192.168.2.0
Router(config-router)#network 192.168.3.0
Router(config-router)#network 192.168.4.0
Router(config-router)#network 192.168.5.0
```

Press **Ctrl-Z** and verify the configuration with **show run**. RIP was just set up to advertise a series of networks. However, the routing protocol is to be changed to IGRP. Using the **no router rip** command removes the RIP process. The **network** commands must still be retyped. The next steps show an alternative method.

Step 10

Issue the **show run** command and hold the output so that the **router rip** commands are displayed. Using the keyboard or mouse, select the **router rip** command and all **network** statements.

Copy the selection.

Use the taskbar to return to Notepad.

Open a new document and paste the selection onto the blank page.

Step 11

In the new document, type the word **no** and put a space in front of the word "router." Press the **End** key, and press **Enter**.

Type **router igrp 100,** but do not press **Enter**. The result should look like this:

```
no router rip
router igrp 100
 network 192.168.1.0
 network 192.168.2.0
 network 192.168.3.0
 network 192.168.4.0
 network 192.168.5.0
```

Step 12

Select the results and copy them.

Use the taskbar to return to the HyperTerminal session.

While you are in global configuration mode, paste the results.

Use the **show run** command to verify the configuration.

Reflection

How can using copy and paste with Notepad be helpful in other editing situations?

_____

_____

Lab 1.4.2: Introductory Lab 2—Capturing HyperTerminal and Telnet Sessions

Estimated Time: 30 Minutes

Objective

This activity describes how to capture HyperTerminal and Telnet sessions.

Note: Mastering these techniques reduces the amount of typing in later labs and while working in the field. These techniques are useful when perusing and testing on a production router while troubleshooting a problem.

Equipment Requirements

This lab requires the following equipment:

- A single router, preferably a 2600 series, and a workstation running a Windows operating system

Step 1

Log in to a router using HyperTerminal.

You can capture the results of the HyperTerminal session in a text file, which you can view, edit, and print using Notepad, WordPad, or Microsoft Word.

Note: This feature captures future screens, not what is currently onscreen. Basically, this is turning on a recording session.

To start a capture session, choose the menu option **Transfer** > **Capture Text**. The Capture Text dialog box appears, as shown in Figure 1-1.

Figure 1-1   Capture Text Dialog Box

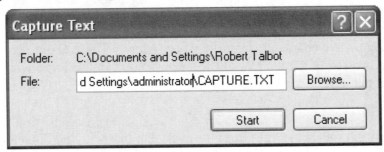

The default filename for a HyperTerminal capture is CAPTURE.TXT, and the default location of this file is C:\Program Files\Accessories\HyperTerminal.

Make sure that the floppy disk is in the A: drive. When the Capture Text dialog box appears, change the File path to **A:\TestRun.txt**.

Click the **Start** button. Anything that appears onscreen after this point is copied to the file.

Step 2

Go to the User privileged configuration mode. Then, issue the **show running config** command and view the entire configuration file.

From the Transfer menu, choose **Capture Text** > **Stop**.

Step 3

Using the Start menu, launch Windows Explorer. You can find Windows Explorer under either Programs or Accessories, depending on which version of Windows you are using.

In the left pane, select the **3½ floppy (A:)** drive. On the right side, you should be able to see the file that was just created.

Double-click the **TestRun.txt** document icon. The result should look something like the following:

```
Router# show running configuration
Building configuration...

Current configuration:
!
version 12.0
service timestamps debug uptime
service timestamps log uptime
no service password-encryption
!
hostname Router
!
enable secret 5 $1$HD2B$6iXb.h6QEJJjtn/NnwUHO.
!
!
ip subnet-zero
no ip domain-lookup
!
interface FastEthernet0/0
no ip address
 --More--
 no ip directed-broadcast
 shutdown
```

You can see unrecognizable characters near the word "More." These characters are a result of the Spacebar being pressed to see the rest of the output. You can use basic word processing techniques to clean that up.

Suggestion

Consider capturing each router configuration for every lab that you do. You can use capture files as you review configuration features and while preparing for certification exams.

Reflection

Are the capture techniques useful if a member of the lab team misses a lab session? Can you use capture techniques to configure an offsite lab?

_____

_____

_____

_____

Lab 1.4.3: Introductory Lab 3—Access Control List Basics and Extended Ping

Estimated Time: 45 Minutes

Objective

This lab activity reviews the basics of standard and extended access lists, which are used extensively in the CCNP curriculum. Use Figure 1-2 as a sample topology in this lab.

Figure 1-2   Sample Topology for Lab 1.4.3

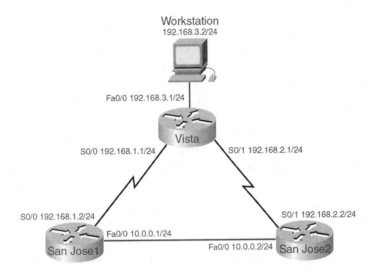

Equipment Requirements

This lab requires the following equipment:

- Three routers, preferably 2600 series, and a workstation running a Windows operating system

Scenario

The LAN users who are connected to the Vista router, shown in Figure 1-2, are concerned about access to their network from hosts on network 10.0.0.0. Use a standard access list to block all access to Vista's LAN from network 10.0.0.0/24.

After you remove the standard access list, use an extended ACL to block network 192.168.3.0 host access to web servers on the 10.0.0.0/24 network.

Step 1

Build and configure the network according to the diagram. Use RIP v1 and enable updates on all active interfaces with the appropriate **network** commands. The commands that are necessary to configure RIP v1 are as follows:

```
SanJose1(config)#router rip
SanJose1(config-router)#network 192.168.1.0
SanJose1(config-router)#network 10.0.0.0
Vista(config)#router rip
Vista(config-router)#network 192.168.1.0
```

```
Vista(config-router)#network 192.168.2.0
SanJose2(config)#router rip
SanJose2(config-router)#network 192.168.2.0
SanJose2(config-router)#network 10.0.0.0
```

Use the **ping** command to verify the work and test connectivity between all interfaces. After you verify connectivity, save your configurations for reuse in Labs 1-4 and 1-5.

Step 2

Check the routing table on Vista using the **show ip route** command. Vista should have all four networks in its table. Troubleshoot if necessary.

Access Control List Basics

Access Control Lists (ACLs) are simple but powerful tools. When the access list is configured, the router processes each statement in the list in the order in which it was created. If an individual packet meets the criteria of a statement, the permit or deny is applied to that packet, and no further list entries are checked. The next packet to be checked starts again at the top of the list.

You cannot reorder statements, skip statements, edit statements, or delete statements from a numbered access list. With numbered access lists, any attempt to delete a single statement results in the deletion of the entire list. Named ACLs (NACLs) do allow for the deletion of individual statements.

The following concepts apply to both standard and extended access lists:

- **Two step process.** First, you create the access list with one or more **access-list** commands while in global configuration mode. Second, other commands, such as the **access-group** command, apply or reference the access list to apply an ACL to an interface. Following is an example:

```
Vista#config t
Vista(config)#access-list 50 deny 10.0.0.0 0.0.0.255
Vista(config)#access-list 50 permit any
Vista(config)#interface fastethernet 0/0
Vista(config-if)#ip access-group 50 out
Vista(config-if)#^Z
```

- **Syntax and keywords.** The basic syntax for creating an access list entry is as follows:

```
router(config)#access-list acl-number {permit | deny}...
```

  The **permit** command allows you to accept packets that match the specified criteria for whatever application the access list is being used. The **deny** command discards packets that match the criteria on that line.

  Two important keywords that you can use with IP addresses and the **access list** command are **any** and **host**. The keyword **any** matches all hosts on all networks, equivalent to **0.0.0.0 255.255.255.255**. You can use the keyword **host** with an IP address to indicate a single host address. The syntax is **host** *ip-address*, such as **host 192.168.1.10**. This is treated the same as 192.168.1.10 0.0.0.0.

- **Implicit deny statement.** Every access list contains a final deny statement that matches all packets. This is called the implicit deny. Because the implicit deny statement is not visible in show command output, it is often overlooked, with serious consequences. As an example, consider the following single line access list:

```
Router(config)#access-list 75 deny host 192.168.1.10
```

Access-list 75 clearly denies all traffic sourced from the host, 192.168.1.10. What might not be obvious is that all other traffic is discarded as well because **deny any** is the final statement in any access list.

- **At least one permit statement is required.** Nothing mandates that an ACL must contain a **deny** statement. If nothing else, the **deny any** statement takes care of that. However, if **permit** statements do not exist, the effect will be the same as if there were only a single **deny any** statement.

- **Wildcard mask.** In identifying IP addresses, ACLs use a wildcard mask instead of a subnet mask. Initially, wildcard masks and subnet masks might look like the same thing, but closer observation reveals that they are different. Remember that a binary 0 in a wildcard bitmask instructs the router to match the corresponding bit in the IP address.

- **In/Out.** When you are deciding whether to apply an ACL to inbound or outbound traffic, always view things from the perspective of the router. Determine whether traffic is coming into the router, inbound, or leaving the router, outbound.

- **Applying ACLs.** Apply extended ACLs as close to the source as possible, thereby conserving network resources. You must apply standard ACLs as close to the destination as possible because the standard ACL can match only at the source address of a packet.

Step 3

On the Vista router, create the following standard ACL and apply it to the LAN interface:

```
Vista#config t
Vista(config)#access-list 50 deny 10.0.0.0 0.0.0.255
Vista(config)#access-list 50 permit any
Vista(config)#interface fastethernet 0/0
Vista(config-if)#ip access-group 50 out
Vista(config-if)#^Z
```

Try **pinging** 192.168.3.2 from SanJose1.

The ping should be successful. This result might be unexpected because all traffic from the 10.0.0.0/8 network was blocked. The ping is successful because, even though it came from SanJose1, it is not sourced from the 10.0.0.0/8 network. A **ping** or **traceroute** from a router uses the closest interface to the destination as the source address. Therefore, the ping is coming from the 192.168.1.0/24, SanJose1's Serial 0/0.

To test the ACL from SanJose1, use the extended **ping** command to specify a specific source interface:

```
SanJose1#ping 192.168.3.2
Sending 5, 100-byte ICMP Echos to 192.168.3.2, timeout is 2 seconds:
!!!!!
Success rate is 100 percent (5/5), round-trip min/avg/max = 4/4/4 ms
```

Step 4

To test the ACL from SanJose1, use the extended **ping** command to specify a source interface as follows. On SanJose1, issue the following commands:

```
SanJose1#ping 192.168.3.2
Sending 5, 100-byte ICMP Echos to 192.168.3.2, timeout is 2 seconds:
!!!!!
Success rate is 100 percent (5/5), round-trip min/avg/max = 4/4/4 ms
SanJose1#
SanJose1#ping
Protocol [ip]:
Target IP address: 192.168.3.2
Repeat count [5]:
Datagram size [100]:
Timeout in seconds [2]:
Extended commands [n]: y
Source address or interface: 10.0.0.1
Type of service [0]:
Set DF bit in IP header? [no]:
Validate reply data? [no]:
Data pattern [0xABCD]:
Loose, Strict, Record, Timestamp, Verbose[none]:
Sweep range of sizes [n]:
Type escape sequence to abort.
Sending 5, 100-byte ICMP Echos to 192.168.3.2, timeout is 2 seconds:
.....
Success rate is 0 percent (0/5)
```

Note: Remember that the extended **ping** command works only in privileged EXEC mode.

Step 5

Standard ACLs are numbered 1 to 99. IOS Release 12.xx also allows standard lists to be numbered 1300 to 1699. Extended ACLs are numbered 100 to 199. IOS Release 12.xx allows lists to be numbered 2000 to 2699. You can use extended ACLs to enforce highly specific criteria for filtering packets. In this step, configure an extended ACL to block access to a web server.

Before proceeding, issue the **no access-list 50** and **no ip access-group 50 out** commands on the Vista router to remove the ACL that was configured previously.

Now, configure both SanJose1 and SanJose 2 to act as web servers by using the **ip http server** command, shown as follows:

```
SanJose1(config)#ip http server
SanJose2(config)#ip http server
```

From the workstation at 192.168.3.2, use a web browser to view the web servers on both routers at 10.0.0.1 and 10.0.0.2. The web login requires that the enable secret password for the router be entered as the password.

After verifying the web connectivity between the workstation and the routers, proceed to Step 6.

Step 6

On the Vista router, enter the following commands:

```
Vista(config)#access-list 101 deny tcp 192.168.3.0 0.0.0.255 10.0.0.0 0.0.0.255 eq www
Vista(config)#access-list 101 deny tcp 192.168.3.0 0.0.0.255 any eq ftp
Vista(config)#access-list 101 permit ip any any
Vista(config)#interface fastethernet 0/0
Vista(config-if)#ip access-group 101 in
```

From the workstation at 192.168.3.2, again attempt to view the web servers at 10.0.0.1 and 10.0.0.2. Both attempts should fail.

Note: You might need to click on the browser REFRESH button so that the screen display does not come from the browser's cache.

Next, browse SanJose1 at 192.168.1.2. Why is this not blocked?

_____

Lab 1.4.4: Implementing Quality of Service with Priority Queuing

Estimated Time: 30 Minutes

Objective

In this lab, you implement quality of service by replacing the default queuing method with priority queuing based on protocol type, on the routers shown in Figure 1-3.

Figure 1-3   Sample Topology for Lab 1.4.4

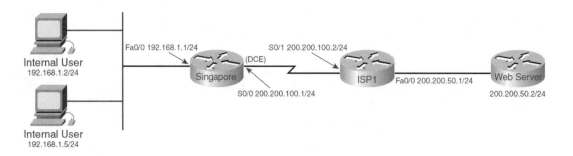

Equipment Requirements

This lab requires the following equipment:

* Three routers, preferably 2600 series, and two workstations running a Windows operating system

Scenario

The International Travel Agency is planning to launch an informational website on a local web server for the general public. You have been hired to configure the network so that all Internet user traffic to the web server is given the highest priority. Other traffic such as Telnet and e-mail are to be allowed over the WAN link, but they are not as important as traffic to the web server. Internet access to the web server is through the standard HTTP port. You decide to use priority queuing.

Step 1

Build and configure the network according to the diagram. If a web server is not available, use a Cisco router with the configuration that follows to simulate a web server.

```
Router(config)#hostname WebServer
WebServer(config)#ip http server
WebServer(config)#ip route 0.0.0.0 0.0.0.0 200.200.50.1
WebServer(config)#interface fastethernet 0/0
WebServer(config-if)#ip address 200.200.50.2 255.255.255.0
WebServer(config-if)#no shutdown
```

A default route is configured because no routing protocol will be enabled. Use the **ping** command to test connectivity between the Singapore and ISP1 routers and between the workstations and their respective gateways.

Step 2

Because no routing protocol will be enabled, configure a default route to the Internet from the Singapore router and a static route from the ISP1 router to the internal user network.

```
Singapore(config)#ip route 0.0.0.0 0.0.0.0 200.200.100.2
ISP1(config)#ip route 192.168.1.0 255.255.255.0 200.200.100.1
```

Now, check that the web server is accessible by connecting from an Internal User workstation with a browser using the web server IP address of 200.200.50.2.

Step 3

Determine which queuing mode is enabled on the Singapore router by using the **show interface serial 0/0** command. A sample output follows:

```
ISP1#show interface s0/0
Serial0/0 is up, line protocol is up
  Hardware is PowerQUICC Serial
  Internet address is 200.200.100.2/24
  MTU 1500 bytes, BW 128 Kbit, DLY 20000 usec,
     reliability 255/255, txload 1/255, rxload 1/255
  Encapsulation HDLC, loopback not set
  Keepalive set (10 sec)
  Last input 00:00:05, output 00:00:02, output hang never
  Last clearing of "show interface" counters never
  Input queue: 0/75/0/0 (size/max/drops/flushes); Total output drops: 0
  Queueing strategy: weighted fair
  Output queue: 0/1000/64/0 (size/max total/threshold/drops)
     Conversations  0/1/32 (active/max active/max total)
     Reserved Conversations 0/0 (allocated/max allocated)
     Available Bandwidth 96 kilobits/sec
  5 minute input rate 0 bits/sec, 0 packets/sec
  5 minute output rate 0 bits/sec, 0 packets/sec
     13041 packets input, 877578 bytes, 0 no buffer
     Received 11437 broadcasts, 0 runts, 0 giants, 0 throttles
     3 input errors, 0 CRC, 3 frame, 0 overrun, 0 ignored, 0 abort
     12200 packets output, 808601 bytes, 0 underruns
     0 output errors, 0 collisions, 10 interface resets
     0 output buffer failures, 0 output buffers swapped out
     9 carrier transitions
     DCD=up  DSR=up  DTR=up  RTS=up  CTS=up
```

Weighted fair queuing (WFQ) is the default queuing mode on interfaces that run at or below E1 speeds (2.048 Mbps or less), and first-in, first-out (FIFO) is the default if the bandwidth is greater than E1 speeds.

1.   What is the queuing mode on the Serial 0/0 interface of the Singapore router?

_____

Note: If the bandwidth of your serial interface is 128 Kb and the queuing mode is FIFO (contrary to the statement above) as shown next, it is probably because **no fair-queue** was automatically configured on the interface with the IOS version that is being used. You can use the **show running-config** command to check whether fair queuing was disabled by default. (See the partial sample output that follows.)

```
ISP1#show interface s0/0
Serial0/0 is up, line protocol is up
  Hardware is PowerQUICC Serial
  Internet address is 200.200.100.2/24
  MTU 1500 bytes, BW 128 Kbit, DLY 20000 usec,
     reliability 255/255, txload 1/255, rxload 1/255
  Encapsulation HDLC, loopback not set
  Keepalive set (10 sec)
```

```
Last input 00:00:06, output 00:00:09, output hang never
Last clearing of "show interface" counters never
Input queue: 0/75/0/0 (size/max/drops/flushes); Total output drops: 0
Queueing strategy: fifo
```

```
---output omitted---

ISP1#show running-config

---output omitted---

interface Serial0/0
 ip address 200.200.100.2 255.255.255.0
 no fair-queue
 clockrate 128000
---output omitted---.
```

Step 4

Priority queuing allows traffic types to be associated with one of four priorities: high, medium, normal, and low. Priority queuing transmits all packets in the high queue first. When the high queue is empty, packets in the medium queue are transmitted. When the medium queue is empty, the high queue is again checked for buffered packets. Because the higher priority queue is always checked before lower priority queued packets are sent, it is possible that lower priority packets will never be transmitted, causing their sessions to time out.

You configure priority queuing based on protocol type by designating HTTP traffic as high priority with all other IP traffic as medium priority on both the ISP1 and Singapore routers. The first step is to define a priority list:

```
Singapore(config)#access-list 101 permit tcp any any eq 80
Singapore(config)#priority-list 1 protocol ip high list 101

Singapore(config)#access-list 102 permit ip any any
Singapore(config)#priority-list 1 protocol ip medium list 102

ISP1(config)#access-list 101 permit tcp any any eq 80
ISP1(config)#priority-list 1 protocol ip high list 101

ISP1(config)#access-list 102 permit ip any any
ISP1(config)#priority-list 1 protocol ip medium list 102
```

Step 5

You must now assign the priority list to the appropriate interface. You can assign only one list per interface:

```
Singapore(config)#interface serial 0/0
Singapore(config-if)#priority-group 1

ISP1(config)#interface serial 0/0
ISP1(config-if)#priority-group 1
```

Step 6

Verify the queuing mode with the **show interface serial 0/0** command on both the ISP1 and Singapore routers. The output should show this: Queueing strategy: priority-list 1.

You can use other **show** commands to verify the queuing mode: **show queueing priority** and **show queueing interface serial 0/0**. Sample output for the commands on the Singapore router is shown here:

```
ISP1#show queueing priority
Current DLCI priority queue configuration:
Current priority queue configuration:
```

```
List    Queue  Args
1       high   protocol ip          list 101
1       medium protocol ip          list 102

ISP1#show queueing interface s0/0
Interface Serial0/0 queueing strategy: priority

Output queue utilization (queue/count)
        high/25 medium/0 normal/12248 low/0
```

You have now successfully configured priority queuing based on protocol type. All traffic that is destined for the web server is now given the highest priority over all other IP traffic. Unfortunately, it is difficult to test priority queuing in a lab environment because it is hard to generate enough non-HTTP traffic from one Internet user workstation to see the effects of priority queuing if the other Internet user is accessing the web server.

Save your configuration files for Singapore, ISP1, and the web server.

Lab 1.5.1: Equal-Cost Load Balancing with RIP

Estimated Time: 45 Minutes

Objective

In this lab, you observe equal-cost load balancing on a per-packet and per-destination basis by using advanced **debug** commands. Use the sample topology shown in Figure 1-4 for the router configuration.

Figure 1-4   Sample Topology Used in Lab 1.5.1

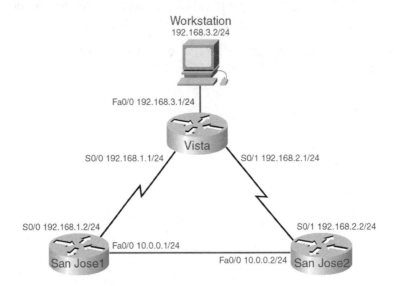

Equipment Requirements

This lab requires three routers configured as shown in Figure 1-4. You cannot use Cisco 2500 series routers in this lab because they do not have FastEthernet interfaces.

Scenario

Vista has two paths to network 10.0.0.0. Use advanced **debug** features to verify that both paths are being used to load balance traffic to 10.0.0.0 and to test both per-packet and per-destination load balancing.

Step 1

Build and configure the network according to the diagram. If you are continuing from the previous lab, remove any configured ACLs. Use RIP v1 and enable updates on all active interfaces with network commands similar to the following:

```
SanJose1(config)#router rip
SanJose1(config-router)#network 192.168.1.0
SanJose1(config-router)#network 10.0.0.0
```

Use the **ping** command to verify the work and test connectivity between all interfaces.

Step 2

Check the routing table on Vista using the **show ip route** command. Vista should have two routes to network 10.0.0.0 in its table. Troubleshoot if necessary.

RIP automatically performs load balancing using equal-cost routes. Notice that both routes have a metric of 1. In this case, it is a hop count. RIP cannot perform unequal-cost load balancing. In the next lab, you see that IGRP can perform unequal-cost load balancing.

Step 3

To configure Vista to load balance on a per-packet basis, both S0/0 and S0/1 must use process switching. Process switching forces the router to look in the routing table for the destination network of each routed packet. In contrast, fast switching performs a table lookup for the first packet only. The router then stores the result in a high-speed cache and uses the cached information to forward all additional packets to the same destination. Fast switching is the default setting.

Enable per-packet process switching on both Vista serial interfaces with the following interface configuration command:

```
Vista(config-if)#no ip route-cache
```

Verify that fast switching is disabled by using the **show ip interface** command:

```
Vista#show ip interface s0/0
Serial0 is up, line protocol is up
  Internet address is 192.168.1.1 255.255.255.0
  Broadcast address is 255.255.255.255
  Address determined by non-volatile memory
  MTU is 1500 bytes
  Helper address is not set
  Directed broadcast forwarding is enabled
  Outgoing access list is not set
  Inbound access list is not set
  Proxy ARP is enabled
  Security level is default
  Split horizon is enabled
  ICMP redirects are always sent
  ICMP unreachables are always sent
  ICMP mask replies are never sent
  IP fast switching is disabled
  <output omitted>
```

Step 4

Because there are two routes to the destination network in the table, half the packets are sent along one path, and half travel over the other path. The path selection alternates with each packet received. Observe this process by using the **debug ip packet** command, which outputs information about IP packets that the router sends and receives:

```
Vista#debug ip packet
```

With the debug running, send a few ping packets to 10.0.0.1 from the workstation at 192.168.3.2, and then return to Vista's console. As the ping packets are sent, the router outputs IP packet information. Stop the debug after a successful ping using the following command:

```
Vista#undebug all
```

Note: You will not be able to see the debug output if you are accessing Vista via Telnet. To display the debug results during a Telnet session, issue the **terminal monitor** command from privileged mode.

Examine the debug output. It can be a little confusing because the ping requests and replies are mixed together, as well as the routing updates. Look for a line of output that includes d=10.0.0.1, which is the destination address. On those lines, look for the interface that the packet was sent out on. The output interface should alternate between Serial0 and Serial1:

```
IP: s=192.168.3.2 (FastEthernet0/0), d=10.0.0.1 (Serial0/1), g=192.168.2.2, len 100, forward
IP: s=192.168.3.2 (FastEthernet0/0), d=10.0.0.1 (Serial0/0), g=192.168.1.2, len 100, forward
IP: s=192.168.3.2 (FastEthernet0/0), d=10.0.0.1 (Serial0/1), g=192.168.2.2, len 100, forward
IP: s=192.168.3.2 (FastEthernet0/0), d=10.0.0.1 (Serial0/0), g=192.168.1.2, len 100, forward
IP: s=192.168.3.2 (FastEthernet0/0), d=10.0.0.1 (Serial0/1), g=192.168.2.2, len 100, forward
```

Step 5

Configure debug to output only information of interest. To do this, configure an access control list (ACL) that debug can use to match packets against. Because the ping requests to the 10.0.0.0 network are the only packets of interest, create a list that filters everything else:

`Vista(config)#access-list 101 permit icmp any 10.0.0.0 0.255.255.255`

Apply the access list filter for the debug output with the following command:

`Vista#debug ip packet 101`

IP packet debugging is on for access list 101.

Repeat the ping to 10.0.0.1 from the workstation, and return to the Vista console to view the output.

Step 6

After you verify per-packet load balancing, configure Vista to use per-destination load balancing. You must configure both of Vista's serial interfaces to use fast switching so that you can use the route cache after the initial table lookup:

`Vista(config-if)#ip route-cache`

With fast switching, the relevant information that is contained in the first packet of a flow is cached so that the CPU does not need to process subsequent packets in the flow. Use the **show ip interface** command to verify that fast switching is enabled.

Step 7

Because the routing table is consulted only once per destination, all packets that are part of a train to a specific host follow the same path. Only when a second destination forces another table lookup or when the cached entry expires is the alternate path used.

Use the **debug ip packet 101** command, and ping 10.0.0.1 from the workstation. Because fast switching is enabled, only one packet is reflected in the output.

1.   Which serial interface was the packet sent out on?

_____

Now, ping 10.0.0.2.

2.   Which serial interface was the packet sent out on?

_____

Although there will not be a reply, send ping packets to the phantom addresses 10.0.0.3 and 10.0.0.4 to see what path the router selects.

Finally, issue the **show ip cache** command to view the contents of the route cache. Notice that mappings exist for 10.0.0.1 and 10.0.0.2, as well as for any other IP addresses on the 10.0.0.0 network for which a ping was executed:

```
Vista#show ip cache
IP routing cache 5 entries, 848 bytes
   14 adds, 9 invalidates, 0 refcounts
Minimum invalidation interval 2 seconds, maximum interval 5 seconds,
   quiet interval 3 seconds, threshold 0 requests
Invalidation rate 0 in last second, 0 in last 3 seconds
Last full cache invalidation occurred 01:40:00 ago

Prefix/Length           Age        Interface      Next Hop
10.0.0.1/32             00:00:15   Serial0/0      192.168.1.2
10.0.0.2/32             00:03:19   Serial0/1      192.168.2.2
10.0.0.3/32             00:00:57   Serial0/0      192.168.1.2
10.0.0.4/32             00:00:43   Serial0/1      192.168.2.2
192.168.3.2/32         00:03:37   FastEthernet0/0 192.168.3.2
```

3.   Briefly explain the meaning of this output.

_____

_____

_____

_____

Note: Save the configuration. You can use it with the next lab.

Lab 1.5.2: Unequal-Cost Load Balancing with IGRP

Estimated Time: 45 Minutes

Objective

In this lab, you observe unequal-cost load balancing on an IGRP network by using advanced **debug** commands on the routers in the sample topology shown in Figure 1-5.

Figure 1-5   Sample Topology for Lab 1.5.2

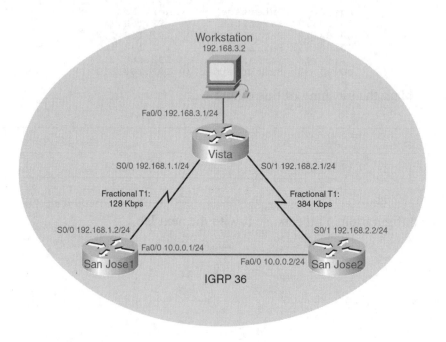

Equipment Requirements

This lab requires three routers configured as shown in Figure 1-5. You cannot use Cisco 2500 series routers in this lab because the 2500 series does not have FastEthernet interfaces.

Scenario

Vista has two paths to network 10.0.0.0, but they have unequal IGRP metrics. Configure unequal-cost load balancing and use advanced **debug** features to verify the work.

Step 1

Build and configure the network according to the diagram. If you are continuing from the previous lab, remove the RIP process (and networks advertised by RIP) with the single command **no router rip**. Configure IGRP with an autonomous system number of 36, and enable updates on all active interfaces with **network** commands similar to the following:

```
SanJose2(config)#router igrp 36
SanJose2(config-router)#network 192.168.2.0
SanJose2(config-router)#network 10.0.0.0
```

Use **ping** to verify the configuration and test connectivity among all interfaces.

Also, because the metric for IGRP includes bandwidth in its calculation, manually configure the bandwidth of serial interfaces to ensure accuracy. For the purposes of this lab, Vista alternative paths to network 10.0.0.0 are not of unequal cost until the appropriate bandwidths are set. Use the following commands to further configure Vista for the correct bandwidth and process switching:

```
Vista(config)#interface s0/0
Vista(config-if)#bandwidth 128
Vista(config-if)#no ip route-cache
Vista(config-if)#interface s0/1
Vista(config-if)#bandwidth 384
Vista(config-if)#no ip route-cache
```

Use the **show interface** command output to verify the correct bandwidth settings and the **show ip interface** command to ensure that fast switching is disabled.

1.   Can you set the bandwidth of Ethernet interfaces manually?

Note: You can enter the **bandwidth** command in interface configuration mode, but it only effects metric computations; in this case, it only affects routing protocols that use bandwidth in their metric computations.

2.   Can you place an Ethernet interface in fast switching mode?

Step 2

Check the routing table on Vista by using the **show ip route** command. Vista should have only one route to network 10.0.0.0 in its table. Troubleshoot if necessary.

Step 3

The variance value determines whether IGRP will accept unequal-cost routes. An IGRP router only accepts routes that are equal to the local best metric for the destination multiplied by the variance value. Therefore, if a router using IGRP has a local best metric for Network A of 10476, and the variance is 3, the router accepts unequal-cost routes with any metric up to 31,428, or 10,476 x 3. This is as long as the advertising router is closer to the destination. An IGRP router only accepts up to four paths to the same network.

Note: An alternate route is added to the route table only if the next-hop router in that path is closer to the destination by having a lower metric value than the current route.

By default, the variance of IGRP is set to 1, which means that only routes that are exactly 1 times the local best metric are installed. Therefore, a variance of 1 disables unequal-cost load balancing.

Configure Vista to enable unequal-cost load balancing using the following commands:

```
Vista(config)#router igrp 36
Vista(config-router)#variance 10
```

1.   According to the help feature, what is the maximum variance multiplier value?

Step 4

Check the Vista routing table again. Vista should have two routes to network 10.0.0.0 with unequal metrics.

1.   What is the IGRP metric for the route to 10.0.0.0 via SanJose1?

_____

2.   What is the IGRP metric for the route to 10.0.0.0 via SanJose2?

_____

Step 5

Now, test unequal-cost load balancing by sending a ping packet to network 10.0.0.0 from Vista while debugging. Remove any existing access lists on Vista. First, configure an access list to restrict debug output to the ping requests from Vista to network 10.0.0.0:

```
Vista(config)#access-list 101 permit icmp any 10.0.0.0 0.255.255.255
```

Then, enable debug using the access list to filter output:

```
Vista#debug ip packet 101
```

Finally, execute the extended **ping** command as follows. Specify the target IP address of 10.0.0.1 and a repeat count of 20. This results in enough pings to see the pattern of usage over the two unequal paths:

```
vista#ping
Protocol [ip]:
Target IP address: 10.0.0.1
Repeat count [5]: 20
Datagram size [100]:
Timeout in seconds [2]:
Extended commands [n]: n
Sweep range of sizes [n]:
Type escape sequence to abort.
Sending 20, 100-byte ICMP Echos to 10.0.0.1, timeout is 2 seconds:
!!!!!!!!!!!!!!!!!!!!!!
Success rate is 100 percent (20/20), round-trip min/avg/max = 32/36/52 ms
```

1.   Are the packets load balanced per destination or per packet?

_____

2.   How is unequal-cost load balancing different from equal-cost load balancing?

_____

Chapter 2

Advanced IP Addressing Management

Lab 2.10.1: Configuring VLSM and IP Unnumbered

Estimated Time: 45 Minutes

Objective

In this lab, you configure VLSM and test its functionality with two different routing protocols—RIP v1 and RIP v2—on the routers shown in Figure 2-1. You also use IP unnumbered in place of VLSM to further conserve addresses.

Figure 2-1   Sample Topology for Lab 2.10.1

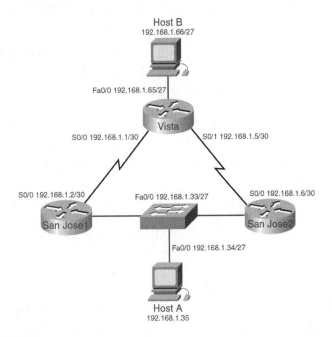

Equipment Requirements

This lab requires three routers configured as shown in Figure 2-1. You cannot use Cisco 2500 series routers in this lab because they do not have FastEthernet interfaces.

Scenario

When the International Travel Agency was much smaller, it wanted to configure its network using a single Class C address, 192.168.1.0, as shown in Figure 2-2. You need to configure the routers with the appropriate addresses. The company requires that at least 25 host addresses be available on each LAN, but it also demands that the maximum number of addresses be conserved for future growth.

Figure 2-2   VLSM Example

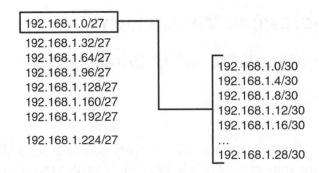

To support 25 hosts on each subnet, a minimum of 5 bits is needed in the host portion of the address. Five bits will yield 30 possible host addresses ($2^5 = 32 - 2$). If you must use 5 bits for hosts, you can add the other 3 bits in the last octet to the default 24-bit Class C mask. Therefore, you can use a 27-bit mask to create the following subnets:

To maximize this address space, the 192.168.1.0 /27 subnet is subnetted further using a 30-bit mask. This creates subnets that you can use on point-to-point links with minimal waste because each subnet can contain only two possible host addresses.

Step 1

Build and configure the network according to the diagram. This configuration requires the use of subnet 0, so the **ip subnet-zero** command might be required. This will depend on which IOS version is being used.

Note: Host A and Host B are not required to complete this lab.

On all three routers, configure RIP v1 and enable updates on all active interfaces with this network command:

```
SanJose1(config)#router rip
SanJose1(config-router)#network 192.168.1.0
```

Use **ping** to verify that each router can ping its directly connected neighbor.

Note: Some remote networks might be unreachable. Proceed to Step 2 anyway.

Step 2

Issue the **show ip route** command on Vista, as shown in the following example:

```
Vista#show ip route
<output omitted>
Gateway of last resort is not set
        192.168.1.0/24 is variably subnetted, 3 subnets, 2 masks
C       192.168.1.64/27 is directly connected, Ethernet0
C       192.168.1.0/30 is directly connected, Serial0
C       192.168.1.4/30 is directly connected, Serial1
```

The 192.168.1.32 /27 subnet is clearly absent from the routing table of Vista.

1.   The other routers also have incomplete tables. Why is this so?

Because RIP v1 with VLSM is being used, routing has broken down on the network. Remember that classful routing protocols, such as RIP v1 and IGRP, do not support VLSM. These protocols do not send subnet masks in their routing updates. For routing to work, RIP v2 must be configured, which does support VLSM.

Step 3

At each of three router consoles, enable RIP v2 updates and turn off automatic route summarization, as shown in the following example:

```
SanJose1(config)#router rip
SanJose1(config)#network 192.168.1.0
SanJose1(config-router)#version 2
SanJose1(config-router)#no auto-summary
```

Configuring **no auto-summary** disables the automatic summarization of subnet routes into network-level routes. This allows subnet information to be sent across classful network boundaries. Note that RIP v1 does not support this feature because it requires VLSM support.

When all three routers are running RIP v2, return to Vista and examine its routing table. It should now be complete, as follows:

```
Vista#show ip route
<output omitted>
Gateway of last resort is not set

     192.168.1.0/24 is variably subnetted, 4 subnets, 2 masks
C       192.168.1.64/27 is directly connected, Ethernet0
R       192.168.1.32/27 [120/1] via 192.168.1.6, 00:00:12, Serial1
                        [120/1] via 192.168.1.2, 00:00:13, Serial0
C       192.168.1.0/30 is directly connected, Serial0
C       192.168.1.4/30 is directly connected, Serial1
```

Notice that Vista has received equal cost routes to 192.168.1.32 /27 from both SanJose1 and SanJose2.

Step 4

Although VLSM has reduced address waste by creating small subnets for point-to-point links, the IP unnumbered feature can make it unnecessary to address these links altogether. Further maximize address use by configuring IP unnumbered on every serial interface in the WAN. To configure IP unnumbered, use the following commands:

```
SanJose1(config)#interface serial 0/0
SanJose1(config-if)#ip unnumbered fastethernet 0/0

Vista(config)#interface serial 0/0
Vista(config-if)#ip unnumbered fastethernet 0/0
Vista(config-if)#interface serial 0/1
Vista(config-if)#ip unnumbered fastethernet 0/0

SanJose2(config)#interface serial 0/0
SanJose2(config-if)#ip unnumbered fastethernet 0/0
```

After the IP unnumbered configuration is complete, each serial interface borrows the address of the local LAN interface. Check the routing table on the Vista router again:

```
Vista#show ip route
<output omitted>

Gateway of last resort is not set

     192.168.1.0/27 is subnetted, 2 subnets
```

```
C        192.168.1.64 is directly connected, Ethernet0
R        192.168.1.32 [120/1] via 192.168.1.34, 00:00:00, Serial1
                      [120/1] via 192.168.1.33, 00:00:08, Serial0
```

Note: If your output does not match this, clear the routing table using the **clear ip route *** command and then issue the **show ip route** command again.

If IP unnumbered were configured on the point-to-point serial links, only the LANs would require addresses in this topology. Because each LAN uses the same 27-bit mask, VLSM would not be required in this case. This would make classful routing protocols, such as RIP v1 and IGRP, viable options.

Lab 2.10.2a: VLSM 1

Estimated Time: 15 Minutes

Objective

Create an addressing scheme using variable-length subnet mask (VLSM) from the sample topology shown in Figure 2-3.

Figure 2-3   Sample Topology for Lab 2.10.2a

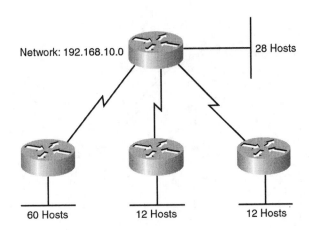

Equipment Requirements

This lab does not require physical hardware. You can create the IP addressing scheme by using Figure 2-3 as a sample topology.

Scenario

The assignment is the Class C address 192.168.10.0, which must support the network shown in the diagram. The use of IP unnumbered or NAT, or /31 subnets (available on point-to-point networks with IOS Release 12.2) is not permitted on this network. Create an addressing scheme that meets the requirements shown in Figure 2-3.

_____

_____

_____

_____

_____

_____

Lab 2.10.2b: VLSM 2

Estimated Time: 15 Minutes

Objective

Create an addressing scheme using subnetting or VLSM from the sample topology shown in Figure 2-4.

Figure 2-4   Sample Topology for Lab 2.10.2b

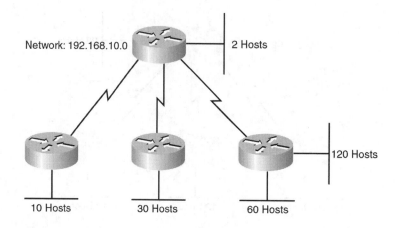

Equipment Requirements

This lab does not require physical hardware. You can create the IP addressing scheme by using Figure 2-4 as a sample topology.

Scenario

The assignment is the Class C address 192.168.10.0, which must support the network shown in the diagram. The use of IP unnumbered, NAT, or /31 subnets (available on point-to-point networks with IOS Release 12.2) are not permitted on this network. Create an addressing scheme that meets the requirements shown in the diagram. First attempt an IP addressing scheme using traditional subnetting. If that proves to be impossible, use VLSM.

_____

_____

_____

_____

_____

Lab 2.10.2c: VLSM 3

Estimated Time: 15 Minutes

Objective

Create an addressing scheme using VLSM from the sample topology shown in Figure 2-5.

Figure 2-5   Sample Topology for Lab 2.10.2c

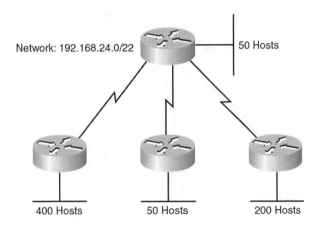

Equipment Requirements

This lab does not require physical hardware. You can create the IP addressing scheme by using Figure 2-5 as a sample topology.

Scenario

The assignment is the CIDR address 192.168.24.0/22, which must support the network shown in the diagram. The use of IP unnumbered or NAT, or /31 subnets (available on point-to-point networks with IOS Release 12.2) is not permitted on this network. Create an addressing scheme that meets the requirements shown in the diagram.

_____

_____

_____

_____

_____

_____

Lab 2.10.2d: VLSM 4

Estimated Time: 15 Minutes

Objective

Create an addressing scheme using VLSM from the sample topology shown in Figure 2-6.

Figure 2-6   Sample Topology for Lab 2.10.2d

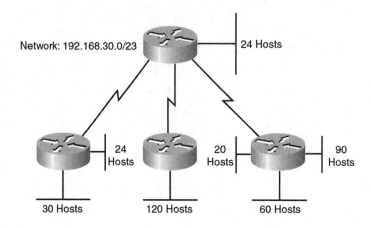

Equipment Requirements

This lab does not require physical hardware. You can create the IP addressing scheme by using Figure 2-6 as a sample topology.

Scenario

The assignment is the CIDR address 192.168.30.0/23, which must support the network shown in the diagram. The use of IP unnumbered or NAT, or /31 subnets (available on point-to-point networks with IOS Release 12.2) is not permitted on this network. Create an addressing scheme that meets the requirements shown in the diagram.

_____

_____

_____

_____

_____

_____

Lab 2.10.3: Using DHCP and IP Helper Addresses

Estimated Time: 45 Minutes

Objective

In this lab, you configure a Cisco router to act as a DHCP server for clients on two separate subnets. You also use the IP helper address feature to forward DHCP requests from a remote subnet. You should configure the routers as shown in Figure 2-7.

Figure 2-7   Sample Topology for 2.10.3

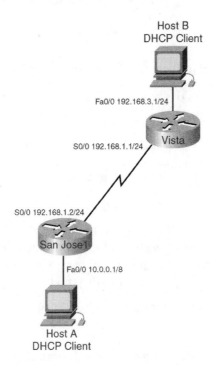

Equipment Requirements

This lab requires three routers configured as shown in Figure 2-7. You cannot use Cisco 2500 series routers in this lab because they do not have FastEthernet interfaces.

Scenario

Clients on the 192.168.3.0/24 network and the 10.0.0.0/8 network require the services of DHCP for automatic IP configuration. Configure SanJose1 to serve both subnets by creating two separate address pools. Finally, configure the FastEthernet interface of the Vista router to forward UDP broadcasts, including DHCP requests, to SanJose1.

Step 1

Build and configure the network according to the diagram. Connect Host A and Host B as shown, but configure these clients to obtain their IP addresses automatically. Because these hosts rely on DHCP, you cannot test them using **ping** until Step 5.

Configure RIP v2 on SanJose1 and Vista. Be sure to enable updates on all active interfaces with the **network** command:

```
SanJose1(config)#router rip
SanJose1(config)#version 2
SanJose1(config-router)#network 192.168.1.0
SanJose1(config-router)#network 10.0.0.0

Vista(config)#router rip
Vista(config-router)#version 2
Vista(config-router)#network 192.168.1.0
Vista(config-router)#network 192.168.3.0
```

Use **ping** and **show ip route** to verify your work and test connectivity between SanJose1 and Vista.

Step 2

Configure SanJose1 to act as a DHCP server for clients on the 10.0.0.0/8 network.

First, verify that SanJose1 can use DHCP services and that it is enabled:

```
SanJose1(config)#service dhcp
```

Next, configure the DHCP address pool for the 10.0.0.0 network. Name the pool **10-net**:

```
SanJose1(config)#ip dhcp pool 10-net
SanJose1(dhcp-config)#network 10.0.0.0 255.0.0.0
```

Step 3

International Travel Agency uses the first ten addresses in this address range to statically address servers and routers. From global configuration mode, exclude addresses from the DHCP pool so that the server does not attempt to assign them to clients. Configure SanJose1 to dynamically assign addresses from the 10-net pool, starting with 10.0.0.11:

```
SanJose1(config)#ip dhcp excluded-address 10.0.0.1 10.0.0.10
```

Step 4

Return to DHCP configuration mode and assign the IP options of the default gateway address, DNS server address, WINS server address, and domain name:

```
SanJose1(dhcp-config)#default-router 10.0.0.1
SanJose1(dhcp-config)#dns-server 10.0.0.3
SanJose1(dhcp-config)#netbios-name-server 10.0.0.4
SanJose1(dhcp-config)#domain-name xyz.net
```

Step 5

The DHCP server is now ready to be tested. Release and renew the IP configuration for Host A. For Windows 9x and Windows Me users, the commands are **winipcfg /release** and **winipcfg /renew**. Windows NT, Windows 2000, and Windows XP will use **ipconfig /release** and **ipconfig /renew**.

Dynamically assign Host A the first available address in the pool, which is 10.0.0.11. Check the configuration of Host A to verify that it received the proper IP address, subnet mask, default gateway, DNS server address, and WINS server address. Use **ipconfig /all** for Windows NT, Windows 2000, and Windows XP. Use the **winipcfg** command with Windows 9x and Windows Me. Troubleshoot if necessary.

Step 6

Because Host B also requires dynamic IP configuration, create a second DHCP pool with address and gateway options that are appropriate to its network, 192.168.3.0/24:

```
SanJose1(config)#ip dhcp pool 192.168.3-net
SanJose1(dhcp-config)#network 192.168.3.0 255.255.255.0
SanJose1(dhcp-config)#default-router 192.168.3.1
SanJose1(dhcp-config)#dns-server 10.0.0.3
SanJose1(dhcp-config)#netbios-name-server 10.0.0.4
SanJose1(dhcp-config)#domain-name xyz.net
```

ITA has recently installed IP phones on the 192.168.3.0 network. These phones require a DHCP server to provide a TFTP server address, 10.0.0.5. The Cisco IOS DHCP server configuration does not provide a keyword for TFTP servers, so configure this option using its raw option number:

```
SanJose1(dhcp-config)#option 150 ip 10.0.0.5
```

Note: When a Cisco IP phone is turned on, it automatically queries for a DHCP server. Then, the DHCP server responds by assigning an IP address to the Cisco IP phone. The IP address of the TFTP server is provided through DHCP option 150.

Step 7

The configuration of the DHCP server is now complete. However, Host B uses a UDP broadcast to find an IP address, and Vista is not configured to forward broadcasts. For DHCP to work, you must configure the FastEthernet interface of the Vista router to forward UDP broadcasts to SanJose1:

```
Vista(config)#interface fastethernet 0/0
Vista(config-if)#ip helper-address 192.168.1.2
```

Step 8

Release and renew the IP configuration of Host B while you are simultaneously logged into the console of SanJose1. Use a second host if necessary.

Verify, using **winipcfg** or **ipconfig /all**, that Host B received the correct IP configuration, and troubleshoot if necessary.

1. An **ip dhcp excluded-address** command was not issued. The DHCP server did not assign Host B 192.168.3.1. Why not?

_____

_____

_____

Issue **show ip dhcp ?** and note the choices:

```
SanJose1#show ip dhcp ?
  binding   DHCP address bindings
  conflict  DHCP address conflicts
  database  DHCP database agents
  import    Show Imported Parameters
  relay     Miscellaneous DHCP relay information
  server    Miscellaneous DHCP server information
```

Try the **conflict** and **binding** options:

```
SanJose1#show ip dhcp binding
IP address        Client-ID/              Lease expiration        Type
                  Hardware address
10.0.0.11         0063.6973.636f.2d30.    Mar 02 1993 02:28 AM    Automatic
                  3030.342e.3961.6432.
                  2e64.3063.302d.4661.
                  302f.30
192.168.3.2       0063.6973.636f.2d30.    Mar 02 1993 03:11 AM    Automatic
                  3030.392e.3433.3566.
                  2e39.6362.312d.4661.
                  302f.30

SanJose1#show ip dhcp conflict
IP address        Detection method    Detection time
192.168.3.1       Ping                Mar 01 1993 03:11 AM
```

2.   How did SanJose1 know to assign Host B an address from the 3-net pool and not the 10-net pool?

_____

_____

_____

_____

Issue the **show ip dhcp server statistics** command. Sample output follows:

```
SanJose1#show ip dhcp server statistics
Memory usage           15650
Address pools          2
Database agents        0
Automatic bindings     2
Manual bindings        0
Expired bindings       0
Malformed messages     0

Message                Received
BOOTREQUEST            0
DHCPDISCOVER           31
DHCPREQUEST            3
DHCPDECLINE            0
DHCPRELEASE            3
DHCPINFORM             0

Message                Sent
BOOTREPLY              0
DHCPOFFER              4
DHCPACK                3
DHCPNAK                0
```

3.   How many DHCPOFFER messages were sent on your network?

_____

_____

_____

Lab 2.10.4a: Network Address Translation—Static NAT and Dynamic NAT

Estimated Time: 45 Minutes

Objective

In this lab, you configure static Network Address Translation (NAT) and dynamic NAT by using the sample topology shown in Figure 2-8.

Figure 2-8   Sample Topology for Lab 2.10.4a

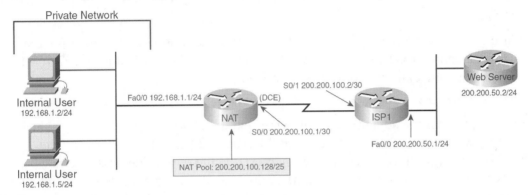

Equipment Requirements

This lab requires three routers configured as shown in Figure 2-8. You cannot use Cisco 2500 series routers in this lab because they do not have FastEthernet interfaces.

Scenario

The International Travel Agency needs approximately 100 private IP addresses translated in a one-to-one fashion with a pool of public IP addresses. To do this, ITA will use NAT translation with a portion of its class C address space allocated by ISP1.

Step 1

Build and configure the network according to the diagram.

Use **ping** to test connectivity between the NAT and ISP1 routers, between the workstations and the default gateway, and between Web Server and ISP1.

Step 2

Because no routing protocol will be enabled, configure a default route to the Internet on the NAT router:

```
NAT(config)#ip route 0.0.0.0 0.0.0.0 200.200.100.2
```

ISP1 needs to be able to reach hosts on the 192.168.0/24 network. However, these hosts will have their IP addresses translated to public IP addresses in the 200.200.100.128/25 network, so a static route to the 200.200.100.128/25 network is required:

```
ISP1(config)#ip route 200.200.100.128 255.255.255.128 200.200.100.1
```

If a router is being used as a web server instead of a PC-based web server, configure a static default route on the Web_Server router:

```
WebServer(config)#ip route 0.0.0.0 0.0.0.0 200.200.50.1
```

Step 3

Create a standard access control list (ACL) that defines all internal users:

```
NAT(config)#access-list 1 permit 192.168.1.0 0.0.0.255
```

Step 4

In this step, configure private and public address spaces to be used for NAT and configure the translation.

You will use the public address space 200.200.100.128/25 as a pool to provide NAT translation for the private IP addresses. To statically map the internal user with IP address 192.168.1.2 pictured in the diagram, enter the following command:

```
NAT(config)#ip nat inside source static 192.168.1.2 200.200.100.252
```

This static mapping has the advantage of allowing "external" users to always access the host 192.168.1.2 by way of the fixed IP address 200.200.100.252 (in addition to letting the 192.168.1.2 internal user have access to the Internet). On the down side, this external accessibility is also viewed as a security vulnerability. To allow the other hosts on the internal (private) network to reach the Internet, you must make translations for those hosts as well. You could make a list of static translations individually, but a simpler alternative is to configure a pool of addresses and let the router make one-to-one dynamic NAT translations for these hosts. For example, to map the nonstatically mapped hosts in the 192.168.1.0/24 network to public IP addresses in the range 200.200.100.129 to 200.200.100.250, proceed as follows:

```
NAT(config)#ip nat pool public 200.200.100.129 200.200.100.250 netmask 255.255.255.128
NAT(config)#ip nat inside source list 1 pool public
```

This provides a dynamic one-to-one NAT translation between public IP addresses in the "public" pool and private IP addresses specified by access list 1. The internal users' IP addresses are configured independently of the NAT translation. Dynamic NAT translations are made for any internal hosts for which no static translation has been defined. The previous configuration reserves IP addresses 200.200.100.251 to 200.200.100.254 for use in further static NAT mappings. You can also use static translations with an internal server to enable external access to it by way of a fixed external IP.

Note: If more than 128 active hosts exist on the private network, static NAT translation and dynamic one-to-one NAT translations prevent more than 128 hosts from accessing the Internet. For these additional hosts to get on the Internet, you must configure "NAT overloading" (see "Lab 2.10.4b: Network Address Translation—Port Address Translation and Port Forwarding").

Step 5

Now, designate the inside NAT interface and the outside NAT interface. In more complex topologies, you can have more than one inside NAT interface:

```
NAT(config)#interface fastethernet 0/0
NAT(config-if)#ip nat inside

NAT(config-if)#interface serial 0/0
NAT(config-if)#ip nat outside
```

You can use several show commands to see if NAT is working: **show ip nat translations**, **show ip nat statistics**, and **show ip nat translations verbose**.

From the two internal user workstations, ping WebServer (200.200.50.2). Then, check that WebServer is accessible by connecting from an internal user workstation using a browser with the WebServer IP address, 200.200.50.2. Issue the three NAT **show** commands listed on the NAT router. Sample output is shown here:

```
NAT#show ip nat translations
Pro Inside global       Inside local      Outside local       Outside global
--- 200.200.100.129     192.168.1.5       ---                 ---
--- 200.200.100.252     192.168.1.2       ---                 ---

NAT#show ip nat statistics
Total active translations: 2 (1 static, 1 dynamic; 0 extended)
Outside interfaces:
  Serial0/0
Inside interfaces:
  FastEthernet0/0
Hits: 131  Misses: 9
Expired translations: 0
Dynamic mappings:
-- Inside Source
[Id: 2] access-list 1 pool public refcount 1
 pool public: netmask 255.255.255.128
        start 200.200.100.129 end 200.200.100.250
        type generic, total addresses 122, allocated 1 (0%), misses 0

NAT#show ip nat translations verbose
Pro Inside global       Inside local      Outside local       Outside global
--- 200.200.100.129     192.168.1.5       ---                 ---
    create 00:02:55, use 00:02:55, left 23:57:04, Map-Id(In): 2,
    flags:
none, use count: 0
--- 200.200.100.252     192.168.1.2       ---                 ---
    create 00:40:36, use 00:02:59,
    flags:
static, use_count: 0
```

Notice that the internal user with IP address 192.168.1.5 had its address dynamically translated to 200.200.100.129, which is the first available address in the "public" pool. You can use the command **clear ip nat translation *** to clear all dynamic NAT translations:

```
NAT#clear ip nat translation *
NAT#show ip nat translations
Pro Inside global       Inside local      Outside local       Outside global
--- 200.200.100.252     192.168.1.2       ---                 ---
```

Save the configurations for NAT and ISP1.

Lab 2.10.4b: Network Address Translation—Port Address Translation and Port Forwarding

Estimated Time: 45 Minutes

Objective

In this lab, port address translation (PAT) and port forwarding are configured using the sample topology shown in Figure 2-9.

Figure 2-9   Sample Topology for Lab 2.10.4b

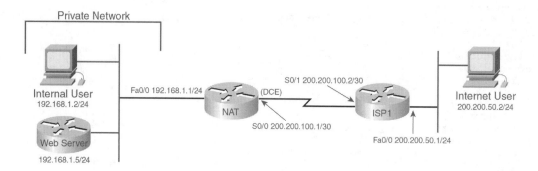

Equipment Requirements

This lab requires three routers configured as shown in Figure 2-9. You cannot use Cisco 2500 series routers in this lab because they do not have FastEthernet interfaces.

Scenario

The International Travel Agency is planning to launch an informational website on a local web server for the general public. However, the one Class C address that has been allocated is not sufficient for the users and devices that the company has on this network. Therefore, a network has been configured to allow all internal company users access to the Internet and all Internet users access to the company's informational web server through static NAT and PAT. You must translate internal user addresses to one legal global address, and all Internet users must access the informational web server through the one legal global address.

Step 1

Build and configure the network according to the diagram. If you are using the configuration files from the previous lab, remove the NAT pool (public) and the static and dynamic NAT configurations. Use a Cisco router as Web_Server if another web server is not available.

Use **ping** to test connectivity between the NAT and ISP1 routers, between the internal user and the NAT router, and between the Internet user and ISP1.

Also check that the WebServer server is accessible by connecting to it from the internal user workstation with a browser using the WebServer IP address, 192.168.1.5.

Step 2

Because no routing protocol will be enabled, configure a default route to the Internet from the NAT router:

```
NAT(config)#ip route 0.0.0.0 0.0.0.0 200.200.100.2
```

If a router is being used as a Web_Server instead of a PC-based web server, configure a static default route on the Web_Server router:

```
WebServer(config)#ip route 0.0.0.0 0.0.0.0 192.168.1.1
```

Step 3

Create a standard ACL that would give all internal users access to the Internet:

```
NAT(config)#access-list 1 permit 192.168.1.0 0.0.0.255
```

Step 4

Because a single inside global address, 200.200.100.1, will be used to represent multiple inside local addresses, 192.168.1.x, simultaneously, apply the access list and configure NAT overload on the serial 0/0 interface of the NAT router. In general, you can use NAT to overload a pool of public addresses, when a single external address is used. This is referred to as PAT.

```
NAT(config)#ip nat inside source list 1 interface s0/0 overload
```

This configuration allows internal users to access the Internet, but it blocks external users from accessing internal hosts.

Step 5

Now, specify the inside and outside NAT interfaces:

```
NAT(config)#interface fastethernet 0/0
NAT(config-if)#ip nat inside

NAT(config-if)#interface serial 0/0
NAT(config-if)#ip nat outside
```

Enter the command **ping 200.200.50.2** from the internal user workstation. Then, on the NAT router, enter the commands **show ip nat translations**, **show ip nat statistics**, and **show ip nat translations verbose**. Sample output follows:

```
NAT#show ip nat translations
Pro Inside global      Inside local      Outside local       Outside global
icmp 200.200.100.1:516 192.168.1.5:516   200.200.50.2:516    200.200.50.2:516
icmp 200.200.100.1:517 192.168.1.5:517   200.200.50.2:517    200.200.50.2:517
icmp 200.200.100.1:518 192.168.1.5:518   200.200.50.2:518    200.200.50.2:518
icmp 200.200.100.1:519 192.168.1.5:519   200.200.50.2:519    200.200.50.2:519
icmp 200.200.100.1:520 192.168.1.5:520   200.200.50.2:520    200.200.50.2:520

NAT#show ip nat statistics
Total active translations: 5 (0 static, 5 dynamic; 5 extended)
Outside interfaces:
  Serial0/0
Inside interfaces:
  FastEthernet0/0
Hits: 25  Misses: 30
Expired translations: 20
Dynamic mappings:
-- Inside Source
[Id: 1] access-list 1 interface Serial0/0 refcount 5
```

```
NAT#show ip nat translations verbose
Pro Inside global      Inside local      Outside local      Outside global
icmp 200.200.100.1:516 192.168.1.5:516    200.200.50.2:516    200.200.50.2:516
    create 00:00:15, use 00:00:15, left 00:00:44, Map-Id(In): 1,
    flags:
extended, use_count: 0
icmp 200.200.100.1:517 192.168.1.5:517    200.200.50.2:517    200.200.50.2:517
    create 00:00:15, use 00:00:15, left 00:00:44, Map-Id(In): 1,
    flags:
extended, use_count: 0
icmp 200.200.100.1:518 192.168.1.5:518    200.200.50.2:518    200.200.50.2:518
    create 00:00:15, use 00:00:15, left 00:00:44, Map-Id(In): 1,
    flags:
extended, use_count: 0
icmp 200.200.100.1:519 192.168.1.5:519    200.200.50.2:519    200.200.50.2:519
    create 00:00:15, use 00:00:15, left 00:00:44, Map-Id(In): 1,
    flags:
extended, use_count: 0
icmp 200.200.100.1:520 192.168.1.5:520    200.200.50.2:520    200.200.50.2:520
    create 00:00:15, use 00:00:15, left 00:00:44, Map-Id(In): 1,
    flags:
extended, use_count: 0
```

Step 6

Internet users need access to the informational web server through 200.200.100.1 through port 80. Configure PAT so that Internet users are directed to the informational web server, 192.168.1.5, when they connect to the IP address 200.200.100.1 through a web browser.

```
NAT(config)#ip nat inside source static tcp 192.168.1.5 80 200.200.100.1 80 extendable
```

The **extendable** keyword at the end of this static NAT command causes the router to reuse the global address of an active translation and save enough information to distinguish it from another translation entry. This command translates external attempts to connect to port 80/IP address 200.200.100.1 to internal attempts to connect to port 80/IP address 192.168.1.5. The process of performing NAT translations based on the value of the incoming port number of an IP packet is called *port forwarding*.

Step 7

Successful configuration of port forwarding is indicated by being able to reach the informational web server from the Internet user workstation with a web browser using the inside global address of 200.200.100.1.

After you successfully connect to the web server with a browser from the Internet user workstation, issue the same three **show** commands from Step 5 on the NAT router to view the translations. Sample output is shown here:

```
NAT#show ip nat translations
Pro Inside global      Inside local      Outside local      Outside global
tcp 200.200.100.1:80   192.168.1.5:80    200.200.50.2:4806  200.200.50.2:4806
tcp 200.200.100.1:80   192.168.1.5:80    200.200.50.2:4809  200.200.50.2:4809
tcp 200.200.100.1:80   192.168.1.5:80    200.200.50.2:4814  200.200.50.2:4814
tcp 200.200.100.1:80   192.168.1.5:80    ---                ---

NAT#show ip nat statistics
Total active translations: 4 (1 static, 3 dynamic; 4 extended)
Outside interfaces:
  Serial0/0
Inside interfaces:
  FastEthernet0/0
Hits: 243  Misses: 30
Expired translations: 34
```

```
Dynamic mappings:
-- Inside Source
[Id: 1] access-list 1 interface Serial0/0 refcount 0

NAT#show ip nat translations verbose
Pro Inside global      Inside local       Outside local       Outside global
tcp 200.200.100.1:80   192.168.1.5:80     200.200.50.2:4806   200.200.50.2:4806
    create 00:01:00, use 00:00:59, left 00:00:00,
    flags:
extended, timing-out, use_count: 0
tcp 200.200.100.1:80   192.168.1.5:80     200.200.50.2:4809   200.200.50.2:4809
    create 00:00:59, use 00:00:59, left 00:00:00,
    flags:
extended, timing-out, use_count: 0
tcp 200.200.100.1:80   192.168.1.5:80     200.200.50.2:4814   200.200.50.2:4814
    create 00:00:41, use 00:00:40, left 00:00:19,
    flags:
extended, timing-out, use_count: 0
tcp 200.200.100.1:80   192.168.1.5:80     ---                 ---
    create 00:11:23, use 00:00:41,
    flags:
static, extended, extendable, use_count: 3
```

You have now successfully configured port address translation (PAT).

Chapter 3

Routing Overview

Lab 3.6.1: Migrating from RIP to EIGRP

Estimated Time: 45 Minutes

Objective

In this lab, configure RIP v2 and then EIGRP on the routers shown in Figure 3-1 so that you can compare their metric calculations.

Figure 3-1   Sample Topology for Lab 3.6.1

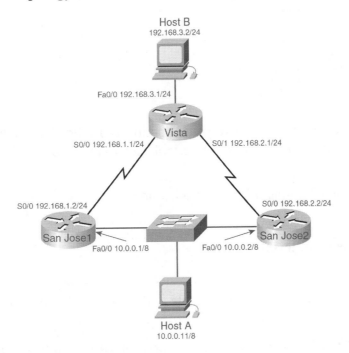

Equipment Requirements

This lab requires three routers configured as shown in Figure 3-1. You cannot use Cisco 2500 series routers in this lab because they do not have Fast Ethernet interfaces.

Scenario

The International Travel Agency (ITA) currently uses RIP v2 as its interior gateway protocol. Migrate its network to EIGRP.

Step 1

Build and configure the network according to the diagram.

Note: Host A and Host B are not required to complete this lab, but they can be used in testing or as Telnet clients. If you use them, the Host A gateway can be either the SanJose1 router or the SanJose2 router.

On all three routers, configure RIP v2 and enable updates on all active interfaces with the **network** command. The following are sample commands for SanJose1:

```
SanJose1(config)#router rip
SanJose1(config-router)#version 2
SanJose1(config-router)#network 192.168.1.0
SanJose1(config-router)#network 10.0.0.0
```

Use **ping** and **show ip route** to verify full connectivity within the network.

Step 2

While you are migrating to EIGRP, leave RIP running on all the routers to avoid a loss of connectivity. On SanJose1 and SanJose2, configure EIGRP for AS 24. Do not configure Vista for EIGRP yet.

```
SanJose1(config)#router eigrp 24
SanJose1(config-router)#network 192.168.1.0
SanJose1(config-router)#network 10.0.0.0
```

and

```
SanJose2(config)#router eigrp 24
SanJose2(config-router)#network 192.168.2.0
SanJose2(config-router)#network 10.0.0.0
```

Step 3

From the Vista console, issue the **show ip route** command. EIGRP has not been configured on this router yet. Therefore, a route has been established to the 10.0.0.0 /8 network through the RIP.

1.   What is the administrative distance of this route?

_____

2.   What is the metric of this route?

_____

Enable **debug** so that changes to the routing table will be reported to the console:

```
Vista#debug ip routing
```

If the connection is through Telnet, enter the **terminal monitor** command so that you can see the logging output.

Now, enable EIGRP on Vista:

```
Vista(config)#router eigrp 24
Vista(config-router)#network 192.168.1.0
Vista(config-router)#network 192.168.2.0
Vista(config-router)#network 192.168.3.0
```

3.   After this configuration is made, did **debug** report changes to the routing table? If so, what were they?

_____

Issue the **show ip route** command again from Vista. There should now be an EIGRP route to network 10.0.0.0 /8.

4.   What is the metric of this route?

_____

5. Because this metric is higher than the metric of the RIP route, why did Vista choose the EIGRP route over the RIP route?

Step 4

To see more with the **debug ip routing** command, force the routing table to rebuild with this command:

```
Vista#clear ip route *
```

1. According to the **debug** output, what are the administrative distances of Vista-connected routes?

---

2. What is the metric for each of the connected routes?

Step 5

To complete the migration from RIP to EIGRP, disable RIP on all three routers using the command **no router rip**.

Next, enter the command **show ip route**:

```
Vista#show ip route
Codes: C - connected, S - static, I - IGRP, R - RIP, M - mobile, B - BGP
       D - EIGRP, EX - EIGRP external, O - OSPF, IA - OSPF inter area
       N1 - OSPF NSSA external type 1, N2 - OSPF NSSA external type 2
       E1 - OSPF external type 1, E2 - OSPF external type 2, E - EGP
       i - IS-IS, L1 - IS-IS level-1, L2 - IS-IS level-2, ia - IS-IS inter area
       * - candidate default, U - per-user static route, o - ODR
       P - periodic downloaded static route

Gateway of last resort is not set

D    10.0.0.0/8 [90/20514560] via 192.168.1.2, 00:00:59, Serial0/0
                [90/20514560] via 192.168.2.2, 00:00:59, Serial0/1
C    192.168.1.0/24 is directly connected, Serial0/0
C    192.168.2.0/24 is directly connected, Serial0/1
C    192.168.3.0/24 is directly connected, FastEthernet0/0
```

Turn off debug before exiting the Vista router:

```
Vista#no debug all
```

Save the configuration files for the next lab.

Lab 3.6.2: Configuring IGRP

Estimated Time: 45 Minutes

Objective

In this lab, configure IGRP for unequal-cost load balancing and tune IGRP timers to improve performance on the routers shown in Figure 3-2.

Figure 3-2   Sample Topology for Lab 3.6.2

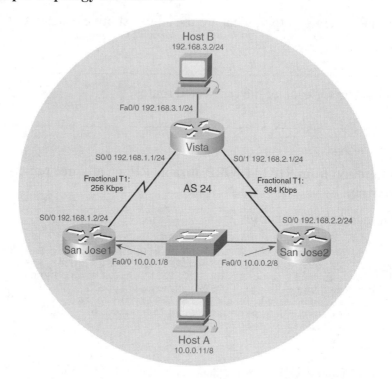

Equipment Requirements

This lab requires three routers configured as shown in Figure 3-2. You cannot use Cisco 2500 series routers in this lab because they do not have Fast Ethernet interfaces.

Scenario

The International Travel Agency (ITA) has asked for IGRP to be implemented in its WAN.

Step 1

Build and configure the network according to the diagram. If the configuration files are used from the previous lab, remove all routing protocols.

Note: Host A and Host B are not required to complete this lab, but you can use them in testing or as Telnet clients. If you use them, the Host A gateway can be either the SanJose1 router or the SanJose2 router.

On all three routers, configure IGRP for AS 24, and enable updates on all active interfaces with the **network** command.

The IGRP metric includes bandwidth in its calculation. Manually configure the bandwidth of serial interfaces so that metrics are accurate. Use the following commands to configure the correct bandwidth settings for each serial interface:

```
SanJose1(config)#interface serial 0/0
SanJose1(config-if)#bandwidth 256

Vista(config)#interface serial 0/0
Vista(config-if)#bandwidth 256
Vista(config-if)#interface serial 0/1
Vista(config-if)#bandwidth 384

SanJose2(config-if)#interface serial 0/0
SanJose2(config-if)#bandwidth 384
```

Use the output from the **show interface** command to verify the correct bandwidth settings. Use **ping** and **show ip route** to verify full connectivity within the network.

Step 2

On Vista, configure unequal-cost load balancing using the **variance 5** command.

Note: A default value of 1 is used for equal-cost load balancing. The following are sample commands for Vista:

```
Vista(config)#router igrp 24
Vista(config-router)#variance 5
```

Use the **show ip route** command to verify that the routers are installing two unequal-cost routes to the same destination:

```
Vista#show ip route
<output omitted>
I    10.0.0.0/8 [100/41072] via 192.168.1.2, 00:00:01, Serial0/0
                [100/28051] via 192.168.2.2, 00:00:00, Serial0/1
C    192.168.1.0/24 is directly connected, Serial0/0
C    192.168.2.0/24 is directly connected, Serial0/1
C    192.168.3.0/24 is directly connected, FastEthernet0/0
```

1.   What has changed in the output of the **show ip route** command? How does the metric of the new route compare with that of the original route?

Step 3

On any router, issue the **show ip protocols** command and check the IGRP invalid, holddown, and flush timers for IGRP.

Note: A route does not become invalid until after 270 seconds and is not flushed from the table until after more than 10 minutes or 630 seconds. Also, the maximum hop count is set at 100 by default.

In small networks, it is advised that the timers for IGRP be adjusted to speed up the convergence process.

Fast IGRP is a specific set of timer settings that result in improved convergence.

To configure Fast IGRP, change the IGRP timers as follows:

- 15 seconds between updates

- 45 seconds for route expiration

- 0 seconds for holddown

- 60 seconds for flushing the route from the table

As part of this configuration, disable the holddown timers completely. This is done so that after the route for a given network has been removed, a new route for that destination network will be accepted immediately. Finally, reduce the IGRP maximum hop count to a number that is appropriate to the ITA network.

Configure Fast IGRP by issuing the following commands on all three routers:

```
SanJose1(config)#router igrp 24
SanJose1(config-router)#timers basic 15 45 0 60
SanJose1(config-router)#no metric holddown
SanJose1(config-router)#metric maximum-hops 10
```

Verify the settings with the **show ip protocols** command.

Step 4

In this step, test the IGRP timer settings by simulating a link failure.

On SanJose1, enable **debug** so that any changes to the routing table are reported to the console:

```
SanJose1#debug ip routing
```

If the connection is through Telnet, enter the **terminal monitor** command so that the logging output is to the Telnet session.

With the connection to SanJose1 open, log in to Vista. Do this on a separate workstation if necessary. On Vista, shut down the Fast Ethernet interface. This removes 192.168.3.0 /24 from the Vista routing table:

```
Vista(config)#interface fastethernet 0/0
Vista(config-if)#shutdown
```

Use **show ip route** to verify that Vista no longer possesses a valid route to 192.168.3.0 /24.

Return to SanJose1 and issue the **show ip route** command.

Note: The route to 192.168.3.0 is still in the SanJose1 table, but it's flagged as possibly being down.

1.   How long will the wait be before this route is removed?

_____

To check the answer, wait for the **debug** output on SanJose1 to report that the route to 192.168.3.0 has been flushed.

2.   If SanJose1 had been configured with default timers, how long would it have taken for the route to be flushed?

_____

Save the configuration files for the next lab.

Lab 3.6.3: Configuring Default Routing with RIP and IGRP

Estimated Time: 45 Minutes

Objective

In this lab, configure a default route and use RIP to propagate this default information to other routers shown in Figure 3-3. When this configuration has reached convergence, migrate the network from RIP to IGRP and configure default routing to work with that protocol as well.

Figure 3-3   Sample Topology for Lab 3.6.3

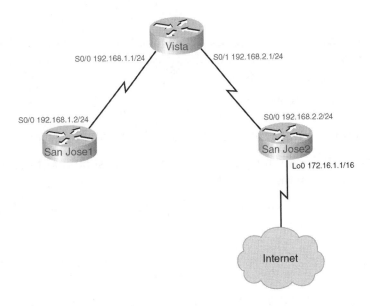

Equipment Requirements

This lab requires three routers configured, as shown in Figure 3-3.

Scenario

The International Travel Agency (ITA) asked for default routing to be configured for its network, which currently uses RIP. The company connects to the Internet through SanJose2. It has been decided to configure a static default route on that router. To aid scalability, SanJose2 will propagate the default route to all other RIP routers.

ITA also asked that the possibility of migrating all routers to IGRP be explored. As a test, configure the three routers in this scenario for IGRP and configure default routing for that protocol as well.

Procedures

Before you begin this lab, you should reload each router after you erase its startup configuration. This prevents problems that residual configuration might cause. After you prepare the equipment, proceed with Step 1.

Step 1

Build and configure the network according to the diagram. If the configurations are used from the previous lab, remove all routing protocols. Do not configure the 172.16.1.1/16 address on SanJose2 yet. This network connects ITA to its ISP and the Internet.

Configure RIP on all three routers. However, be sure not to configure the SanJose2 RIP process to include the 172.16.0.0/16 network.

Use **ping** and **show ip route** to verify full connectivity within the network, excluding 172.16.0.0/16.

Step 2

Configure SanJose2 to simulate the existence of an outside network. For this scenario, you need to simulate the link between ITA and its provider by configuring a loopback interface with an IP address. Enter the following commands on SanJose2:

```
SanJose2(config)#interface loopback0
SanJose2(config-if)#ip address 172.16.1.1 255.255.0.0
```

Note: If 172.16.1.1 is **pinged** from the SanJose2 console, the loopback interface replies.

From the Vista console, attempt to ping 172.16.1.1. This ping should fail because the 172.16.0.0/17 network is not in the Vista table.

1.   If no default route exists, what does a router do with a packet destined for a network that is not in its table?

Step 3

Next, configure SanJose2 with a 0.0.0.0/0 default route pointed at the simulated ISP. Issue the following command on SanJose2:

```
SanJose2(config)#ip route 0.0.0.0 0.0.0.0 loopback0
```

This command statically configures the default route. The default route directs traffic destined for networks that are not in the routing table to the simulated WAN link loopback 0.

Depending on the IOS version, you might need to specifically configure RIP to propagate this 0.0.0.0/0 route. Enter the following commands on SanJose2:

```
SanJose2(config)#router rip
SanJose2(config-router)#default-information originate
```

Step 4

Now check the routing tables of SanJose1 and Vista using the **show ip route** command. Verify that they both have received and installed a route to 0.0.0.0/0 in their tables.

1.   On Vista, what is the metric of this route?

2.   On SanJose1, what is the metric of this route?

SanJose1 and Vista still do not have routes to 172.16.0.0/16 in their tables. From Vista, ping 172.16.1.1. This ping should be successful.

3. Why does the ping to 172.16.1.1 work, even though there is no route to 172.16.0.0/16 in the Vista table?

Check to be sure that SanJose1 can also ping 172.16.1.1. Troubleshoot if necessary.

Note: If default route propagation does not occur as expected, two options are available as a last resort:

*   Save the configuration files and reboot the routers.

*   Remove the RIP process on each router with the **no router rip** command and reconfigure the RIP.

Step 5

With default routing now working, migrate the network from RIP to IGRP for testing purposes. Issue the following command on all three routers:

```
SanJose1(config)#no router rip
```

With RIP removed from each router configuration, configure IGRP on all three routers using AS 24, as follows:

```
SanJose1(config)#router igrp 24
SanJose1(config-router)#network 192.168.1.0

Vista(config)#router igrp 24
Vista(config-router)#network 192.168.1.0
Vista(config-router)#network 192.168.2.0

SanJose2(config)#router igrp 24
SanJose2(config-router)#network 192.168.2.0
```

Use **ping** and **show ip route** to verify that IGRP is working properly. Do not worry about the 172.16.1.1 loopback address on SanJose2 yet.

Step 6

Check the SanJose2 routing table. The static default route to 0.0.0.0/0 should still be there. The **default-information originate** command might have been required to propagate this route with RIP, based on the IOS version. The **default-information originate** command is not available in an IGRP configuration. Therefore, use the **ip default-network** method to propagate default information in IGRP.

On SanJose2, issue the following commands:

```
SanJose2(config)#router igrp 24
SanJose2(config-router)#network 172.16.0.0
SanJose2(config-router)#exit
SanJose2(config)#ip default-network 172.16.0.0
```

These commands configure IGRP to update neighbor routers about the network 172.16.0.0/16, which includes the simulated ISP link, loopback 0. Not only will IGRP advertise this network, but the **ip default-network** command also will flag this network as a candidate default route. A candidate default route is flagged with an asterisk in the routing table. When a network is flagged as a default, that flag will stay with the route as it passes from neighbor to neighbor by IGRP.

Check the routing tables of SanJose1 and Vista. If they do not yet have the 172.16.0.0/16 route with an asterisk, wait for another IGRP update. This could take 90 seconds. The **clear ip route *** command could also be issued on all three routers to force them to immediately send new updates.

When the 172.16.0.0/16 route appears as a candidate default in all three routing tables, proceed to the next step.

Note: If default route propagation does not occur as expected, two options are available as a last resort:

- Save the configuration files and reboot the routers.

- Remove the IGRP process on each router with the **no router igrp 24** command and reconfigure IGRP.

Step 7

SanJose1 and Vista know the 172.16.0.0/16 network explicitly. To test the default route, you need to create a second loopback interface on SanJose2. Issue the following commands on SanJose2:

```
SanJose2(config)#interface loopback1
SanJose2(config-if)#ip address 10.0.0.1 255.0.0.0
```

This loopback interface simulates another external network, but one that is not explicitly identified in the routing table for SanJose1 or Vista.

Return to SanJose1 and check its routing table using the **show ip route** command.

1. Is there a route to the 10.0.0.0/8 network?

_____

From SanJose1, ping 10.0.0.1. This ping should be successful.

2. If there is no route to 10.0.0.0/8 and no route to 0.0.0.0/0, why does this ping succeed?

_____

Save the configuration files for the next lab.

Lab 3.6.4: Configuring Floating Static Routes

Estimated Time: 45 Minutes

Objective

In this lab, configure a floating static route on the routers shown in Figure 3-4.

Figure 3-4   Sample Topology for Lab 3.6.4

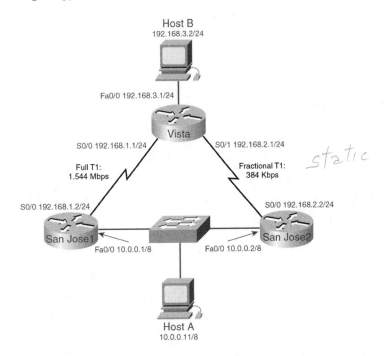

Equipment Requirements

This lab requires three routers configured as shown in Figure 3-4. You cannot use Cisco 2500 series routers in this lab because they do not have Fast Ethernet interfaces.

Scenario

The International Travel Agency (ITA) uses a combination of static routing and RIP in the core of its network. One of the ITA key boundary routers, Vista, has two routes to the 10.0.0.0/8 network. RIP only advertises one of these routes. If the other path is configured statically using the default administrative distance, the static route will be preferred over the RIP route. The lower administrative distance is preferred. However, ITA wants the RIP route to be preferred because the RIP route has a higher bandwidth. Therefore, you must override the default administrative distance of the static route to create a floating static route.

Procedures

Before you begin this lab, reload each router after you erase its startup configuration. This prevents problems that residual configurations might causes. After you prepare the equipment, proceed with Step 1.

Step 1

Build and configure the network according to the diagram. Be sure to configure Host B. Do not configure a routing protocol. If the configuration files are used from the previous lab, remove all routing protocols and static routes.

Use **ping** to verify that directly connected devices can reach each other.

Step 2

Configure routing on the three routers. SanJose1 and Vista will run RIP, so issue the following commands on the appropriate router:

```
SanJose1(config)#router rip
SanJose1(config-router)#network 192.168.1.0
SanJose1(config-router)#network 10.0.0.0
...
Vista(config)#router rip
Vista(config-router)#network 192.168.1.0
Vista(config-router)#network 192.168.3.0
```

SanJose2 will reach Vista using a static route. Enter the following command on SanJose2:

```
SanJose2(config)#ip route 192.168.3.0 255.255.255.0 192.168.2.1
```

Verify that Host B can ping the serial interfaces of SanJose1 (192.168.1.2) and SanJose2 (192.168.2.2). Troubleshoot if necessary.

Step 3

Check the Vista routing table. It should have a route to the 10.0.0.0/8 network.

1.   Which interface will Vista use to reach the 10.0.0.0/8 network?

_192.168.1.2_

Now that the RIP route to the 10.0.0.0/8 network is verified as operational, configure a static route on Vista that will use SanJose2 to get to 10.0.0.0/8 by using the following command:

```
Vista(config)#ip route 10.0.0.0 255.0.0.0 192.168.2.2
```

When Vista has been configured with this static route, check its routing table using the **show ip route** command. Only the static route to the 10.0.0.0/8 network should be in the Vista routing table.

2.   What happened to the RIP route?

got replaced

Remember that ITA wants Vista configured to use the SanJose2 link to 10.0.0.0/8 only if the other route goes down. Therefore, the static route on Vista must be configured so that it floats. Floating means that the route remains in the configuration but is not installed in the routing table until a route with a better metric is lost.

Before you can configure a floating static route on Vista, remove the first static route using the following command:

```
Vista(config)#no ip route 10.0.0.0 255.0.0.0 192.168.2.2
```

When you have verified that this static route is no longer part of Vista configuration, issue the following command to create a floating static route:

```
Vista(config)#ip route 10.0.0.0 255.0.0.0 192.168.2.2 130
```

_120_

The integer 130 at the end of this command overrides the default administrative distance for the static route. By default, a static route that uses the next-hop router IP address as a gateway has an administrative distance of 1. In this scenario, you must increase the administrative distance so that it is higher than the RIP administrative distance of 120. Only by increasing the default route administrative distance above 120 will the RIP route be preferred. Vista will install the static route only if the RIP route fails.

Add the following floating static route to SanJose1 in case the link between SanJose1 and Vista fails:

```
SanJose1(config)#ip route 192.168.3.0 255.255.255.0 10.0.0.2 130
```
d   *via*

Step 4

After you reconfigure the static route to be a floating static route, check the Vista routing table again. Only the RIP route to 10.0.0.0/8 should be in the table. Verify that routing is working by pinging Host A 10.0.0.11 from Host B. Troubleshoot if necessary.

Although you cannot see the floating static route in the Vista table, it remains in the configuration file. Observe how Vista reacts to a link failure by issuing the following command:

```
Vista#debug ip routing
```

If the connection is through Telnet, enter the **terminal monitor** command so that the logging output is to the Telnet session.

Verify that the routers are configured correctly and disconnect the SanJose1 Ethernet connection to the 10.0.0.0/8 network. The **debug** output on Vista should send a change notification after a few seconds. The full process of deleting the old route and installing the new one takes several minutes. Vista waits until its holddown timer expires before it installs the floating static route to 10.0.0.0/8 via SanJose2.

```
01:38:38: RT: metric change to 10.0.0.0 via 192.168.1.2, rip metric [120/1]
          new metric [120/-1]
01:38:38: RT: delete route to 10.0.0.0 via 192.168.1.2, rip metric [120/4294967295]
01:38:38: RT: no routes to 10.0.0.0, entering holddown
01:42:33: RT: garbage collecting entry for 10.0.0.0
01:42:33: RT: add 10.0.0.0/8 via 192.168.2.2, static metric [130/0]
```

Check the Vista routing table to ensure that the static route has been installed. As a final test, ping 10.0.0.1 and 10.0.0.2 from Host B. The ping to 10.0.0.2 should be successful. Why is the ping to 10.0.0.1 not successful?

not directly connected & broken link at the static route.

SanJose1 (config)# int fa0/0 no keepalive

Vista ip route 10.0.0.1 255.255.255.255 192.168.1.2 5 ← Lowest

then even if patch cable from SJ1 to switch is broken host b should be able to ping to san jose1 s0/0.

(no applicable for serial int's). (can misinform Vista. So don't use ✱ in a production setting.

Chapter 4

Routing Information Protocol Version 2

Lab 4.4.1: Routing Between RIP v1 and RIP v2

Estimated Time: 45 Minutes

Objective

In this lab, configure RIP v1 and RIP v2 routing protocols per Figure 4-1. You configure RIP v2 to accept RIP v1 updates.

Figure 4-1   Lab Equipment and IP Addressing Scheme for Routing Between RIP v1 and RIP v2

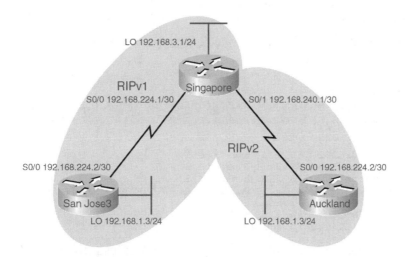

Equipment Requirements

This lab requires three routers configured as shown in Figure 4-1.

Scenario

RIP v1 is presently running between SanJose3, Singapore, and Auckland. New routers that support RIP v2 and variable-length subnet mask (VLSM) have been installed at the Singapore and Auckland headquarters. However, you will install an upgrade of the SanJose3 router, which presently does not support RIP v2, at a later time. You must configure RIP v2 between Auckland and Singapore. You will then need to configure Singapore to receive RIP v1 updates so that the SanJose3 router can communicate with Auckland.

Step 1

Before you begin this lab, reload the routers after you erase their startup configuration. Doing so prevents problems that residual configurations might cause. Build the network according to the diagram and configure all routers with RIP v1. Test connectivity between the routers and troubleshoot as necessary. A ping should be successful from one end of the network to the other.

Step 2

Verify that RIP v1 is running. You can use several commands to verify that RIP v1 is enabled and running. Two of the commands are shown here:

```
SanJose3#show ip protocols
Routing Protocol is "rip"
  Sending updates every 30 seconds, next due in 14 seconds
  Invalid after 180 seconds, hold down 180, flushed after 240
  Outgoing update filter list for all interfaces is
  Incoming update filter list for all interfaces is
  Redistributing: rip
  Default version control: send version 1, receive any version
    Interface        Send  Recv  Triggered RIP  Key-chain
    Serial0/0        1     1 2
    Loopback0        1     1 2
  Routing for Networks:
    192.168.1.0
    192.168.224.0
  Routing Information Sources:
    Gateway          Distance      Last Update
    192.168.224.1        120         00:00:22
Distance: (default is 120)
```

You can use the **debug ip rip** command to check the type of updates the router is receiving and sending:

```
SanJose3#debug ip rip
RIP protocol debugging is on
00:21:28: RIP: sending v1 update to 255.255.255.255 via Serial0/0 (192.168.224.2
00:21:28: RIP: sending v1 update to 255.255.255.255 via Loopback0 (192.168.1.3)
00:21:28: RIP: build update entries
00:21:28:         network 192.168.3.0 metric 2
00:21:28:         network 192.168.224.0 metric 1
00:21:28:         network 192.168.240.0 metric 2
00:21:28:         network 192.168.252.0 metric 3
00:21:41: RIP: received v1 update from 192.168.224.1 on Serial0/0
00:21:41:         192.168.3.0 in 1 hops
00:21:41:         192.168.240.0 in 1 hops
00:21:41:         192.168.252.0 in 2 hops
```

Notice that all RIP v1 updates are sent using broadcast addresses through all the interfaces. The advertisements are also classful. That is, no mask information is carried in a RIP v1 update. RIP v1 does not support classless interdomain routing (CIDR) and VLSM.

Turn **debug** off if it is enabled and check that a route to 192.168.1.0 exists in the routing tables of the Singapore and Auckland routers.

Step 3

Configure RIP v2 on the Singapore and Auckland routers:

```
Singapore(config)#router rip
Singapore(config-router)#version 2

Auckland(config)#router rip
Auckland(config-router)#version 2
```

Issue a **show running-config** command on either Singapore or Auckland and notice that RIP version 2 replaced RIP version 1. Issue the **clear ip route *** command to flush the routing table.

Check the routing table of the Singapore and Auckland routers.

1.   Is there still a route to 192.168.1.0 on either router?

By default, RIP v1 accepts RIP v2 updates. However, RIP v2 does not accept RIP v1 updates. Therefore, you must configure RIP v2 to accept RIP v1 updates.

When you issue **debug ip rip** on the SanJose3 and Singapore routers, you can view RIP v1 accepting RIP v2 updates and RIP v2 ignoring RIP v1 updates. Sample output is shown here:

```
SanJose3#debug ip rip
RIP protocol debugging is on
01:12:28: RIP: received v2 update from 192.168.224.1 on Serial0/0
01:12:28:       192.168.3.0/24 via 0.0.0.0 in 1 hops
01:12:28:       192.168.240.0/24 via 0.0.0.0 in 1 hops
01:12:28:       192.168.252.0/24 via 0.0.0.0 in 2 hops
01:12:32: RIP: sending v1 update to 255.255.255.255 via Serial0/0(192.168.224.2)
01:12:32: RIP: build update entries
01:12:32:        network 192.168.1.0 metric 1
01:12:32: RIP: sending v1 update to 255.255.255.255 via Loopback0 (192.168.1.3)
01:12:32: RIP: build update entries
01:12:32:        network 192.168.3.0 metric 2
01:12:32:        network 192.168.224.0 metric 1
01:12:32:        network 192.168.240.0 metric 2
01:12:32:        network 192.168.252.0 metric 3
Singapore#debug ip rip
RIP protocol debugging is on
01:49:40: RIP: sending v2 update to 224.0.0.9 via Serial0/0 (192.168.224.1)
01:49:40: RIP: build update entries
01:49:40:        192.168.3.0/24 via 0.0.0.0, metric 1, tag 0
01:49:40:        192.168.240.0/24 via 0.0.0.0, metric 1, tag 0
01:49:40:        192.168.252.0/24 via 0.0.0.0, metric 2, tag 0
01:49:40: RIP: sending v2 update to 224.0.0.9 via Serial0/1 (192.168.240.1)
01:49:40: RIP: build update entries
01:49:40:        192.168.3.0/24 via 0.0.0.0, metric 1, tag 0
01:49:40:        192.168.224.0/24 via 0.0.0.0, metric 1, tag 0
01:49:40: RIP: sending v2 update to 224.0.0.9 via Loopback0 (192.168.3.1)
01:49:40: RIP: build update entries
01:49:40:        192.168.224.0/24 via 0.0.0.0, metric 1, tag 0
01:49:40:        192.168.240.0/24 via 0.0.0.0, metric 1, tag 0
01:49:40:        192.168.252.0/24 via 0.0.0.0, metric 2, tag 0
01:49:40: RIP: ignored v2 packet from 192.168.3.1 (sourced from one of our addresses)
01:49:45: RIP: received v2 update from 192.168.240.2 on Serial0/1
01:49:45:        192.168.252.0/24 via 0.0.0.0 in 1 hops
01:40:45: RIP: ignored v1 packet from 192.168.224.2 (illegal version)
```

Step 4

Configure RIP v2 to accept RIP v1 updates:

```
Singapore(config-if)#interface serial 0/0
Singapore(config-if)#ip rip receive version 1
```

Issue the **clear ip route *** command to flush the routing table. Check the Singapore and Auckland routing tables again.

1.   Is there a route for network 192.168.1.0?

Enable the **debug ip rip** command on Singapore to see RIP v2 now accepting RIP v1 updates. Sample output is shown here:

```
Singapore#debug ip rip
RIP protocol debugging is on
02:05:09: RIP: received v1 update from 192.168.224.2 on Serial0/0
02:05:09:       192.168.1.0 in 1 hops
02:05:22: RIP: received v2 update from 192.168.240.2 on Serial0/1
02:05:22:       192.168.252.0/24 via 0.0.0.0 in 1 hops
02:05:33: RIP: sending v2 update to 224.0.0.9 via Serial0/0 (192.168.224.1)
```

2. Remember that RIP v1 updates are sent through a broadcast. How are RIP v2 updates sent?

    _____

3. What are the steps to verify that RIP v2 supports CIDR/VLSM by examining the **debug ip rip** output?

    _____

Lab 4.4.2: RIP v2 MD5 Authentication

Estimated Time: 20 Minutes

Objective

In this lab, configure RIP v2 authentication per Figure 4-2.

Figure 4-2   Lab Equipment and IP Addressing Scheme for RIP v2 MD5 Authentication

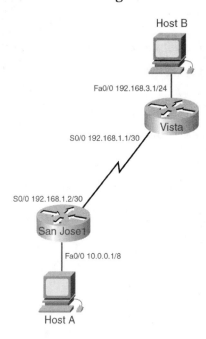

Equipment Requirements

This lab requires you to configure three routers, as shown in Figure 4-2. You cannot use Cisco 2500 series routers in this lab because they do not have Fast Ethernet interfaces.

Scenario

RIP v1 is running between SanJose1 and Vista. Currently, no authentication exists between the two routers. You must use RIP v2 to provide authentication. The default authentication in every RIP v2 packet is plain text authentication. However, the Cisco IOS implementation of RIP v2 provides a higher level of security with MD5 authentication. After you view the default authentication, the routers are upgraded to MD5 authentication. Make sure that the IOS versions on the individual routers are compatible.

Step 1

Before you begin this lab, reload the routers after you erase their startup configuration. Doing so prevents problems that residual configurations might cause. Build the network according to the diagram. Configure the routers with RIP v1 and advertise all networks. Test connectivity and routing between the routers. Troubleshoot the network if required.

Step 2

Verify that RIP v1 is running. Debug commands can be useful when you are verifying RIP operation. Type the **debug ip rip** command on each router. The following is sample output of the **debug ip rip** on Vista:

```
00:30:58: RIP: sending v1 update to 255.255.255.255 via Serial0/0 (192.168.1.1)
00:30:58: RIP: build update entries
00:30:58:       network 192.168.3.0 metric 1
00:30:58: RIP: sending v1 update to 255.255.255.255 via FastEthernet0/0 (192.168.3.1)
00:30:58: RIP: build update entries
00:30:58:       network 10.0.0.0 metric 2
00:30:58:       network 192.168.1.0 metric 1
00:30:58: RIP: received v1 update from 192.168.1.2 on Serial0/0
00:30:58:       10.0.0.0 in 1 hops
00:31:24: RIP: received v1 update from 192.168.1.2 on Serial0/0
00:31:24:       10.0.0.0 in 1 hops
```

Stop all previous debugs.

1.   Which version of RIP are the routers running?

2.   Which **show** command can you use to verify which version of RIP is running?

Step 3

Configure RIP v2 on SanJose1 and Vista:

```
Vista(config)#router rip
Vista(config-router)#version 2

SanJose1(config)#router rip
SanJose1(config-router)#version 2
Again, use the debug ip rip command to verify that RIP v2 is running on SanJose1.
00:42:03: RIP: received v2 update from 192.168.1.1 on Serial0/0
00:42:03:       192.168.3.0/24 via 0.0.0.0 in 1 hops
00:42:04: RIP: sending v2 update to 224.0.0.9 via Serial0/0 (192.168.1.2)
00:42:04: RIP: build update entries
00:42:04:       10.0.0.0/8 via 0.0.0.0, metric 1, tag 0
00:42:04: RIP: sending v2 update to 224.0.0.9 via FastEthernet0/0 (10.0.0.1)
00:42:04: RIP: build update entries
00:42:04:       192.168.1.0/24 via 0.0.0.0, metric 1, tag 0
00:42:04:       192.168.3.0/24 via 0.0.0.0, metric 2, tag 0
00:42:04: RIP: ignored v2 packet from 10.0.0.1 (sourced from one of our address
```

1.   Which version of RIP updates are being sent and received?

Notice that RIP is no longer using broadcasts on 255.255.255.255 to send updates. RIP v2 uses the multicast address 224.0.0.9 to send routing messages. RIP v2 also supports CIDR/VLSM by providing the subnet mask information to its neighbors.

Turn off debugging.

Step 4

Configure authentication on SanJose1 and Vista. Define the key first:

```
Vista(config)#key chain private
Vista(config-keychain)#key 1
Vista(config-keychain-key)#key-string 234
```

```
SanJose1(config)#key chain private
SanJose1(config-keychain)#key 1
SanJose1(config-keychain-key)#key-string 234
Enable the authentication on the interfaces.
Vista(config)#interface serial 0/0
Vista(config-if)#ip rip authentication key-chain private

SanJose1(config)#interface serial 0/0
SanJose1(config-if)#ip rip authentication key-chain private
```

Execute the **debug ip rip** command again on Vista and examine the output:

```
01:10:31: RIP: sending v2 update to 224.0.0.9 via Serial0/0 (192.168.1.1)
01:10:31: RIP: build update entries
01:10:31:       192.168.3.0/24 via 0.0.0.0, metric 1, tag 0
01:10:31: RIP: sending v2 update to 224.0.0.9 via FastEthernet0/0 (192.168.3.1)
01:10:31: RIP: build update entries
01:10:31:       10.0.0.0/8 via 0.0.0.0, metric 2, tag 0
01:10:31:       192.168.1.0/24 via 0.0.0.0, metric 1, tag 0
01:10:31: RIP: ignored v2 packet from 192.168.3.1 (sourced from one of our addresses)
01:10:35: RIP: received packet with text authentication 234
01:10:35: RIP: received v2 update from 192.168.1.2 on Serial0/0
01:10:35:       10.0.0.0/8 via 0.0.0.0 in 1 hops
```

Step 5

The Cisco implementation of RIP v2 supports MD5 authentication. This provides a higher level of security over clear text. You need to configure both router interfaces with MD5 authentication. The key number and key string must match on both sides; otherwise, authentication fails:

```
Vista(config)#interface serial0/0
Vista(config-if)#ip rip authentication mode md5
```

Examine the debug output on Vista before applying the MD5 authentication on the SanJose1 router:

```
1:21:11: RIP: ignored v2 packet from 192.168.1.2 (invalid authentication)
01:21:28: RIP: sending v2 update to 224.0.0.9 via Serial0/0 (192.168.1.1)
01:21:28: RIP: build update entries
01:21:28:       192.168.3.0/24 via 0.0.0.0, metric 1, tag 0
01:21:28: RIP: sending v2 update to 224.0.0.9 via FastEthernet0/0 (192.168.3.1)
01:21:28: RIP: build update entries
01:21:28:       10.0.0.0/8 via 0.0.0.0, metric 2, tag 0
01:21:28:       192.168.1.0/24 via 0.0.0.0, metric 1, tag 0
```

Clear the routing table on Vista. Type the command **show ip route**.

1.   Is the RIP route still there? Why or why not?

Note: It might take several moments for the correct result to be displayed.

Enable MD5 authentication on SanJose1:

```
SanJose1(config)#interface serial0/0
SanJose1(config-if)#ip rip authentication mode md5
```

Examine the **debug** output:

```
01:30:06: RIP: sending v2 update to 224.0.0.9 via FastEthernet0/0 (10.0.0.1)
01:30:06: RIP: build update entries
01:30:06:       192.168.1.0/24 via 0.0.0.0, metric 1, tag 0
01:30:06:       192.168.3.0/24 via 0.0.0.0, metric 2, tag 0
01:30:06: RIP: ignored v2 packet from 10.0.0.1 (sourced from one of our addresses)
01:30:11: RIP: received packet with MD5 authentication
01:30:11: RIP: received v2 update from 192.168.1.1 on Serial0/0
01:30:11:       192.168.3.0/24 via 0.0.0.0 in 1 hops
```

Display the routing table.

2. Is the RIP route there?

_____

If a route is missing, troubleshoot.

3. Use the **show ip rip database** command to verify that RIP v2 is being routed. List three other commands used in this context.

_____

_____

Chapter 5

EIGRP

Lab 5.7.1: EIGRP

Estimated Time: 30 Minutes

Objective

In this lab, you configure EIGRP on three Cisco routers within the International Travel Agency WAN per Figure 5-1. You also observe the basic behaviors of the protocol.

Figure 5-1   Lab Equipment and IP Addressing Scheme to Configure EIGRP

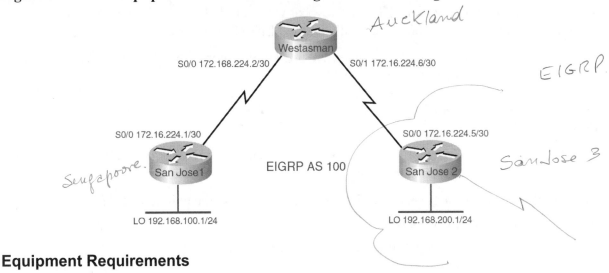

Equipment Requirements

This lab requires three routers to be configured, as shown in Figure 5-1.

Scenario

The International Travel Agency is implementing EIGRP between its overseas headquarters and its North American headquarters. You must configure EIGRP at all three locations to allow the SanJose1 headquarters to connect to the SanJose2 headquarters.

Step 1

Before you begin this lab, reload the routers after you erase their startup configuration. Doing so prevents problems that residual configurations might cause. Build and configure the network according to the diagram, but *do not* configure EIGRP yet.

Use **ping** to test connectivity between serial interfaces. SanJose1 and SanJose2 cannot ping each other until you have enabled EIGRP.

Step 2

Configure EIGRP for AS 100 on all routers, as shown here:

```
SanJose1(config)#router eigrp 100
SanJose1(config-router)#network 192.168.100.0
SanJose1(config-router)#network 172.16.0.0
```

```
Westasman(config)#router eigrp 100
Westasman(config-router)#network 172.16.0.0

SanJose2(config)#router eigrp 100
SanJose2(config-router)#network 192.168.200.0
SanJose2(config-router)#network 172.16.0.0
```

Step 3

After you enable EIGRP on each of the three routers, verify the operation using the **show ip route** command on the Westasman router. The Westasman router should have routes to all networks.

1.   Based on the output of this command, which routes were learned by way of EIGRP?

_____

The Westasman router received EIGRP routes that were internal to the EIGRP domain, 192.168.100.0 and 192.168.200.0. Internally learned EIGRP routes were denoted by a D.

2.   The administrative distance of an external EIGRP route is 170. What is the administrative distance of an internal EIGRP route?

_____

Step 4

Now that you have configured EIGRP, use **show** commands to view EIGRP neighbors and topology tables on the Westasman router.

From the Westasman router, issue the **show** command to view the neighbor table:

```
Westasman#show ip eigrp neighbors
```

1.   How many EIGRP neighbors are listed in the output?

_____

To view the topology table, issue the **show ip eigrp topology all-links** command.

2.   A passive route is one that is stable and available for use. How many routes are in passive mode?

_____

3.   What is the feasible distance and the reported distance for the LANs (loopback addresses) that are on the SanJose1 and SanJose2 routers?

_____

To view more specific information about a topology table entry, use an IP address with the **show ip eigrp topology** command:

```
Westasman#show ip eigrp topology 192.168.200.0
```

4.   Does it show which router originated the route?

_____

Finally, use **show** commands to view key EIGRP statistics. On the Westasman router, issue the **show ip eigrp traffic** command to see the EIGRP packet types. Then, enter the **show ip eigrp interfaces** command.

5.   List the five EIGRP packet types and the number sent and received for each.

_____

6.   Which interfaces are participating in the EIGRP routing process?

_____

Lab 5.7.2: Configuring EIGRP Fault Tolerance

Estimated Time: 30 Minutes

Objective

In this lab, you configure EIGRP over a full mesh topology (see Figure 5-2). Then, you test it to observe DUAL replacing a successor with a feasible successor after a link failure.

Figure 5-2   Lab Equipment and IP Address Scheme for EIGRP Fault Tolerance

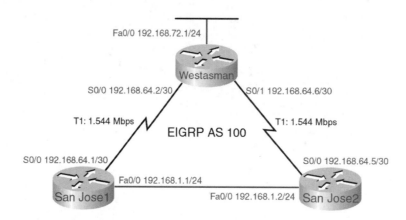

Equipment Requirements

This lab requires three routers to be configured, as shown in Figure 5-2. You cannot use Cisco 2500 series routers in this lab because they do not have Fast Ethernet interfaces.

Scenario

The International Travel Agency wants to run EIGRP on its core, branch, and regional routers. You are to configure and test EIGRP for its ability to install alternate routes in the event of link failure.

Step 1

Before you begin this lab, reload the routers after you erase their startup configuration. Doing so prevents problems that residual configurations might cause. Build and configure the network according to the diagram, configuring EIGRP as indicated for AS 100. If you are using the configuration files from the previous lab, be sure to change IP addresses according to the diagram. Also, remove all loopback interfaces.

Set the bandwidth for each serial interface to reflect the diagram. Use the **show interface** command to verify the configuration.

Use **ping** and **show ip route** to verify the configuration and test connectivity among all routers.

Step 2

Verify that EIGRP maintains all routes to destination networks in its topology table.

From the SanJose2 router, issue the **show ip eigrp topology all-links** command:

```
SanJose2#show ip eigrp topology all-links
IP-EIGRP Topology Table for AS(100)/ID(192.168.64.5)

Codes: P - Passive, A - Active, U - Update, Q - Query, R - Reply,
       r - reply Status, s - sia Status

P 192.168.72.0/24, 1 successors, FD is 2297856, serno 53
        via 192.168.64.6 (2297856/128256), Serial0/0
        via 192.168.1.1 (2300416/2297856), FastEthernet0/0
P 192.168.64.0/30, 1 successors, FD is 2273792, serno 50
        via 192.168.64.6 (2681856/2169856), Serial0/0
P 192.168.64.0/24, 1 successors, FD is 1761792, serno 52
        via Summary (2169856/0), Null0
        via 192.168.1.1 (2172416/2169856), FastEthernet0/0, serno 48
P 192.168.64.4/30, 1 successors, FD is 2169856, serno 51
        via Connected, Serial0/0
P 192.168.1.0/24, 1 successors, FD is 28160, serno 2
        via Connected, FastEthernet0/0
```

The router topology table for SanJose2 includes two paths to the 192.168.72.0 network. Use **show ip route** to determine which path is installed in the SanJose2 routing table.

1. Which route is installed?

_____

2. According to the output of the **show ip eigrp topology all-links** command, what is the feasible distance (FD) for the route 192.168.72.0?

_____

Both paths to 192.168.72.0 are listed in the topology table with their computed distance and reported distance in parentheses. The computed distance is listed first.

3. What is the reported distance (RD) of the route to 192.168.72.0 by way of 192.168.1.1?

_____

4. Is this RD greater than, less than, or equal to the FD of the route?

_____

Step 3

To display debugging information about EIGRP feasible successor metrics (FSM) and to observe how EIGRP deals with the loss of a successor to a route, use the **debug eigrp fsm** command.

On the SanJose2 router, issue the command **debug eigrp fsm**.

Next, shut down or unplug the router serial connection to SanJose2. This causes the SanJose2 router to lose its preferred route to 192.168.72.0 by way of 192.168.64.6.

Examine the **debug eigrp fsm** output for information regarding the route to 192.168.72.0, as shown in the following example:

```
<output omitted>
11:15:55: DUAL: Destination 192.168.72.0/24
11:15:55: DUAL: Find FS for dest 192.168.72.0/24. FD is 2297856, RD is 2297856
11:15:55: DUAL:        192.168.64.6 metric 4294967295/4294967295
11:15:55: DUAL:        192.168.1.1 metric 2300416/2297856 not found Dmin is 2300416
11:15:55: DUAL: Dest 192.168.72.0/24 entering active state.
11:15:55: DUAL: Set reply-status table. Count is 1.
<output omitted>
```

```
11:15:55: DUAL: rcvreply: 192.168.72.0/24 via 192.168.1.1 metric 2300416/2297856
11:15:55: DUAL: reply count is 1
11:15:55: DUAL: Clearing handle 1, count now 0
11:15:55: DUAL: Freeing reply status table
11:15:55: DUAL: Find FS for dest 192.168.72.0/24. FD is 4294967295, RD is 4294967295
  found
11:15:55: DUAL: Removing dest 192.168.72.0/24, nexthop 192.168.64.6
11:15:55: DUAL: RT installed 192.168.72.0/24 via 192.168.1.1
11:15:55: DUAL: Send update about 192.168.72.0/24.  Reason: metric chg
11:15:55: DUAL: Send update about 192.168.72.0/24.  Reason: new if
<output omitted>
```

The highlighted portion of the sample output shows DUAL attempting to locate a feasible successor (FS) for 192.168.72.0. In this case, DUAL failed to find a feasible successor, and the router entered the active state. After querying its EIGRP neighbors, SanJose2 locates and installs a route to 192.168.72.0/24 by way of 192.168.1.1.

Step 4

Verify that the new route has been installed by using the **show ip route** command.

Bring the SanJose2 router serial interface back up; 192.168.64.6 will be restored as the preferred route to the 192.168.72.0 network.

Save the configuration files for the routers.

Lab 5.7.3: Configuring EIGRP Summarization

Estimated Time: 25 Minutes

Objective

In this lab, you configure EIGRP and test the operation over discontiguous subnets by disabling automatic route summarization. Discontiguous subnets are subnets that are out of order. Finally, you manually configure EIGRP to use specific summary routes. (See Figure 5-3.)

Figure 5-3   Lab Equipment and IP Address Scheme for EIGRP Summarization

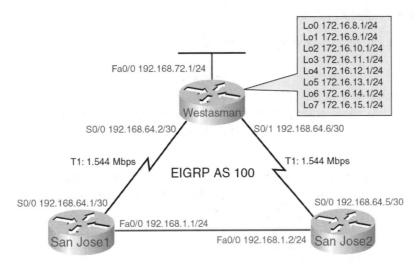

Equipment Requirements

This lab requires three routers to be configured, as shown in Figure 5-3. You cannot use Cisco 2500 series routers in this lab because they do not have Fast Ethernet interfaces.

Scenario

The International Travel Agency uses VLSM to conserve IP addresses. All LANs are addressed using contiguous subnets, but the company would like to examine the effects of discontiguous subnets using EIGRP for future reference. The existence of multiple networks is simulated by loopback interfaces on the Westasman router. The WAN links are addressed using 192.168.64.0 with a 30-bit mask.

Because this scheme creates discontiguous subnets, the default summarization behavior of EIGRP should result in incomplete routing tables. You should resolve the problem by disabling the default summarization in EIGRP while maintaining a route summary at the Westasman router with manual route summarization.

Step 1

Before you begin this lab, reload the routers after you erase their startup configuration. This prevents problems that residual configurations might cause. Build and configure the network according to the diagram. Add the loopback interfaces if you use the configuration files from the previous lab. This configuration requires the use of subnet 0. Therefore, check if this is enabled or enter the **ip subnet-zero** command, depending on which IOS version is used. Configure the Westasman router with eight loopback interfaces using the IP addresses from the diagram. These interfaces simulate the existence of multiple networks behind the Westasman router. Configure EIGRP as indicated for AS 100.

Use **ping** to verify that all serial interfaces can ping each other.

Note: Until the additional configurations are complete, not all networks will appear in the routing table for each router.

Step 2

Use **show ip route** to check the routing table for SanJose1 and SanJose2.

1.   Are any routes missing? If so, which ones?

_____

SanJose1 and SanJose2 will install a summary route to 192.168.64.0/24 by way of Null0. EIGRP routers create these summary routes automatically. Because the local router has generated the summary, there is no next hop for the route. Therefore, the router maps this summary route to its null interface.

2.   Look again at the routing tables for SanJose1 and SanJose2. What subnet masks appear on each router for the route 192.168.64.0? What are the corresponding next-hop interfaces?

_____

_____

Examine the routing table on Westasman.

3.   Are any routes missing? If so, which ones?

_____

For all subnets to appear in the routing table, you must disable the default behavior of EIGRP that automatically summarizes routes.

Step 3

Disable the automatic summarization feature on EIGRP.

On each router, issue the following commands:

```
Westasman(config)#router eigrp 100
Westasman(config-router)#no auto-summary
```

After you issue these commands on all three routers, return to the SanJose1 router and type the **show ip route** command.

1.   Has anything changed in the SanJose1 routing table?

_____

Finally, to provide the most prescriptive routing updates, use the wildcard mask option for advertising networks in EIGRP. For a given classful network, you need to advertise all subnets with their exact subnet masks. You complete this through the wildcard mask. If just one subnet is advertised without the mask option, then all other subnets are advertised. To illustrate this on Westasman, enter the following commands:

```
Westasman(config)#router eigrp 100
Westasman(config-router)#no network 172.16.0.0
Westasman(config-router)#network 172.16.8.0 0.0.0.255
```

Now, enter **show ip route** on SanJose1:

```
SanJose1#show ip route

<output omitted>

Gateway of last resort is not set

D    192.168.72.0/24 [90/2297856] via 192.168.64.2, 00:02:27, Serial0/0
     172.16.0.0/24 is subnetted, 1 subnets
D       172.16.8.0 [90/2297856] via 192.168.64.2, 00:02:27, Serial0/0
     192.168.64.0/30 is subnetted, 2 subnets
C       192.168.64.0 is directly connected, Serial0/0
D       192.168.64.4 [90/2172416] via 192.168.1.2, 00:03:31, FastEthernet0/0
C    192.168.1.0/24 is directly connected, FastEthernet0/0
```

Next, enter the command **network 172.16.9.0** in EIGRP 100 configuration mode on Westasman. Then, enter **show ip route** again on SanJose1:

```
SanJose1#show ip route
<output omitted>

Gateway of last resort is not set

D    192.168.72.0/24 [90/2297856] via 192.168.64.2, 00:05:55, Serial0/0
     172.16.0.0/24 is subnetted, 8 subnets
D       172.16.12.0 [90/2297856] via 192.168.64.2, 00:00:06, Serial0/0
D       172.16.13.0 [90/2297856] via 192.168.64.2, 00:00:06, Serial0/0
D       172.16.14.0 [90/2297856] via 192.168.64.2, 00:00:06, Serial0/0
D       172.16.15.0 [90/2297856] via 192.168.64.2, 00:00:06, Serial0/0
D       172.16.8.0 [90/2297856] via 192.168.64.2, 00:05:55, Serial0/0
D       172.16.9.0 [90/2297856] via 192.168.64.2, 00:00:07, Serial0/0
D       172.16.10.0 [90/2297856] via 192.168.64.2, 00:00:07, Serial0/0
D       172.16.11.0 [90/2297856] via 192.168.64.2, 00:00:07, Serial0/0
     192.168.64.0/30 is subnetted, 2 subnets
C       192.168.64.0 is directly connected, Serial0/0
D       192.168.64.4 [90/2172416] via 192.168.1.2, 00:07:00, FastEthernet0/0
C    192.168.1.0/24 is directly connected, FastEthernet0/0
```

The wildcard mask option in EIGRP allows prescriptive subnet advertisements, as long as each advertised subnet has the mask applied in the configuration.

Before proceeding to Step 4, remove the **network 172.16.8.0 0.0.0.255** and **network 172.16.9.0** commands on Westasman and apply the **network 172.16.0.0** command.

Step 4

Now that auto summarization is disabled, the International Travel Agency's routers should build complete routing tables. Unfortunately, this means that the Westasman router is advertising eight routes that should be summarized for efficiency. Use the manual summarization feature of EIGRP to summarize these addresses.

The Westasman router should be advertising eight subnets:

- 172.16.8.0

- 172.16.9.0

- 172.16.10.0

- 172.16.11.0

- 172.16.12.0

- 172.16.13.0

- 172.16.14.0

- 172.16.15.0

The first 21 bits of these addresses are the same. Therefore, you can create a summary route for all subnets by using a /21 prefix, which is 255.255.248.0 in dotted decimal notation.

Because the Westasman router must advertise the summary route to the SanJose1 and SanJose2 routers, enter the following commands on the Westasman router:

```
Westasman(config)#interface s0/0
Westasman(config-if)#ip summary-address eigrp 100 172.16.8.0 255.255.248.0
Westasman(config-if)#interface s0/1
Westasman(config-if)#ip summary-address eigrp 100 172.16.8.0 255.255.248.0
```

These commands configure EIGRP to advertise summary routes for AS 100 through the serial 0/0 and 0/1 interfaces. Verify this configuration by issuing **show ip protocols**.

1. Which metric is the Westasman router using for its address summarization?

_____

After you verify manual address summarization on the Westasman router, check the routing tables on SanJose1 and SanJose2.

2. What has happened in the SanJose1 and SanJose2 routing tables since you looked at them in Step 3?

_____

From the SanJose1 or SanJosse2 router, verify that 192.168.72.1 can be pinged.

You should be able to ping 172.16.15.1 from the SanJose1 router.

3. Is there a route to 172.16.15.0 in the SanJose1 routing table? Explain.

_____

_____

Lab 5.8.1: EIGRP Challenge Lab

Estimated Time: 25 Minutes

Objective

In this lab, you configure an EIGRP network with Network Address Translation (NAT) and Dynamic Host Configuration Protocol (DHCP) services provided by the routers. You configure EIGRP interface address summarization to reduce the number of routes in the EIGRP routing tables. (See Figure 5-4.)

Figure 5-4   Configuring EIGRP with NAT

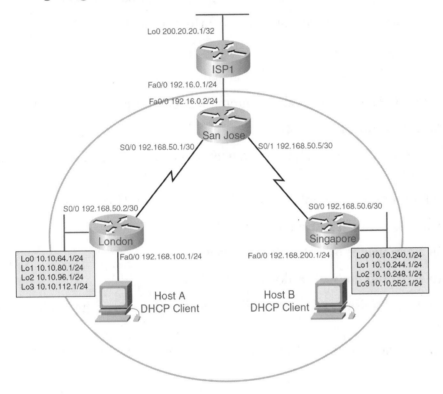

Equipment Requirements

This lab requires you to configure three routers, as shown in Figure 5-4. You cannot use Cisco 2500 series routers in this lab because they do not have Fast Ethernet interfaces.

Scenario

The International Travel Agency is currently running EIGRP between its overseas and North American headquarters. The ISP recently raised the price on the static IP addresses. To alleviate costs, you must implement address conservation technologies, such as NAT and DHCP. You also must implement interface address summarization to reduce routing table size. To simplify default routing procedures, SanJose should propagate a persistent default route to both overseas headquarters.

Design Considerations

Before you begin this lab, reload each router after you erase its startup configuration. This prevents problems that residual configurations might cause. Build and configure the network according to the diagram, but do not configure EIGRP until you have confirmed the connectivity between directly connected networks. The respective loopback addresses simulate local networks, so you do not need to make physical connections.

Implementation Requirements

To achieve a successful lab, the following requirements must be met:

- A successful ping must be made to every interface from every router.
- Advertise a persistent default route from SanJose through EIGRP.
- Configure NAT on SanJose.
- Configure DHCP service on the London and Singapore routers.
- Configure EIGRP interface address summarization on London and Singapore.

Implementation Completion Tests

The following are some commands that you can use to determine whether the goals of this lab were accomplished:

- Successful **pings** to the loopback interface of ISP1 from Host A and Host B
- **show run** and **show ip route** for each router
- **show ip eigrp neighbor** of the SanJose router
- **show ip eigrp topology all-links** of the SanJose router
- **show ip dhcp binding** and **show ip dhcp server statistics** of the London and Singapore routers
- **show ip nat translations** and **show ip nat statistics** of the SanJose router

Chapter 6

OSPF

Lab 6.9.1: Configuring OSPF

Estimated Time: 40 Minutes

Objective

In this lab, you configure OSPF on three Cisco routers, shown in the topology example in Figure 6-1. First, configure loopback interfaces to provide stable OSPF router IDs. Then, configure the OSPF process and enable OSPF on the appropriate interfaces. After OSPF is enabled, tune the update timers and configure authentication.

Figure 6-1   Configuring Basic OSPF

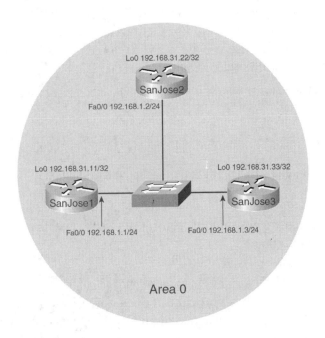

Equipment Requirements

To complete this lab, you need the following Cisco equipment:

- Three Cisco 2600 series routers

- One Cisco switch that has at least four ports

- Three Ethernet cables

Scenario

The backbone of the International Travel Agency (ITA) WAN, located in San Jose, consists of three routers connected using an Ethernet core. Configure these core routers as members of

OSPF Area 0. Because the core routers connect to the Internet, you need to implement security, preventing unauthorized routers from joining Area 0. Also, within the core, you must realize the network failures quickly.

Step 1

Make sure to load a clean IOS image on each router or manually erase any configurations on the routers before starting this lab.

Build and configure the network according to Figure 6-1, but do not configure OSPF yet. A switch or hub is required to connect the three routers through Ethernet.

Use **ping** to verify the work and test connectivity between the Fast Ethernet interfaces.

Step 2

On each router, configure a loopback interface with a unique IP address. Cisco routers use the highest loopback IP address as the OSPF router ID. In the absence of a loopback interface, the router uses the highest IP address among its active interfaces, which might force a router to change router IDs if an interface goes down. Because loopback interfaces are immune to physical and data link problems, you should use them to derive the router ID. To avoid conflicts with registered network addresses, use private network ranges for the loopback interfaces. Configure the core routers using the following commands:

```
SanJose1(config)#interface loopback 0
SanJose1(config-if)#ip address 192.168.31.11 255.255.255.255

SanJose2(config)#interface loopback 0
SanJose2(config-if)#ip address 192.168.31.22 255.255.255.255

SanJose3(config)#interface loopback 0
SanJose3(config-if)#ip address 192.168.31.33 255.255.255.255
```

Step 3

Now that loopback interfaces are configured, configure OSPF. Use the following commands as an example to configure each router:

```
SanJose1(config)#router ospf 1
SanJose1(config-router)#network 192.168.1.0 0.0.0.255 area 0
```

Note: An OSPF process ID is locally significant. It does not need to match neighboring routers. The ID is required to identify a unique instance of an OSPF database because multiple processes can run concurrently on a single router.

Step 4

After you enable OSPF routing on each of the three routers, verify its operation using **show** commands. You can use several important **show** commands to gather OSPF information. First, issue the **show ip protocols** command on any of the three routers, as follows:

```
SanJose1#show ip protocols
Routing Protocol is "ospf 1"
  Sending updates every 0 seconds
  Invalid after 0 seconds, hold down 0, flushed after 0
  Outgoing update filter list for all interfaces is
  Incoming update filter list for all interfaces is
  Redistributing: ospf 1
  Routing for Networks:
    192.168.1.0
  Routing Information Sources:
    Gateway          Distance      Last Update
```

```
   192.168.31.11          110        00:01:16
Distance: (default is 110)
```

Note: The update timers are set to 0. Updates are not sent at regular intervals. Updates are event driven.

Next, use the **show ip ospf** command, as follows, to get more details about the OSPF process, including the router ID:

```
SanJose1#show ip ospf
 Routing Process "ospf 1" with ID 192.168.31.11
 Supports only single TOS(TOS0) routes
 SPF schedule delay 5 secs, Hold time between two SPFs 10 secs
 Minimum LSA interval 5 secs. Minimum LSA arrival 1 secs
 Number of external LSA 0. Checksum Sum 0x0
 Number of DCbitless external LSA 0
 Number of DoNotAge external LSA 0
 Number of areas in this router is 1. 1 normal 0 stub 0 nssa
 External flood list length 0
    Area BACKBONE(0)
        Number of interfaces in this area is 1
        Area has no authentication
        SPF algorithm executed 5 times
        Area ranges are
        Number of LSA 4. Checksum Sum 0x1CAC4
        Number of DCbitless LSA 0
        Number of indication LSA 0
        Number of DoNotAge LSA 0
        Flood list length 0
```

1. What address is the router using as its router ID?

    192.168.31.33 (SanJose3) *I am*

The loopback interface should be seen as the router ID. To see the OSPF neighbors, use the **show ip ospf neighbor** command. The output of this command displays all known OSPF neighbors, including their router IDs, their interface addresses, and their adjacency status. Also, issue the **show ip ospf neighbor detail** command, which outputs even more information, as follows:

```
SanJose1#show ip ospf neighbor
Neighbor ID     Pri   State           Dead Time   Address         Interface
192.168.31.22    1    FULL/BDR        00:00:36    192.168.1.2 FastEthernet0/0
192.168.31.33    1    FULL/DR         00:00:33    192.168.1.3 FastEthernet0/0

SanJose1#show ip ospf neighbor detail
 Neighbor 192.168.31.22, interface address 192.168.1.2
    In the area 0 via interface FastEthernet0/0
    Neighbor priority is 1, State is FULL, 6 state changes
    DR is 192.168.1.3 BDR is 192.168.1.2
    Options 2
    Dead timer due in 00:00:34
    Index 2/2, retransmission queue length 0, number of
retransmission 2
    First 0x0(0)/0x0(0) Next 0x0(0)/0x0(0)
    Last retransmission scan length is 1, maximum is 1
    Last retransmission scan time is 0 msec, maximum is 0 msec
 Neighbor 192.168.31.33, interface address 192.168.1.3
    In the area 0 via interface FastEthernet0/0
    Neighbor priority is 1, State is FULL, 6 state changes
    DR is 192.168.1.3 BDR is 192.168.1.2
    Options 2
   Dead timer due in 00:00:30
    Index 1/1, retransmission queue length 0, number of
retransmission 1
    First 0x0(0)/0x0(0) Next 0x0(0)/0x0(0)
    Last retransmission scan length is 1, maximum is 1
    Last retransmission scan time is 0 msec, maximum is 0 msec
```

2. Based on the output of this command, which router is the designated router (DR) on this network?

192.168.1.3   San Jose 3 me

3. Which router is the backup designated router (BDR)?

192.168.1.2   San Jose 2

Most likely, the router with the highest router ID is the DR, the router with the second-highest router ID is the BDR, and the other router is a DROTHER.

Because you can connect each interface on a given router to a different network, some of the key OSPF information is interface specific. Issue the **show ip ospf interface** command for the Fast Ethernet interface on the router, as follows:

```
SanJose1#show ip ospf interface fa0/0
FastEthernet0/0 is up, line protocol is up
  Internet Address 192.168.1.1/24, Area 0
  Process ID 1, Router ID 192.168.31.11, Network Type BROADCAST,
Cost: 1
  Transmit Delay is 1 sec, State DROTHER, Priority 1
  Designated Router (ID) 192.168.31.33, Interface address
192.168.1.3
  Backup Designated router (ID) 192.168.31.22, Interface address
192.168.1.2
  Timer intervals configured, Hello 10, Dead 40, Wait 40,
Retransmit 5
    Hello due in 00:00:09
  Index 1/1, flood queue length 0
  Next 0x0(0)/0x0(0)
  Last flood scan length is 0, maximum is 1
  Last flood scan time is 0 msec, maximum is 0 msec
  Neighbor Count is 2, Adjacent neighbor count is 2
    Adjacent with neighbor 192.168.31.22  (Backup Designated
Router)
    Adjacent with neighbor 192.168.31.33  (Designated Router)
  Suppress hello for 0 neighbor(s)
```

4. Based on the output of this command, to which OSPF network type is the Ethernet interface on the router connected?

network Type: Broadcast

5. What is the Hello update timer set to?

Hello: 10

6. What is the Dead timer set to?

Dead: 40

Ethernet networks are known to OSPF as broadcast multiaccess networks. The default timer values are 10-second Hello updates and 40-second dead intervals.

Step 5

You decide to adjust the OSPF timers so that the core routers can detect network failures in less time. Doing so increases traffic, but this is less of a concern on the high-speed core Ethernet segment than on a busy WAN link. You also decide that the need for quick convergence at the core outweighs the extra traffic. Manually change the Hello and Dead intervals on SanJose1, as follows:

```
SanJose1(config)#interface fastethernet 0/0
SanJose1(config-if)#ip ospf hello-interval 5
SanJose1(config-if)#ip ospf dead-interval 20
```

These commands set the Hello update timer to 5 seconds and the Dead interval to 20 seconds. Although the Cisco IOS does not require it, configure the Dead interval to four times the Hello interval. This ensures that routers experiencing temporary link problems can recover and are not declared dead unnecessarily, causing a ripple of updates and recalculations throughout the internetwork.

After you change the timers on SanJose1, issue the **show ip ospf neighbor** command.

1. Does SanJose1 still show that it has OSPF neighbors?

No   Timer mismatch. no syncro.

To find out what happened to SanJose1's neighbors, use the IOS **debug** feature by entering the command **debug ip ospf events**, as follows:

```
SanJose1#debug ip ospf events
OSPF events debugging is on
SanJose1#
00:08:25: OSPF: Rcv hello from 192.168.31.22 area 0 from
FastEthernet0/0 192.168.1.2
00:08:25: OSPF: Mismatched hello parameters from 192.168.1.2
00:08:25: Dead R 40 C 20, Hello R 10 C 5  Mask R 255.255.255.0
C 255.255.255.0
SanJose1#
00:08:32: OSPF: Rcv hello from 192.168.31.33 area 0 from
FastEthernet0/0 192.168.1.3
00:08:32: OSPF: Mismatched hello parameters from 192.168.1.3
00:08:32: Dead R 40 C 20, Hello R 10 C 5  Mask R 255.255.255.0
C 255.255.255.0
```

Note: If you connect to SanJose1 with a Telnet session, use the **terminal monitor** command to see the **debug** output.

2. According to the **debug** output, what is preventing SanJose1 from forming relationships with the other two OSPF routers in Area 0?

mismatched hello parameter

The Hello and Dead intervals must be the same before routers within an area can form neighbor adjacencies.

Turn off **debug** using **undebug all**, or just **u all**:

```
SanJose1#undebug all
All possible debugging has been turned off
```

The Hello and Dead intervals are declared in Hello packet headers. For OSPF routers to establish a relationship, their Hello and Dead intervals must match.

Configure the SanJose2 and SanJose3 Hello and Dead timers to match the timers on SanJose1. Before continuing, check the OSPF neighbor table to verify that these routers can now communicate.

Step 6

Whether intentional or by accident, no unauthorized routers that are exchanging updates within Area 0 are wanted. This is accomplished by adding encrypted authentication to each OSPF packet header. Select message digest (MD5) authentication. This mode of authentication sends a message digest, or hash, in place of the password. You must configure OSPF neighbors with the same message digest key number, encryption type, and password to authenticate using the hash.

To configure a message digest password for SanJose1 to use on its Ethernet interface, use the following commands:

```
SanJose1(config)#interface fastethernet 0/0
SanJose1(config-if)#ip ospf message-digest-key 1 md5 itsasecret
SanJose1(config-if)#router ospf 1
SanJose1(config-router)#area 0 authentication message-digest
```

After entering these commands, wait 20 seconds, and then issue the **show ip ospf neighbor** command on SanJose1.

1.   Does SanJose1 still show that it has OSPF neighbors?

NO... yet; other router need to put same pwd

Use the **debug ip ospf events** command to determine why SanJose1 does not see its neighbors:

```
SanJose1#debug ip ospf events
OSPF events debugging is on
SanJose1#
00:49:32: OSPF: Send with youngest Key 1
SanJose1#
00:49:33: OSPF: Rcv pkt from 192.168.31.33, FastEthernet0/0 :
Mismatch Authentication type. Input packet specified type
0, we use type 2
00:49:33: OSPF: Rcv pkt from 192.168.31.22, FastEthernet0/0 :
Mismatch Authentication type. Input packet specified type, we use type 2
SanJose1#u all
All possible debugging has been turned off
```

Again, OSPF routers do not communicate unless certain configurations match. In this case, the routers are not communicating because the authentication fields in the OSPF packet header are different.

Correct this problem by configuring authentication on the other two routers. Remember that you must use the same key number, encryption type, and password on each router.

After you complete the configurations, verify that the routers can communicate by using the **show ip ospf neighbors** command:

```
SanJose1#show ip ospf neighbors
Neighbor ID       Pri   State        Dead Time    Address
Interface
192.168.31.33      1    FULL/DR      00:00:16     192.168.1.3
FastEthernet0/0
192.168.31.22      1    FULL/BDR     00:00:15     192.168.1.2
FastEthernet0/0
```

Step 7

Save the configuration files for each router. You will use these configurations to begin the next lab. At the conclusion of each lab, copy the configuration file for each router and save it for future reference.

Lab 6.9.2a: Examining the DR/BDR Election Process

Estimated Time: 30 Minutes

Objective

In this lab, observe the OSPF DR and BDR election processing, for the topology shown in Figure 6-2, using **debug** commands. Then, assign each OSPF interface a priority value to force the election of a specific router as a DR.

Figure 6-2   Examining the DR and BDR Election Process

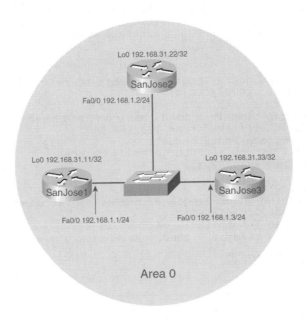

Equipment Requirements

To complete this lab, you need the following Cisco equipment:

- Three Cisco 2600 series routers
- One Cisco switch that has at least four ports
- Three Ethernet cables

Scenario

The backbone of the International Travel Agency enterprise network consists of three routers connected using an Ethernet core. SanJose1 has more memory and processing power than the other core routers. Unfortunately, other core routers are continually elected as the DR under the default settings. In the interest of optimization, ensure that SanJose1 is elected as the DR because it is best suited to handle associated extra duties, including management of link-state advertisements (LSAs) for Area 0. Investigate and correct this situation.

Step 1

Build and configure the network according to Figure 6-2. Use the configuration files from the previous lab if they are available. Configure OSPF on all Ethernet interfaces. You need a switch or a hub to connect the three routers through Ethernet. Be sure to configure each router with the loopback interface and IP address shown in Figure 6-2.

Use **ping** to verify the work and test connectivity between the Ethernet interfaces.

Step 2

Use the **show ip ospf neighbor detail** command as follows to verify that the OSPF routers have formed adjacencies:

Note: The routers are still using authentication for the previous lab setup.

```
SanJose3#show ip ospf neighbor detail
 Neighbor 192.168.31.11, interface address 192.168.1.1
    In the area 0 via interface FastEthernet0/0
    Neighbor priority is 1, State is FULL, 12 state changes
    DR is 192.168.1.3 BDR is 192.168.1.2
    Options 2
    Dead timer due in 00:00:17
    Index 2/2, retransmission queue length 0, number of retransmission 1
    First 0x0(0)/0x0(0) Next 0x0(0)/0x0(0)
    Last retransmission scan length is 1, maximum is 1
    Last retransmission scan time is 0 msec, maximum is 0 msec
 Neighbor 192.168.31.22, interface address 192.168.1.2
    In the area 0 via interface FastEthernet0/0
    Neighbor priority is 1, State is FULL, 6 state changes
    DR is 192.168.1.3 BDR is 192.168.1.2
    Options 2
    Dead timer due in 00:00:15
    Index 1/1, retransmission queue length 0, number of retransmission 5
    First 0x0(0)/0x0(0) Next 0x0(0)/0x0(0)
    Last retransmission scan length is 1, maximum is 1
    Last retransmission scan time is 0 msec, maximum is 0 msec
```

1.   Which router is the DR? Why?

   1.3   router IP is highest.

_____

2.   Which router is the BDR? Why?

   1.2   "   "   " is 2nd highest.

_____

Recall that router IDs determine the DR and BDR.

Step 3

If the network is configured according to Figure 6-2, SanJose1 will not be the DR. Temporarily shut down the Fast Ethernet interface on SanJose3, which has the highest router ID, 192.168.31.33, and observe the DR/BDR election process. To observe the election, issue the following **debug** command on SanJose1:

```
SanJose1#debug ip ospf adj
```

Now that OSPF adjacency events will be logged to SanJose1 console, remove SanJose3 from the OSPF network by shutting down its Fast Ethernet interface as follows:

```
SanJose3(config)#interface fastethernet 0/0
SanJose3(config-if)#shutdown
```

```
Watch the debug output on SanJose1:
SanJose1#
00:48:47: OSPF: Rcv hello from 192.168.31.22 area 0 from
FastEthernet0/0 192.168.1.2
00:48:47: OSPF: Neighbor change Event on interface FastEthernet0/0
00:48:47: OSPF: DR/BDR election on FastEthernet0/0
```

```
00:48:47: OSPF: Elect BDR 192.168.31.11
00:48:47: OSPF: Elect DR 192.168.31.22
00:48:47: OSPF: Elect BDR 192.168.31.11
00:48:47: OSPF: Elect DR 192.168.31.22
00:48:47:       DR: 192.168.31.22 (Id)   BDR: 192.168.31.11 (Id)
00:48:47: OSPF: Remember old DR 192.168.31.33 (id)
00:48:47: OSPF: End of hello processing
```

1.   Who is elected DR? Why?

SJ2,   SJ 2 is higher than SJ1.

The former BDR is promoted to DR.

In the **debug** output, look for a statement about remembering the "old DR." Unless SanJose1 and SanJose2 are powered off, they will remember that SanJose3 was the old DR. When SanJose3 comes back online, these routers will allow SanJose3 to reassume its role as DR:

```
SanJose1#
00:51:32: OSPF: Rcv hello from 192.168.31.22 area 0 from
FastEthernet0/0 192.168.1.2
00:51:32: OSPF: End of hello processing
00:51:33: OSPF: Rcv hello from 192.168.31.33 area 0 from
FastEthernet0/0 192.168.1.3
00:51:33: OSPF: 2 Way Communication to 192.168.31.33 on
FastEthernet0/0, state 2WAY
00:51:33: OSPF: Neighbor change Event on interface FastEthernet0/0
00:51:33: OSPF: DR/BDR election on FastEthernet0/0
00:51:33: OSPF: Elect BDR 192.168.31.11
00:51:33: OSPF: Elect DR 192.168.31.33
00:51:33:       DR: 192.168.31.33 (Id)   BDR: 192.168.31.11 (Id)
00:51:33: OSPF: Send DBD to 192.168.31.33 on FastEthernet0/0 seq
0x21CF opt 0x2 flag 0x7 len 32
00:51:33: OSPF: Send with youngest Key 1
00:51:33: OSPF: Remember old DR 192.168.31.22 (id)
00:51:33: OSPF: End of hello processing
```

Step 4

At this point, SanJose1 should have assumed the role of BDR. Bring SanJose3 back online, and observe the new election process.

1.   SanJose3 assumes its former role as DR. Who is elected BDR? Why?

BDR is SJ1   192.168.1.1,   BDR dosen't loose

SanJose1 remains the BDR even though SanJose2 has the higher router ID.   _its appointment after elected .(when I went down)._

Step 5   _Manual: DR_

You can manipulate a router to become the DR by using two methods. You can change the router ID to a higher number, but that might confuse the loopback addressing system and affect elections on other interfaces. The same router ID is used for every network of which a router is a member. For example, if an OSPF router has an exceptionally high router ID, it could win the election on every multiaccess interface and, as a result, do triple or quadruple duty as a DR.

Instead of reconfiguring router IDs, manipulate the election by configuring OSPF priority values. Because priorities are interface-specific values, they provide finer control of the OSPF internetwork by allowing a router to be the DR in one network and a DROTHER in another. Priority values are the first consideration in the DR election, with the highest priority winning. Values can range from 0 to 255. A value of 0 indicates that the interface will not participate in an election. Use the **show ip ospf interface** command as follows to examine the current priority values of the Ethernet interfaces on the three routers:

```
SanJose1#show ip ospf interface
FastEthernet0/0 is up, line protocol is up
  Internet Address 192.168.1.1/24, Area 0
  Process ID 1, Router ID 192.168.31.11, Network Type BROADCAST, Cost: 1
  Transmit Delay is 1 sec, State BDR, Priority 1
  Designated Router (ID) 192.168.31.33, Interface address 192.168.1.3
  Backup Designated router (ID) 192.168.31.11, Interface address 192.168.1.1
  Timer intervals configured, Hello 5, Dead 20, Wait 20, Retransmit 5
    Hello due in 00:00:03
  Index 1/1, flood queue length 0
  Next 0x0(0)/0x0(0)
  Last flood scan length is 1, maximum is 2
  Last flood scan time is 0 msec, maximum is 0 msec
  Neighbor Count is 2, Adjacent neighbor count is 2
    Adjacent with neighbor 192.168.31.33   (Designated Router)
    Adjacent with neighbor 192.168.31.22
  Suppress hello for 0 neighbor(s)
  Message digest authentication enabled
    Youngest key id is 1
```

1.   What is the priority value of these interfaces?

_____ Priority 1 _____

The default priority is 1. Because all have equal priority, the router ID determines the DR and BDR.

Modify the priority values so that SanJose1 becomes the DR and SanJose2 becomes the BDR, regardless of their router ID. Use the following commands:

```
SanJose1(config)#interface fastethernet 0/0
SanJose1(config-if)#ip ospf priority 200
SanJose2(config)#interface fastethernet 0/0
SanJose2(config-if)#ip ospf priority 100
```

To reset the election process, write the configuration for each router to NVRAM and reload SanJose1, SanJose2, and SanJose3. Issue the following commands at each router:

```
SanJose1#copy running-config startup-config
SanJose1#reload
```
No router ospf 1   (to simulate the reload)

When the routers finish reloading, try to observe the OSPF election on SanJose1 by using the **debug ip ospf adj** command. Also, verify the configuration by issuing the **show ip ospf interface** command at both SanJose1 and SanJose2:

```
SanJose1#debug ip ospf adj
00:01:20: OSPF: Rcv hello from 192.168.31.22 area 0 from
FastEthernet0/0 192.168.1.2
00:01:20: OSPF: Neighbor change Event on interface FastEthernet0/0
00:01:20: OSPF: DR/BDR election on FastEthernet0/0
00:01:20: OSPF: Elect BDR 192.168.31.22
00:01:20: OSPF: Elect DR 192.168.31.11
00:01:20:       DR: 192.168.31.11 (Id)   BDR: 192.168.31.22 (Id)
00:01:20: OSPF: End of hello processing

SanJose2#show ip ospf interface
FastEthernet0/0 is up, line protocol is up
  Internet Address 192.168.1.2/24, Area 0
  Process ID 1, Router ID 192.168.31.22, Network Type BROADCAST, Cost: 1
  Transmit Delay is 1 sec, State BDR, Priority 100
  Designated Router (ID) 192.168.31.11, Interface address 192.168.1.1
  Backup Designated router (ID) 192.168.31.22, Interface address 192.168.1.2
  Timer intervals configured, Hello 5, Dead 20, Wait 20,
Retransmit 5
```

```
   Hello due in 00:00:03
Index 1/1, flood queue length 0
Next 0x0(0)/0x0(0)
Last flood scan length is 1, maximum is 1
Last flood scan time is 0 msec, maximum is 0 msec
Neighbor Count is 2, Adjacent neighbor count is 2
   Adjacent with neighbor 192.168.31.33
   Adjacent with neighbor 192.168.31.11   (Designated Router)
Suppress hello for 0 neighbor(s)
Message digest authentication enabled
   Youngest key id is 1
```

After the election is complete, verify that SanJose1 and SanJose2 have assumed the correct roles by using the **show ip ospf neighbor detail** command. Troubleshoot if necessary:

```
SanJose3#show ip ospf neighbor detail
Neighbor 192.168.31.22, interface address 192.168.1.2
   In the area 0 via interface FastEthernet0/0
   Neighbor priority is 100, State is FULL, 6 state changes
   DR is 192.168.1.1 BDR is 192.168.1.2
   Options 2
   Dead timer due in 00:00:17
   Index 2/2, retransmission queue length 0, number of retransmission 0
   First 0x0(0)/0x0(0) Next 0x0(0)/0x0(0)
   Last retransmission scan length is 0, maximum is 0
   Last retransmission scan time is 0 msec, maximum is 0 msec
Neighbor 192.168.31.11, interface address 192.168.1.1
   In the area 0 via interface FastEthernet0/0
   Neighbor priority is 200, State is FULL, 6 state changes
   DR is 192.168.1.1 BDR is 192.168.1.2
   Options 2
   Dead timer due in 00:00:19
   Index 1/1, retransmission queue length 0, number of retransmission 2
   First 0x0(0)/0x0(0) Next 0x0(0)/0x0(0)
   Last retransmission scan length is 1, maximum is 1
   Last retransmission scan time is 0 msec, maximum is 0 msec
```

Note that the order in which routers join an area can have the most significant effect on which routers are elected as DR and BDR. An election is necessary only when a DR or BDR does not exist in the network. As a router starts its OSPF process, it checks the network for an active DR and BDR. If they exist, the new router becomes a DROTHER, regardless of its priority or router ID. Remember: The roles of DR and BDR were created for efficiency. New routers in the network should not force an election when adjacencies are already optimized. However, there is an exception: A known bug in some IOS versions allows a "new" router with higher election credentials to force an election and assume the role of DR.

Lab 6.9.2b: Configuring Point-to-Multipoint OSPF over Frame Relay

Estimated Time: 45 Minutes

Objective

In this lab, configure OSPF as a point-to-multipoint network type so that it operates efficiently over a hub-and-spoke Frame Relay topology. For this lab, assemble a router topology as shown in Figure 6-3, or as an alternative, use the sample topology shown in Figure 6-4. In Figure 6-3, the routers connect to an Adtran Atlas 550 to simulate the Frame Relay connection. For Figure 6-4, the routers connect to each other via serial interfaces and use a router configured as a Frame Relay switch to simulate the Frame Relay connection.

Figure 6-3 **Configuring Point-to-Multipoint OSPF over Frame Relay with an Adtran Atlas 550**

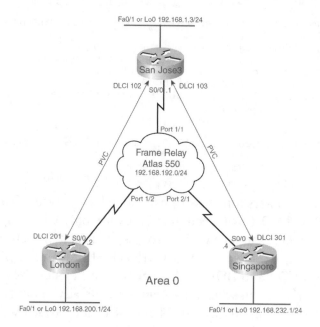

Equipment Requirements

To complete this lab, you need the following Cisco equipment:

- Four Cisco 2600 series routers or three Cisco 2600 routers and an one Adtran Atlas 550 Frame Relay emulator

- Three serial cables

Figure 6-4 **Configuring Point-to-Multipoint OSPF over Frame Relay with a Frame Relay Switch**

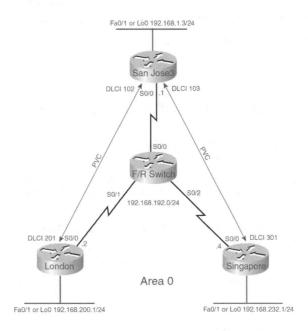

Scenario

The International Travel Agency has connected two regional headquarters to San Jose using Frame Relay in a hub-and-spoke topology. You are to configure OSPF routing over this type of network, which is known for introducing complications into OSPF adjacency relationships. To avoid these complications, manually override the nonbroadcast multiaccess (NBMA) OSPF network type and configure OSPF to run as a point-to-multipoint network. In this environment, no DR or BDR is elected.

Step 1

Cable the network according to Figure 6-3 or Figure 6-4. Configure the Fast Ethernet or Loopback interface for each router as shown, but leave the serial interfaces and OSPF routing unconfigured for now. Before proceeding to Step 2, load a fresh IOS image on the San Jose, London, and Singapore routers. No configuration should be set for any of the interfaces; erase any configurations that are currently on the routers.

Until you configure Frame Relay, **ping** is not useful for testing connectivity.

Note: This lab requires another router or device to act as a Frame Relay switch. Figure 6-3 assumes that an Adtran Atlas 550 will be used, which is preconfigured. Figure 6-4 assumes that a router will be configured with at least three serial interfaces as a Frame Relay switch. See the configuration at the end of this lab for an example of how to configure a router as a Frame Relay switch. If desired, copy the configuration to a 2600 router for use in this lab.

The Adtran Atlas 550 has a fixed internal configuration that is used for all CCNP 1-4 Version 3.0 labs. The Atlas Frame Relay configuration implements a full mesh topology. To implement a hub-and-spoke topology for this lab, both Frame Relay maps on London reference DLCI 201.

Similarly, both Frame Relay maps on Singapore reference DLCI 301. DLCI 201 on London and DLCI 301 on Singapore cause the Atlas to switch frames to the hub router, SanJose3. Using Frame Relay maps on the spoke routers automatically disables Frame Relay inverse ARP on the serial interfaces, thus preventing inadvertent dynamic Frame Relay maps from being formed directly between the spoke routers (which would circumvent the hub router).

Step 2

SanJose3 acts as the hub in this hub-and-spoke network. It reaches London and Singapore through two separate PVCs. Configure Frame Relay on SanJose3's serial interface, as follows:

```
SanJose3(config)#interface serial 0/0
SanJose3(config-if)#encapsulation frame-relay
SanJose3(config-if)#ip address 192.168.192.1 255.255.255.0
SanJose3(config-if)#no shutdown
SanJose3(config-if)#frame-relay map ip 192.168.192.2 102 broadcast
SanJose3(config-if)#frame-relay map ip 192.168.192.4 103 broadcast
SanJose3(config-if)#ip ospf network point-to-multipoint
```

Notice that this configuration includes **frame-relay map** commands, which are also used on multipoint Frame Relay subinterfaces. These commands are used here with the **broadcast** keyword so that Frame Relay can process broadcast traffic. Without this configuration, OSPF multicast traffic would not be forwarded correctly by the SanJose3 router.

Configure the serial interface for London as follows:

```
London(config)#interface serial 0/0
London(config-if)#encapsulation frame-relay
London(config-if)#ip address 192.168.192.2 255.255.255.0
London(config-if)#no shutdown
London(config-if)#frame-relay map ip 192.168.192.1 201 broadcast
London(config-if)#frame-relay map ip 192.168.192.4 201 broadcast
London(config-if)#ip ospf network point-to-multipoint
```

Finally, configure the serial interface for Singapore as follows:

```
Singapore(config)#interface serial 0/0
Singapore(config-if)#encapsulation frame-relay
Singapore(config-if)#ip address 192.168.192.4 255.255.255.0
Singapore(config-if)#no shutdown
Singapore(config-if)#frame-relay map ip 192.168.192.1 301 broadcast
Singapore(config-if)#frame-relay map ip 192.168.192.2 301 broadcast
Singapore(config-if)#ip ospf network point-to-multipoint
```

Verify Frame Relay operation with a **ping** command from each router to the other two. Use **show frame-relay pvc** and **show frame-relay map** to troubleshoot connectivity problems. Rebooting the Frame Relay switch might also solve connectivity issues:

```
SanJose3#show frame-relay pvc

PVC Statistics for interface Serial0/0 (Frame Relay DTE)

              Active      Inactive      Deleted       Static
  Local         2            0             0            0
  Switched      0            0             0            0
  Unused        0            1             0            0

DLCI = 102, DLCI USAGE = LOCAL, PVC STATUS = ACTIVE, INTERFACE = Serial0/0

  input pkts 111          output pkts 112         in bytes 10936
  out bytes 6259          dropped pkts 0          in pkts dropped 0
  out pkts dropped 0           out bytes dropped 0
  in FECN pkts 0          in BECN pkts 0          out FECN pkts 0
  out BECN pkts 0         in DE pkts 0            out DE pkts 0
  out bcast pkts 19       out bcast bytes 1428
  pvc create time 00:10:58, last time pvc status changed 00:08:38
```

```
DLCI = 103, DLCI USAGE = LOCAL, PVC STATUS = ACTIVE, INTERFACE = Serial0/0

  input pkts 65           output pkts 56          in bytes 5136
  out bytes 3752          dropped pkts 0          in pkts dropped 0
  out pkts dropped 0           out bytes dropped 0
  in FECN pkts 0          in BECN pkts 0          out FECN pkts 0
  out BECN pkts 0         in DE pkts 0            out DE pkts 0
  out bcast pkts 19       out bcast bytes 1428
  pvc create time 00:11:01, last time pvc status changed 00:08:41

DLCI = 104, DLCI USAGE = UNUSED, PVC STATUS = INACTIVE, INTERFACE = Serial0/0

  input pkts 0            output pkts 0           in bytes 0
  out bytes 0             dropped pkts 0          in pkts dropped 0
  out pkts dropped 0           out bytes dropped 0
  in FECN pkts 0          in BECN pkts 0          out FECN pkts 0
  out BECN pkts 0         in DE pkts 0            out DE pkts 0
  out bcast pkts 0        out bcast bytes 0
  switched pkts 0
  Detailed packet drop counters:
  no out intf 0           out intf down 0         no out PVC 0
  in PVC down 0           out PVC down 0          pkt too big 0
  shaping Q full 0        pkt above DE 0          policing drop 0
  pvc create time 00:10:22, last time pvc status changed 00:09:49

SanJose3#show frame-relay map
Serial0/0 (up): ip 192.168.192.2 dlci 102(0x66,0x1860), static,
          broadcast,
          CISCO, status defined, active
Serial0/0 (up): ip 192.168.192.4 dlci 103(0x67,0x1870), static,
          broadcast,
          CISCO, status defined, active
```

Step 3

Configure OSPF to run over this point-to-multipoint network. Issue the following commands at the appropriate router:

```
London(config)#router ospf 1
London(config-router)#network 192.168.200.0 0.0.0.255 area 0
London(config-router)#network 192.168.192.0 0.0.0.255 area 0

SanJose3(config)#router ospf 1
SanJose3(config-router)#network 192.168.1.0 0.0.0.255 area 0
SanJose3(config-router)#network 192.168.192 0.0.0.255 area 0

Singapore(config)#router ospf 1
Singapore(config-router)#network 192.168.232.0 0.0.0.255 area 0
Singapore(config-router)#network 192.168.192.0 0.0.0.255 area 0
```

Verify the OSPF configuration by issuing the **show ip route** command at each of the routers:

```
London#show ip route
Codes: C - connected, S - static, I - IGRP, R - RIP, M - mobile, B - BGP
       D - EIGRP, EX - EIGRP external, O - OSPF, IA - OSPF inter area
       N1 - OSPF NSSA external type 1, N2 - OSPF NSSA external type 2
       E1 - OSPF external type 1, E2 - OSPF external type 2, E - EGP
       i - IS-IS, L1 - IS-IS level-1, L2 - IS-IS level-2, ia - IS-IS inter area
       * - candidate default, U - per-user static route, o - ODR
       P - periodic downloaded static route

Gateway of last resort is not set

     192.168.192.0/24 is variably subnetted, 3 subnets, 2 masks
C       192.168.192.0/24 is directly connected, Serial0/0
O       192.168.192.1/32 [110/781] via 192.168.192.1, 00:10:04, Serial0/0
O       192.168.192.4/32 [110/845] via 192.168.192.1, 00:10:04, Serial0/0
C    192.168.200.0/24 is directly connected, Loopback0
     192.168.232.0/32 is subnetted, 1 subnets
O       192.168.232.1 [110/846] via 192.168.192.1, 00:10:04, Serial0/0
     192.168.1.0/32 is subnetted, 1 subnets
O       192.168.1.3 [110/782] via 192.168.192.1, 00:10:04, Serial0/0
```

If each router has a complete table—including routes to 192.168.1.0 /24, 192.168.200.0 /24, and 192.168.232.0 /24—OSPF has been successfully configured to operate over Frame Relay.

Test these routes by pinging the Fast Ethernet interfaces of each router from London's console.

Finally, issue the **show ip ospf neighbor detail** command at any router console:

```
SanJose3#show ip ospf neighbor

Neighbor ID      Pri  State        Dead Time   Address        Interface
192.168.200.1     1   FULL/  -     00:01:39    192.168.192.2  Serial0/0
192.168.232.1     1   FULL/  -     00:01:36    192.168.192.4  Serial0/0

SanJose3#show ip ospf neighbor detail
 Neighbor 192.168.200.1, interface address 192.168.192.2
    In the area 0 via interface Serial0/0
    Neighbor priority is 1, State is FULL, 6 state changes
    DR is 0.0.0.0 BDR is 0.0.0.0
    Options is 0x42
    Dead timer due in 00:01:49
    Neighbor is up for 00:12:25
    Index 2/2, retransmission queue length 0, number of retransmission 1
    First 0x0(0)/0x0(0) Next 0x0(0)/0x0(0)
    Last retransmission scan length is 1, maximum is 1
    Last retransmission scan time is 0 msec, maximum is 0 msec
 Neighbor 192.168.232.1, interface address 192.168.192.4
    In the area 0 via interface Serial0/0
    Neighbor priority is 1, State is FULL, 6 state changes
    DR is 0.0.0.0 BDR is 0.0.0.0
    Options is 0x42
    Dead timer due in 00:01:46
    Neighbor is up for 00:12:25
    Index 1/1, retransmission queue length 0, number of retransmission 1
    First 0x0(0)/0x0(0) Next 0x0(0)/0x0(0)
    Last retransmission scan length is 1, maximum is 1
    Last retransmission scan time is 0 msec, maximum is 0 msec
```

1.   Is there a DR for this network? Why or why not?

There is no DR. The configuration of OSPF point-to-multipoint network type on serial interfaces creates a logical multiaccess network over physical point-to-point links. No efficiency would be realized by electing a DR.

Router as Frame Relay Switch Configuration

You can use the following example to configure a router as the Frame Relay switch:

```
Frame-Switch#show run
version 12.0
service timestamps debug uptime
service timestamps log uptime
no service password-encryption
!
hostname Frame-Switch
!
ip subnet-zero
no ip domain-lookup
!
ip audit notify log
ip audit po max-events 100
frame-relay switching
!
process-max-time 200
!
interface Serial0/0
 no ip address
 no ip directed-broadcast
```

```
 encapsulation frame-relay
 clockrate 56000
 cdp enable
 frame-relay intf-type dce
 frame-relay route 103 interface Serial0/2 301
 frame-relay route 102 interface Serial0/1 201
!
interface Serial0/1
  no ip address
 no ip directed-broadcast
 encapsulation frame-relay
 clockrate 56000
 cdp enable
 frame-relay intf-type dce
 frame-relay route 201 interface Serial0/0 102
!
interface Serial0/2
 no ip address
 no ip directed-broadcast
 encapsulation frame-relay
 clockrate 56000
 cdp enable
  frame-relay intf-type dce
 frame-relay route 301 interface Serial0/0 103
!
interface Serial0/3
 no ip address
 no ip directed-broadcast
 shutdown
!
ip classless
no ip http server
!
line con 0
 password cisco
 login
 transport input none
line aux 0
line vty 0 4
 password cisco
 login
!
no scheduler allocate
end
```

Lab 6.9.3: Configuring Multiarea OSPF

Estimated Time: 60 Minutes

Objective

In this lab, configure a multiarea OSPF operation, interarea summarization, external route summarization, and default routing for the network scenario shown in Figure 6-5.

Figure 6-5   Multiarea OSPF Scenario

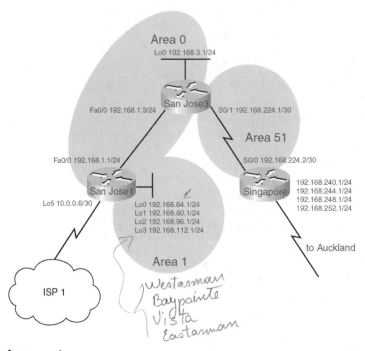

Equipment Requirements

To complete this lab, you need the following Cisco equipment:

* Three Cisco 2600 series routers

* One serial cable

* One Ethernet cable

Scenario

The International Travel Agency (ITA) maintains a complex OSPF environment. The task is to optimize OSPF routing, which creates the need to design and configure multiarea OSPF on the key routers that connect Asian regional headquarters to San Jose corporate headquarters and its local sites.

Step 1

Build and configure the network according to Figure 6-5, but do not configure a routing protocol yet. Before proceeding to Step 2, load a fresh IOS image on both San Jose and Singapore routers. No configuration should be set for any of the interfaces; erase any configurations that are currently on the routers.

Note: Ignore the ISP1 cloud for now. Also, the Singapore-to-Auckland networks 192.168.240.0/24, 192.168.244.0/244, 192.168.248.0/24, and 192.168.252.0/24 will be configured as static routes to Null0 in Steps 5 and 6, so defer those until then.

Configure each router with the loopback address indicated in Figure 6-5. Be sure to configure SanJose1 with additional loopbacks of Lo0, Lo1, Lo2, and Lo3. These loopback interfaces simulate the serial links to local San Jose sites: Westasman, Baypointe, Vista, and Eastasman.

Use **ping** to test connectivity between all interfaces. Each router should be able to ping its link partner.

Step 2

Configure multiarea OSPF. On SanJose1, configure Fast Ethernet 0/0 as a member of Area 0 and all other interfaces as members of Area 1 by using the following commands:

```
SanJose1(config)#router ospf 1
SanJose1(config-router)#network 192.168.1.0 0.0.0.255 area 0
SanJose1(config-router)#network 192.168.64.0 0.0.63.255 area 1
```

The last command conveniently enables all loopback interfaces on SanJose1 to participate in the OSPF process.

On SanJose3, configure E0 and Lo0 as members of Area 0, but configure Serial 0/0 as part of Area 51, as follows:

```
SanJose3(config)#router ospf 1
SanJose3(config-router)#network 192.168.1.0 0.0.0.255 area 0
SanJose3(config-router)#network 192.168.224.0 0.0.0.3 area 51
SanJose3(config-router)#network 192.168.3.0 0.0.0.255 area 0
```

Finally, on Singapore, configure Serial 0/0 to belong to Area 51, as follows:

```
Singapore(config)#router ospf 1
Singapore(config-router)#network 192.168.224.0 0.0.0.3 area 51
```

Issue the **show ip ospf** command on all three routers:

```
SanJose3#show ip ospf
 Routing Process "ospf 1" with ID 192.168.3.1
 Supports only single TOS(TOS0) routes
 It is an area border router
 SPF schedule delay 5 secs, Hold time between two SPFs 10 secs
 Minimum LSA interval 5 secs. Minimum LSA arrival 1 secs
 Number of external LSA 0. Checksum Sum 0x0
 Number of DCbitless external LSA 0
 Number of DoNotAge external LSA 0
 Number of areas in this router is 2. 2 normal 0 stub 0 nssa
 External flood list length 0
    Area BACKBONE(0)
        Number of interfaces in this area is 2
        Area has no authentication
        SPF algorithm executed 6 times
        Area ranges are
        Number of LSA 8. Checksum Sum 0x42B0C
        Number of DCbitless LSA 0
        Number of indication LSA 0
        Number of DoNotAge LSA 0
        Flood list length 0
    Area 51
        Number of interfaces in this area is 1
        Area has no authentication
        SPF algorithm executed 4 times
        Area ranges are
```

```
Number of LSA 8. Checksum Sum 0x59B4F
Number of DCbitless LSA 0
Number of indication LSA 0
Number of DoNotAge LSA 0
Flood list length 0
```

1. According to the output of the **show ip ospf** command, which of these routers is an area border router (ABR)?

    SJ3

ABRs connect one or more adjacent OSPF areas to the backbone area.

2. Are there autonomous system border routers (ASBRs)?

    NO, external protocol.

ASBRs connect external, non-OSPF networks to the OSPF internetwork.

Issue the **show ip ospf neighbor detail** command on SanJose3:

```
SanJose3#show ip ospf neighbor detail
 Neighbor 192.168.112.1, interface address 192.168.1.1
    In the area 0 via interface FastEthernet0/0
    Neighbor priority is 1, State is FULL, 6 state changes
    DR is 192.168.1.1 BDR is 192.168.1.3
    Options 2
    Dead timer due in 00:00:33
    Index 1/1, retransmission queue length 0, number of retransmission 2
    First 0x0(0)/0x0(0) Next 0x0(0)/0x0(0)
    Last retransmission scan length is 1, maximum is 1
    Last retransmission scan time is 0 msec, maximum is 0 msec
 Neighbor 192.168.252.1, interface address 192.168.224.2
    In the area 51 via interface Serial0/0
    Neighbor priority is 1, State is FULL, 6 state changes
    DR is 0.0.0.0 BDR is 0.0.0.0
    Options 2
    Dead timer due in 00:00:32
    Index 1/2, retransmission queue length 0, number of retransmission 1
    First 0x0(0)/0x0(0) Next 0x0(0)/0x0(0)
    Last retransmission scan length is 1, maximum is 1
    Last retransmission scan time is 0 msec, maximum is 0 msec
```

3. Is there a DR election on the 192.168.1.0/24 network? *(SJ1)* Why or why not?

    DR is 192.168.1.1   BDR is 192.168.1.3.

    'cause loopback (in SJ1) has preference over physical int's

---

4. Is there a DR election on the 192.168.224.0/30 *Singapore* network? Why or why not?

    NO,

    point-to-point. No multi access broadcast segment

These are different types of OSPF networks. The Ethernet core network is designated as broadcast, and the WAN link between SanJose3 and Singapore is designated as point-to-point. On a point-to-point link, you do not need to elect a DR to reduce the number of adjacencies because only two routers exist in the network. The Ethernet segment has only two routers. However, a DR and BDR are elected because neighbor routers could join the area.

Ethernet core net is broadcast
Wan Link SJ3 - Singapore is p-to-p

Step 3

Check the routing table on each router. The output should show OSPF interarea routes, which are denoted by an O, and other routes denoted by an IA:

```
Singapore#show ip route
Codes: C - connected, S - static, I - IGRP, R - RIP, M - mobile,
B - BGP
       D - EIGRP, EX - EIGRP external, O - OSPF, IA - OSPF inter area
       N1 - OSPF NSSA external type 1, N2 - OSPF NSSA external type 2
       E1 - OSPF external type 1, E2 - OSPF external type 2, E - EGP
       i - IS-IS, L1 - IS-IS level-1, L2 - IS-IS level-2, ia -
IS-IS inter area
       * - candidate default, U - per-user static route, o - ODR
       P - periodic downloaded static route
Gateway of last resort is not set
     192.168.224.0/30 is subnetted, 1 subnets
C       192.168.224.0 is directly connected, Serial0/0
     192.168.64.0/32 is subnetted, 1 subnets
O IA    192.168.64.1 [110/783] via 192.168.224.1, 00:00:28, Serial0/0
     192.168.80.0/32 is subnetted, 1 subnets
O IA    192.168.80.1 [110/783] via 192.168.224.1, 00:00:28, Serial0/0
     192.168.96.0/32 is subnetted, 1 subnets
O IA    192.168.96.1 [110/783] via 192.168.224.1, 00:00:28, Serial0/0
     192.168.112.0/32 is subnetted, 1 subnets
O IA    192.168.112.1 [110/783] via 192.168.224.1, 00:00:28, Serial0/0
O IA 192.168.1.0/24 [110/782] via 192.168.224.1, 00:01:31, Serial0/0
     192.168.3.0/32 is subnetted, 1 subnets
O IA    192.168.3.1 [110/782] via 192.168.224.1, 00:01:31, Serial0/0
```

1.   What does IA stand for?

Inter Area. (routes)

Check the codes listed with the routing table. Interarea routes point to networks in separate areas within the same OSPF AS.

Verify that the routing tables are complete. Notice that SanJose1's loopback interfaces appear in the other routing tables of other routers with a 32-bit mask. Any route with a 32-bit mask is called a host route because it is a route to a host, not to a network. OSPF does not advertise loopback interfaces as if they were connected to a network.

2.   How many host routes are in Singapore's table?

_4   /32's_

There should be a host route for every remote loopback advertised through OSPF.

Verify connectivity. From Singapore, ping SanJose3's Lo0 interface (192.168.3.1) and SanJose1's Lo2 interface (192.168.96.1).

Step 4

To reduce routing table entries, you must implement interarea route summarization throughout the internetwork. Start by configuring SanJose1 to summarize the networks for Area 1 and advertise this summary route to Area 0.

On SanJose1, enter the following commands to perform interarea summarization:

```
SanJose1(config)#router ospf 1
SanJose1(config-router)#area 1 range 192.168.64.0 255.255.192.0
```

When you finish configuring the summary address, check the routing tables of SanJose3 and Singapore. If the expected changes do not occur, save and reload the routers.

```
Singapore#show ip route

<output omitted>

     192.168.224.0/30 is subnetted, 1 subnets
C       192.168.224.0 is directly connected, Serial0/0
O IA 192.168.1.0/24 [110/782] via 192.168.224.1, 00:01:38, Serial0/0
     192.168.3.0/32 is subnetted, 1 subnets
O IA    192.168.3.1 [110/782] via 192.168.224.1, 00:01:38, Serial0/0
O IA 192.168.64.0/18 [110/783] via 192.168.224.1, 00:00:02, Serial0/0
```

1.   What happened to the host routes?

   got summarized.

2.   How many host routes does Singapore have?

   one

3.   Singapore should still be able to ping 192.168.96.1. Why?

   'cause of it is between summary range

4.   What is the destination IP network of the ICMP request?

   192.168.96.0

Singapore should have only one host route of 192.168.3.1/32 from SanJose3 Lo0. A host route points to one host. A network route points to multiple hosts in one broadcast domain. A summarized route points to a numerically contiguous series of networks.

Step 5

You must configure Singapore to redistribute external routes from Auckland into the OSPF AS. For the purposes of this lab, simulate the Auckland connection by configuring a static route in Singapore to the Auckland LAN (192.168.248.0/24). Use the following commands:

```
Singapore(config)#ip route 192.168.248.0 255.255.255.0 null0
Singapore(config)#router ospf 1
Singapore(config-router)#redistribute static
```

Because the route to 192.168.248.0/24 is imaginary, null0 is used as the exit interface. The **redistribute static** command imports the static route into OSPF. Routes that are originated from anything except OSPF are considered external to the OSPF database. By default, when Singapore redistributes into Area 51, it creates and advertises Type 2 (E2) external routes by using Type 5 LSAs.

The use of static routes to a null interface is a commonly used routing trick. Typically, this technique is used to initialize or advertise a supernet route so that packets destined to an unknown subnet of a classful network are forwarded to "this" router for handling. This technique is particularly useful when you are configuring Border Gateway Protocol (BGP).

Issue the **show ip ospf** command on Singapore:

```
Singapore#show ip ospf
 Routing Process "ospf 1" with ID 192.168.252.1
 Supports only single TOS(TOS0) routes
 It is an autonomous system boundary router
 Redistributing External Routes from,
    static
 SPF schedule delay 5 secs, Hold time between two SPFs 10 secs
 Minimum LSA interval 5 secs. Minimum LSA arrival 1 secs
 Number of external LSA 1. Checksum Sum 0x8650
 Number of DCbitless external LSA 0
 Number of DoNotAge external LSA 0
 Number of areas in this router is 1. 1 normal 0 stub 0 nssa
 External flood list length 0
    Area 51
        Number of interfaces in this area is 1
        Area has no authentication
        SPF algorithm executed 4 times
        Area ranges are
        Number of LSA 5. Checksum Sum 0x3A27A
        Number of DCbitless LSA 0
        Number of indication LSA 0
        Number of DoNotAge LSA 0
        Flood list length 0
```

1.   According to the output of this command, what type of OSPF router is Singapore?

_____ ASBR _____

Recall that ASBRs connect external networks to the OSPF autonomous system.

Now, check the routing table of SanJose1. The routing table should have an E2 route to 192.168.248.0/24:

```
SanJose1#show ip route
<output omitted>
        192.168.224.0/30 is subnetted, 1 subnets
O IA    192.168.224.0 [110/782] via 192.168.1.3, 00:04:39, FastEthernet0/0
        192.168.64.0/30 is subnetted, 1 subnets
C        192.168.64.0 is directly connected, Loopback0
        192.168.80.0/30 is subnetted, 1 subnets
C        192.168.80.0 is directly connected, Loopback1
        192.168.96.0/30 is subnetted, 1 subnets
C        192.168.96.0 is directly connected, Loopback2
O E2 192.168.248.0/24 [110/20] via 192.168.1.3, 00:03:57, FastEthernet0/0
        192.168.112.0/30 is subnetted, 1 subnets
C        192.168.112.0 is directly connected, Loopback3
C       192.168.1.0/24 is directly connected, FastEthernet0/0
        192.168.3.0/32 is subnetted, 1 subnets
O        192.168.3.1 [110/2] via 192.168.1.3, 00:08:08, FastEthernet0/0
```

2.   What is the metric, or OSPF cost, of this route?

_____

Check the routing table of SanJose3. This router should also have the external route.

3.   What is the metric of SanJose3's route to 192.168.248.0/24?

_____ 110/20 _____

SanJose1 and SanJose3 should have the same cost. This might be surprising, because SanJose1 has an additional network to traverse.

A second link to the external network is about to come online. If the network is designed so that OSPF routers can have multiple external routes to the same destination, consider using Type 1

(E1) external routes. Type 2 (E2) external routes have static metrics throughout the OSPF autonomous system (AS). Type 1 routes consider metrics internal and external to the AS for accurate route selection when multiple external routes exist. The decision is made that Singapore should advertise external routes as Type 1 (E1). To configure Type 1, use the following commands on Singapore:

```
Singapore(config)#router ospf 1
Singapore(config-router)#redistribute static metric-type 1
```

After you reconfigure Singapore, check SanJose3's table again. SanJose3's route to 192.168.248.0/24 should now be Serial 0/1.

4.   What is the metric of this route?

_____

Check SanJose1's route to 192.168.248.0/24.

5.   What is the metric of Singapore's route?

                        110/801

_____

Typically, the cost of a route increases with every hop. Type2 (E2) routes ignore internal OSPF metrics. Type1 (E1) routes accumulate costs while being propagated through the OSPF AS. With one exit point for the AS, Type2 (E2) routes might be adequate.

Step 6

Over time, notice that as the Auckland office grows, many more Type 1, or Fast Ethernet 0/1, networks are propagated through the internetwork. To optimize the internetwork by reducing the routing table size, implement classless interdomain routing (CIDR) to advertise all Auckland networks with one route. Create routes to these Auckland networks with three more static routes as follows:

```
Singapore(config)#ip route 192.168.240.0 255.255.255.0 null0
Singapore(config)#ip route 192.168.244.0 255.255.255.0 null0
Singapore(config)#ip route 192.168.252.0 255.255.255.0 null0
```

Configure Singapore to advertise all Auckland networks with a summary route:

```
Singapore(config)#router ospf 1
Singapore(config-router)#summary-address 192.168.240.0 255.255.240.0
```

After you configure the summary, check the routing tables on SanJose1 and SanJose3. Both routers should receive and install the supernet route, 192.168.240.0/20.

Note: On routers that have large routing tables, use the command **show ip route supernet** to show only aggregate routes:

```
SanJose3#show ip route
<output omitted>
     192.168.224.0/30 is subnetted, 1 subnets
C       192.168.224.0 is directly connected, Serial0/1
C    192.168.1.0/24 is directly connected, FastEthernet0/0
C    192.168.3.0/24 is directly connected, Loopback0
O E1 192.168.240.0/20 [110/801] via 192.168.224.2, 00:00:05, Serial0/1
O IA 192.168.64.0/18 [110/2] via 192.168.1.1, 00:05:36, FastEthernet0/0

SanJose1#show ip route supernet
<output omitted>
O E1 192.168.240.0/20 [110/802] via 192.168.1.3, 00:01:08, FastEthernet0/0
```

SJ3: O IA 192.168.64.0/18 (110/2) via 192.168.1.1   (before summarizing)

1.   Is 192.168.248.0/24 still in SanJose1 or SanJose3's routing table?

No   *110/801*

It should not be present because 192.168.248.0/24 is included in the range 192.168.240.0/20.

Internet connectivity is by way of ISP1 through SanJose1. The link is not active yet, but OSPF is configured in advance. Simulate the link with a loopback interface, as follows:

```
SanJose1(config)#interface lo5
SanJose1(config-if)#ip address 10.0.0.6 255.255.255.252
```

Use the following commands to create and advertise a default route on SanJose1:

```
SanJose1(config)#router ospf 1
SanJose1(config-router)#default-information originate always
```

The **always** keyword instructs OSPF to advertise the default route whether or not the router has one in the routing table. In this case, the router will install a gateway of last resort, as displayed in the output. Check the routing tables on SanJose3 and Singapore. Both should now have a default route of 0.0.0.0/0:

```
SanJose3#show ip route
<output omitted>
Gateway of last resort is 192.168.1.1 to network 0.0.0.0
     192.168.224.0/30 is subnetted, 1 subnets
C       192.168.224.0 is directly connected, Serial0/1
C    192.168.1.0/24 is directly connected, FastEthernet0/0
C    192.168.3.0/24 is directly connected, Loopback0
O*E2 0.0.0.0/0 [110/1] via 192.168.1.1, 00:00:09, FastEthernet0/0
O E1 192.168.240.0/20 [110/801] via 192.168.224.2, 00:00:09, Serial0/1
O IA 192.168.64.0/18 [110/2] via 192.168.1.1, 00:00:09, FastEthernet0/0
```

2.   What type of OSPF route is the default?

E2   External Type 2

---

3.   What is the metric of this route on SanJose3?

110/1   → 1

---

4.   What is the metric of this route on Singapore?

110/1   → 1

The default route is considered External Type2 (E2). The default cost of 1 will be retained throughout the AS.

Verify that default routing is working by asking Singapore to ping a host that is not represented in its routing table. From Singapore, ping 10.0.0.6. If the default route is working, Singapore should receive replies. Troubleshoot if necessary.

Save these configuration files for each router.

Lab 6.9.4: Configuring a Stub Area and a Totally Stubby Area

Estimated Time: 45 Minutes

Objective

In this lab, you configure an OSPF stub area and a totally stubby area by using the sample topology shown in Figure 6-6 as a guide.

Figure 6-6   Sample Topology for Configuring a Stub Area and a Totally Stubby Area

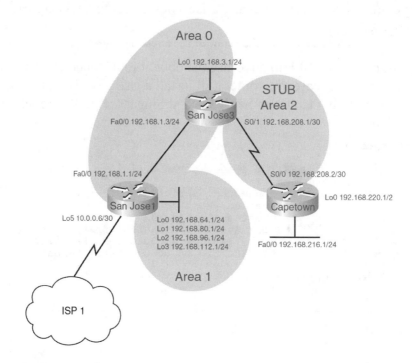

Equipment Requirements

To complete this lab, you need the following Cisco equipment:

* Three Cisco 2600 series routers

* One serial cable

* One Ethernet cable

Scenario

You need to upgrade the Capetown router because you suspect that it is not keeping up with the growth of the OSPF internetwork. You perform diagnostics and discover that the router could benefit from more memory due to the large routing table. The router could also use a faster processor because of frequent Shortest Path First calculations. You decide to create a smaller and more stable routing table using a stub or totally stubby area configuration.

Step 1

Build and configure the network according to Figure 6-6. Configure multiarea OSPF according to Figure 6-6. However, do not configure a stub area yet. Use the configuration files from the previous lab if they are available, and make adjustments as necessary.

Note: You can ignore the loopback, Lo5, on SanJose1 for now.

Configure each router with the loopback address as indicated in Figure 6-6. Be sure to configure SanJose1 with additional loopbacks using Lo0, Lo1, Lo2, and Lo3. These loopback interfaces simulate the serial links to other local San Jose sites:

```
Capetown#show ip route
<output omitted>
Gateway of last resort is not set
     192.168.208.0/30 is subnetted, 1 subnets
C        192.168.208.0 is directly connected, Serial0/0
     192.168.64.0/32 is subnetted, 1 subnets
O IA    192.168.64.1 [110/66] via 192.168.208.1, 00:20:04, Serial0/0
C    192.168.216.0/24 is directly connected, FastEthernet0/0
     192.168.80.0/32 is subnetted, 1 subnets
O IA    192.168.80.1 [110/66] via 192.168.208.1, 00:20:04, Serial0/0
     192.168.96.0/32 is subnetted, 1 subnets
O IA    192.168.96.1 [110/66] via 192.168.208.1, 00:20:04, Serial0/0
     192.168.112.0/32 is subnetted, 1 subnets
O IA    192.168.112.1 [110/66] via 192.168.208.1, 00:20:05, Serial0/0
C    192.168.220.0/24 is directly connected, Loopback0
O IA 192.168.1.0/24 [110/65] via 192.168.208.1, 00:20:05, Serial0/0
     192.168.3.0/32 is subnetted, 1 subnets
O IA    192.168.3.1 [110/65] via 192.168.208.1, 00:20:07, Serial0/0
```

Use **ping** and **show ip route** to test connectivity between all interfaces. Each router should be able to ping all network interfaces.

Step 2

Create a loopback interface as follows to simulate the serial interface connecting to ISP1:

```
SanJose1(config)#interface lo5
SanJose1(config-if)#ip address 10.0.0.6 255.255.255.252
```

Configure SanJose1 as follows to redistribute an external route into the OSPF domain:

```
SanJose1(config)#ip route 10.0.0.0 255.0.0.0 null0
SanJose1(config)#router ospf 1
SanJose1(config-router)#redistribute static
```

Check the routing tables of all three routers. They should be complete:

```
Capetown#show ip route
<output omitted>
Gateway of last resort is not set
     192.168.208.0/30 is subnetted, 1 subnets
C        192.168.208.0 is directly connected, Serial0/0
     192.168.64.0/32 is subnetted, 1 subnets
O IA    192.168.64.1 [110/66] via 192.168.208.1, 00:07:32, Serial0/0
C    192.168.216.0/24 is directly connected, FastEthernet0/0
     192.168.80.0/32 is subnetted, 1 subnets
O IA    192.168.80.1 [110/66] via 192.168.208.1, 00:07:32, Serial0/0
O E2 10.0.0.0/8 [110/20]via 192.168.208.1, 00:00:35, Serial0/0
     192.168.96.0/32 is subnetted, 1 subnets
O IA    192.168.96.1 [110/66] via 192.168.208.1, 00:07:32, Serial0/0
     192.168.112.0/32 is subnetted, 1 subnets
O IA    192.168.112.1 [110/66] via 192.168.208.1, 00:07:32, Serial0/0
C    192.168.220.0/24 is directly connected, Loopback0
O IA 192.168.1.0/24 [110/65] via 192.168.208.1, 00:07:34, Serial0/0
     192.168.3.0/32 is subnetted, 1 subnets
O IA    192.168.3.1 [110/65] via 192.168.208.1, 00:07:34, Serial0/0
```

SanJose3 and Capetown should also have a Type 2 external route to 10.0.0.0/8. They will not have a specific route to the loopback network, 10.0.0.4/30. That network has not clearly been advertised.

Step 3

Capetown has several interarea (IA) routes and one external (E2) route. In complex OSPF networks, many external and interarea routes can needlessly weigh down some routers. Capetown is in a stub area, an area with one egress point. Capetown does not need external routing information, or even interarea summaries. Capetown just needs a default route to the ABR, SanJose3.

By configuring Area 2 as a stub area, SanJose3 automatically produces a default route into Area 2. Use the following commands to configure the stub area:

```
SanJose3(config)#router ospf 1
SanJose3(config-router)#area 2 stub
```

Also, configure Capetown as follows:

```
Capetown(config)#router ospf 1
Capetown(config-router)#area 2 stub
```

Verify that Area 2 is a stub by issuing the **show ip ospf** command:

```
CapeTown#show ip ospf
 Routing Process "ospf 1" with ID 192.168.220.1
 Supports only single TOS(TOS0) routes
 SPF schedule delay 5 secs, Hold time between two SPFs 10 secs
 Minimum LSA interval 5 secs. Minimum LSA arrival 1 secs
 Number of external LSA 0. Checksum Sum 0x0
 Number of DCbitless external LSA 0
 Number of DoNotAge external LSA 0
 Number of areas in this router is 1. 0 normal 1 stub 0 nssa
 External flood list length 0
    Area 2
        Number of interfaces in this area is 2
        It is a stub area
        Area has no authentication
        SPF algorithm executed 6 times
        Area ranges are
        Number of LSA 9. Checksum Sum 0x428E6
        Number of DCbitless LSA 0
        Number of indication LSA 0
        Number of DoNotAge LSA 0
        Flood list length 0
```

1.   According to the output of this command, what type of OSPF area is Area 2?

STUB

Now, check Capetown's routing table. Notice that the ABR, SanJose3, has generated a default route, 0.0.0.0/0, on the stub area and it now appears in Capetown's table:

```
Capetown#show ip route
<output omitted>
Gateway of last resort is 192.168.208.1 to network 0.0.0.0

     192.168.208.0/30 is subnetted, 1 subnets
C        192.168.208.0 is directly connected, Serial0/0
     192.168.64.0/32 is subnetted, 1 subnets
O IA    192.168.64.1 [110/66] via 192.168.208.1, 00:01:01, Serial0/0
C    192.168.216.0/24 is directly connected, FastEthernet0/0
     192.168.80.0/32 is subnetted, 1 subnets
O IA    192.168.80.1 [110/66] via 192.168.208.1, 00:01:01, Serial0/0
     192.168.96.0/32 is subnetted, 1 subnets
```

```
O IA    192.168.96.1 [110/66] via 192.168.208.1, 00:01:01, Serial0/0
     192.168.112.0/32 is subnetted, 1 subnets
O IA    192.168.112.1 [110/66] via 192.168.208.1, 00:01:02, Serial0/0
C     192.168.220.0/24 is directly connected, Loopback0
O IA 192.168.1.0/24 [110/65] via 192.168.208.1, 00:01:02, Serial0/0
     192.168.3.0/32 is subnetted, 1 subnets
O IA    192.168.3.1 [110/65] via 192.168.208.1, 00:01:03, Serial0/0
O*IA 0.0.0.0/0 [110/65] via 192.168.208.1, 00:01:03, Serial0/0
```

2.   What type of OSPF route is Capetown's default route?

_____INTERAREA_____

Recall that interarea (IA) routes point to networks in different areas within the same OSPF AS.

Because Area 2 is a stub area, all external routes, Type 5 LSAs, have been prevented from reaching internal routers.

3.   Look carefully at Capetown's routing table. Does it still have a route to 10.0.0.0/8?

_____NO_____

All external routes are filtered from stub areas and replaced with a default route.

Step 4

The stub area configuration is not making a substantial impact on Area 2. Because Capetown can use the default route to its ABR for all nonlocal area traffic, you decide to filter Type 3 and Type 4 interarea routes from Area 2. To do this, you must configure Area 2 as a totally stubby area, which is a Cisco proprietary feature.

Use the following commands on SanJose3, the ABR, to configure Area 2 as a totally stubby area:

```
SanJose3(config)#router ospf 1
SanJose3(config-router)#no area 2 stub
SanJose3(config-router)#area 2 stub no-summary
```

The **no-summary** keyword at the ABR keeps interarea routes from entering stub Area 2, creating a totally stubby area. Only the ABR needs the additional configuration. The role of Area 2 internal routers has not changed.

Return to Capetown and check its routing table:

```
Capetown#show ip route
<output omitted>
Gateway of last resort is 192.168.208.1 to network 0.0.0.0

     192.168.208.0/30 is subnetted, 1 subnets
C        192.168.208.0 is directly connected, Serial0/0
C     192.168.216.0/24 is directly connected, FastEthernet0/0
C     192.168.220.0/24 is directly connected, Loopback0
O*IA 0.0.0.0/0 [110/65] via 192.168.208.1, 00:00:25, Serial0/0
```

1.   What has changed?

_____Interareas route have been replaced by a default route_____

2.   Does Area 2 still have connectivity to 10.0.0.0/8? Test with **ping 10.0.0.6**.

_____yes, 1 way U-ping_____

A default route has also replaced interarea routes.

Capetown should get a positive response by forwarding ICMP requests to SanJose3 using the default route 0.0.0.0/0. SanJose3 has a default route to network 10.0.0.0/8, and SanJose1 has a directly connected route to 10.0.0.4/30 with the loopback interface 10.0.0.6/30.

Lab 6.9.5: Configuring an NSSA

Estimated Time: 45 Minutes

Objective

In this lab, you configure an OSPF NSSA for the topology shown in Figure 6-7 so that you can import external routing information while retaining the benefits of a stub area.

Figure 6-7   NSSA Topology Scenario

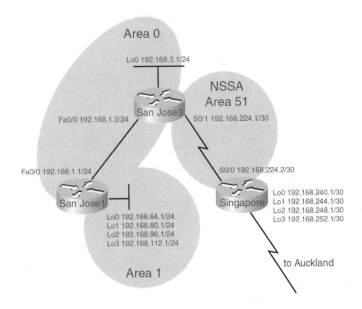

Equipment Requirements

To complete this lab, you need the following Cisco equipment:

- Three Cisco 2600 series routers

- One serial cable

- One Ethernet cable

Scenario

The implementation of a totally stubby area in Area 2 was successful. Now, implement this area in Area 51 for more efficient routing and greater route stability. A stub or totally stubby area will not work because the Singapore router in Area 51 has the added responsibility of redistributing external routes from Auckland using Type 5 LSAs. To meet every need, you decide to configure Area 51 as a not so stubby area (NSSA).

Step 1

Build and configure the network according to Figure 6-7. Also, configure multiarea OSPF according to Figure 6-7. However, do not configure NSSA yet. Use the configuration files from the previous lab if they are available, and make adjustments as necessary. In this case, it is easiest to just remove and reapply the OSPF process. Reboot after reconfiguring OSPF if you have problems.

Note: This lab requires the use of subnet 0.

Configure each router with the loopback address indicated in Figure 6-7. Be sure to configure SanJose1 and Singapore with additional loopbacks (Lo0, Lo1, Lo2, Lo3). On SanJose1, these loopback interfaces simulate the serial links to local San Jose sites: Westasman, Baypointe, Vista, and Eastasman. On Singapore, the loopbacks simulate Auckland networks.

Use **ping** and **show ip route** to test connectivity between all interfaces. Each router should be able to ping all network interfaces, as the following shows:

```
SanJose3#show ip route
<output omitted>
     192.168.224.0/30 is subnetted, 1 subnets
C       192.168.224.0 is directly connected, Serial0/0
     192.168.64.0/32 is subnetted, 1 subnets
O IA    192.168.64.1 [110/2] via 192.168.1.1, 00:03:49, FastEthernet0/0
     192.168.80.0/32 is subnetted, 1 subnets
O IA    192.168.80.1 [110/2] via 192.168.1.1, 00:03:49, FastEthernet0/0
     192.168.96.0/32 is subnetted, 1 subnets
O IA    192.168.96.1 [110/2] via 192.168.1.1, 00:03:49, FastEthernet0/0
     192.168.112.0/32 is subnetted, 1 subnets
O IA    192.168.112.1 [110/2] via 192.168.1.1, 00:03:49, FastEthernet0/0
C    192.168.1.0/24 is directly connected, FastEthernet0/0
C    192.168.3.0/24 is directly connected, Loopback0
```

Step 2

Configure Singapore as follows to redistribute connected routes into the OSPF domain:

```
Singapore(config)#router ospf 1
Singapore(config-router)#redistribute connected subnets
```

This command advertises Singapore's loopbacks as external networks. Check the routing tables of all three routers. They should be complete. SanJose1 and SanJose3 should also have Type 2 external routes to the Auckland networks, as the following shows:

```
SanJose1#show ip route
<output omitted>
     192.168.224.0/30 is subnetted, 1 subnets
O IA    192.168.224.0 [110/782] via 192.168.1.3, 00:11:16, FastEthernet0/0
     192.168.240.0/30 is subnetted, 1 subnets
O E2    192.168.240.0 [110/20] via 192.168.1.3, 00:04:54, FastEthernet0/0
O E2 192.168.244.0/24 [110/20] via 192.168.1.3, 00:09:34, FastEthernet0/0
     192.168.64.0/30 is subnetted, 1 subnets
C       192.168.64.0 is directly connected, Loopback0
     192.168.80.0/30 is subnetted, 1 subnets
C       192.168.80.0 is directly connected, Loopback1
     192.168.96.0/30 is subnetted, 1 subnets
C       192.168.96.0 is directly connected, Loopback2
O E2 192.168.248.0/24 [110/20] via 192.168.1.3, 00:09:35, FastEthernet0/0
     192.168.112.0/30 is subnetted, 1 subnets
C       192.168.112.0 is directly connected, Loopback3
C    192.168.1.0/24 is directly connected, FastEthernet0/0
O E2 192.168.252.0/24 [110/20] via 192.168.1.3, 00:09:38, FastEthernet0/0
     192.168.3.0/32 is subnetted, 1 subnets
192.168.3.1 [110/2] via 192.168.1.3, 00:11:19, FastEthernet0/0
```

Step 3

The following shows that Singapore has several interarea (IA) routes:

```
Singapore#show ip route
<output omitted>
Gateway of last resort is not set
     192.168.224.0/30 is subnetted, 1 subnets
C       192.168.224.0 is directly connected, Serial0/0
     192.168.240.0/30 is subnetted, 1 subnets
C       192.168.240.0 is directly connected, Loopback0
C    192.168.244.0/24 is directly connected, Loopback1
     192.168.64.0/32 is subnetted, 1 subnets
O IA    192.168.64.1 [110/66] via 192.168.224.1, 00:00:48, Serial0/0
     192.168.80.0/32 is subnetted, 1 subnets
O IA    192.168.80.1 [110/66] via 192.168.224.1, 00:00:48, Serial0/0
     192.168.96.0/32 is subnetted, 1 subnets
O IA    192.168.96.1 [110/66] via 192.168.224.1, 00:00:49, Serial0/0
C    192.168.248.0/24 is directly connected, Loopback2
     192.168.112.0/32 is subnetted, 1 subnets
O IA    192.168.112.1 [110/66] via 192.168.224.1, 00:00:49, Serial0/0
O IA 192.168.1.0/24 [110/65] via 192.168.224.1, 00:00:49, Serial0/0
C    192.168.252.0/24 is directly connected, Loopback3
     192.168.3.0/32 is subnetted, 1 subnets
O IA    192.168.3.1 [110/65] via 192.168.224.1, 00:00:49, Serial0/0
```

In Lab 6.9.4, "Configuring a Stub Area and a Totally Stubby Area," Capetown's table was minimized by configuring Area 2 as a stub. Attempt to repeat this configuration with the following commands on Singapore:

```
Singapore(config)#router ospf 1
Singapore(config-router)#area 51 stub
```

1. What does the router output when you enter this command?

    Stub command is invalid when it is ASBR

Because Singapore imports routes that are external to OSPF, it is considered an ASBR and ASBRs cannot be members of a stub area. Stub areas do not permit Type 5 LSAs. Issue the **show ip ospf database** command on Singapore. Note that OSPF router IDs are used as references in managing the link-state database. You might have to remove and reinstall the OSPF process, or possibly reboot the routers, to get the desired result:

```
Singapore#show ip ospf database

        OSPF Router with ID (192.168.252.1) (Process ID 1)

                Router Link States (Area 51)
Link ID         ADV Router      Age     Seq#        Checksum Link count
192.168.3.1     192.168.3.1     817     0x80000004 0xF239    2
192.168.252.1   192.168.252.1   1307    0x80000002 0xB918    2

                Summary Net Link States (Area 51)
Link ID         ADV Router      Age     Seq#        Checksum
192.168.1.0     192.168.3.1     1262    0x80000003 0xABB6
192.168.3.1     192.168.3.1     1308    0x80000001 0x8FD1
192.168.64.1    192.168.3.1     1258    0x80000001 0xF72B
192.168.80.1    192.168.3.1     1258    0x80000001 0x47CB
192.168.96.1    192.168.3.1     1258    0x80000001 0x966C
192.168.112.1   192.168.3.1     1258    0x80000001 0xE50D

                Type-5 AS External Link States
Link ID         ADV Router      Age     Seq#        Checksum Tag
192.168.224.0   192.168.252.1   429     0x80000001 0x7D74    0
192.168.240.0   192.168.252.1   432     0x80000001 0xCC15    0
192.168.244.0   192.168.252.1   713     0x80000001 0xB228    0
192.168.248.0   192.168.252.1   713     0x80000001 0x8650    0
192.168.252.0   192.168.252.1   713     0x80000001 0x5A78    0
```

2.   According to the output of this command, what link IDs are included under Type 5 AS external link states?

_192.168.240.0 , x.x.244.0, x.x.248.0, x.x.252.0_

All Auckland network routes, loopbacks, are Type 5 external links.

The workaround for this situation is to configure Area 51 as an NSSA. Enter the following commands:

```
Singapore(config)#router ospf 1
Singapore(config-router)#area 51 nssa

SanJose3(config)#router ospf 1
SanJose3(config-router)#area 51 nssa
```

Now, use the **show ip ospf database** command on Singapore. Because stub areas do not support Type 5 LSAs, external routes are redistributed and advertised as Type 7 LSAs. The output of this command should verify that Type 7 LSAs have replaced Type 5 LSAs:

```
Singapore#show ip ospf database

        OSPF Router with ID (192.168.252.1) (Process ID 1)

                Router Link States (Area 51)
Link ID         ADV Router      Age         Seq#        Checksum Link count
192.168.3.1     192.168.3.1     10          0x80000006  0x9A87   2
192.168.252.1   192.168.252.1   10          0x80000004  0x5B6E   2

                Summary Net Link States (Area 51)
Link ID         ADV Router      Age         Seq#        Checksum
192.168.1.0     192.168.3.1     137         0x80000004  0x4F0C
192.168.3.1     192.168.3.1     137         0x80000002  0x3327
192.168.64.1    192.168.3.1     138         0x80000002  0x9B80
192.168.80.1    192.168.3.1     138         0x80000002  0xEA21
192.168.96.1    192.168.3.1     138         0x80000002  0x3AC1
192.168.112.1   192.168.3.1     138         0x80000002  0x8962
                                 ← TYPE 7 now
                Type-7 AS External Link States (Area 51)
Link ID         ADV Router      Age         Seq#        Checksum Tag
192.168.224.0   192.168.252.1   19          0x80000001  0xA0FA   0
192.168.240.0   192.168.252.1   20          0x80000001  0xEF9B   0
192.168.244.0   192.168.252.1   21          0x80000001  0xD5AE   0
192.168.248.0   192.168.252.1   21          0x80000001  0xA9D6   0
192.168.252.0   192.168.252.1   21          0x80000001  0x7DFE   0
```

Enter the **show ip route** command on Singapore. Next, you see how the routing table changes with the **no-summary** option in OSPF.

NSSA routers receive updates from the ABR the same way that stub area routers do. Singapore's routing table should look similar to the way Capetown's table did when it was in a stub area. See Lab 6.9.4. SanJose3 continues to flood Area 51 with summary link and Type 3 and Type 4 LSAs. Because your goal is to reduce the burden on Area 51 routers, reconfigure SanJose3 as follows to filter interarea summary LSAs:

```
SanJose3(config)#router ospf 1
SanJose3(config-router)#area 51 nssa no-summary
```

Again, check Singapore's routing table:

```
Singapore#show ip route
<output omitted>
Gateway of last resort is 192.168.224.1 to network 0.0.0.0

    192.168.224.0/30 is subnetted, 1 subnets
```

```
C        192.168.224.0 is directly connected, Serial0/0
         192.168.240.0/30 is subnetted, 1 subnets
C        192.168.240.0 is directly connected, Loopback0
C        192.168.244.0/24 is directly connected, Loopback1
C        192.168.248.0/24 is directly connected, Loopback2
C        192.168.252.0/24 is directly connected, Loopback3
O*IA 0.0.0.0/0 [110/65] via 192.168.224.1, 00:00:04, Serial0/0
```

3.   What has changed?

All IA routes were replaced w default route 0.0.0.0 (don't sumarize)

All interarea (IA) routes are replaced with the 0.0.0.0/0 default route. Area 51 is now acting like Area 2 when it was configured as totally stubby. See Lab 6.9.4. The primary difference is that an NSSA can redistribute external routes.

NSSAs allow the OSPF link-state databases to be minimized within an area, yet still import external routes as Type 7 LSAs. The NSSA ABR, in this case SanJose3, must convert these Type 7s into Type 5s, which will overflow into Area 0. On SanJose3, issue the **show ip ospf database** command, as follows:

```
SanJose3#show ip ospf database

        OSPF Router with ID (192.168.3.1) (Process ID 1)

                Router Link States (Area 0)
Link ID         ADV Router      Age     Seq#        Checksum Link count
192.168.3.1     192.168.3.1     170     0x80000007  0x45B2   2
192.168.112.1   192.168.112.1   1711    0x80000008  0x148A   1

                Net Link States (Area 0)
Link ID         ADV Router      Age     Seq#        Checksum
192.168.1.1     192.168.112.1   1712    0x80000001  0xA10A

                Summary Net Link States (Area 0)
Link ID         ADV Router      Age     Seq#        Checksum
192.168.64.1    192.168.112.1   1238    0x80000005  0xE7CA
192.168.80.1    192.168.112.1   1238    0x80000005  0x376B
192.168.96.1    192.168.112.1   1238    0x80000005  0x860C
192.168.112.1   192.168.112.1   1238    0x80000005  0xD5AC
192.168.224.0   192.168.3.1     1748    0x80000001  0x92E5

                Router Link States (Area 51)
Link ID         ADV Router      Age     Seq#        Checksum
Link count
192.168.3.1     192.168.3.1     165     0x8000000B  0x908C   2
192.168.252.1   192.168.252.1   278     0x80000004  0x5B6E   2

                Summary Net Link States (Area 51)
Link ID         ADV Router      Age     Seq#        Checksum
0.0.0.0         192.168.3.1     172     0x80000001  0x12B6

                Type-7 AS External Link States (Area 51)
Link ID         ADV Router      Age     Seq#        Checksum Tag
192.168.224.0   192.168.252.1   287     0x80000001  0xA0FA   0
192.168.240.0   192.168.252.1   287     0x80000001  0xEF9B   0
192.168.244.0   192.168.252.1   287     0x80000001  0xD5AE   0
192.168.248.0   192.168.252.1   287     0x80000001  0xA9D6   0
192.168.252.0   192.168.252.1   287     0x80000001  0x7DFE   0

                Type-5 AS External Link States
Link ID         ADV Router      Age     Seq#        Checksum Tag
192.168.240.0   192.168.3.1     161     0x80000001  0x5A35   0
192.168.244.0   192.168.3.1     163     0x80000001  0x4048   0
192.168.248.0   192.168.3.1     163     0x80000001  0x1470   0
192.168.252.0   192.168.3.1     163     0x80000001  0xE798   0
```

4.   Does SanJose3's database include link IDs that use Type 7 LSAs?

Yes

5.   Does SanJose3's database include link IDs that use Type 5 LSAs?

Yes

SanJose3 converts the Type 7 LSAs from Singapore and reproduces them as Type 5 LSAs to SanJose1.

Issue the **show ip route** command on SanJose3:

```
SanJose3#show ip route
<output omitted>
Gateway of last resort is not set
     192.168.224.0/30 is subnetted, 1 subnets
C        192.168.224.0 is directly connected, Serial0/0
     192.168.240.0/30 is subnetted, 1 subnets
O N2    192.168.240.0 [110/20] via 192.168.224.2, 00:03:23, Serial0/0
O N2 192.168.244.0/24 [110/20] via 192.168.224.2, 00:03:23, Serial0/0
     192.168.64.0/32 is subnetted, 1 subnets
O IA    192.168.64.1 [110/2] via 192.168.1.1, 00:03:23, FastEthernet0/0
     192.168.80.0/32 is subnetted, 1 subnets
O IA    192.168.80.1 [110/2] via 192.168.1.1, 00:03:23, FastEthernet0/0
     192.168.96.0/32 is subnetted, 1 subnets
O IA    192.168.96.1 [110/2] via 192.168.1.1, 00:03:24, FastEthernet0/0
O N2 192.168.248.0/24 [110/20] via 192.168.224.2, 00:03:24, Serial0/0
     192.168.112.0/32 is subnetted, 1 subnets
IA    192.168.112.1 [110/2] via 192.168.1.1, 00:03:30, FastEthernet0/0
C     192.168.1.0/24 is directly connected, FastEthernet0/0
O N2 192.168.252.0/24 [110/20] via 192.168.224.2, 00:03:30, Serial0/0
C     192.168.3.0/24 is directly connected, Loopback0
```

6.   According to the output of this command, what kind of OSPF route is the external route to 192.168.248.0/24?

Type 7

NSSA Type 2 (N2) routes are learned through Type 7 LSAs.

Finally, check SanJose1's routing table. You should still install the external route to 192.168.248.0/24. Issue the **show ip ospf database** command on SanJose1:

```
SanJose1#show ip ospf database

        OSPF Router with ID (192.168.112.1) (Process ID 1)
                Router Link States (Area 0)
Link ID            ADV Router         Age        Seq#          Checksum
Link count
192.168.3.1        192.168.3.1        390        0x80000007 0x45B2    2
192.168.112.1      192.168.112.1      1931       0x80000008 0x148A    1

                Net Link States (Area 0)
Link ID            ADV Router         Age        Seq#          Checksum
192.168.1.1        192.168.112.1      1931       0x80000001 0xA10A

                Summary Net Link States (Area 0)
Link ID            ADV Router         Age        Seq#          Checksum
192.168.64.1       192.168.112.1      1456       0x80000005 0xE7CA
192.168.80.1       192.168.112.1      1457       0x80000005 0x376B
192.168.96.1       192.168.112.1      1457       0x80000005 0x860C
192.168.112.1      192.168.112.1      1457       0x80000005 0xD5AC
192.168.224.0      192.168.3.1        1967       0x80000001 0x92E5

                Router Link States (Area 1)
Link ID            ADV Router         Age        Seq#          Checksum
```

```
Link count
192.168.112.1    192.168.112.1    1457          0x80000006 0x39FE    4

                 Summary Net Link States (Area 1)
Link ID          ADV Router       Age          Seq#        Checksum
192.168.1.0      192.168.112.1    1924         0x80000009 0xA14D
192.168.3.1      192.168.112.1    1919         0x80000001 0x9B57
192.168.224.0    192.168.112.1    1919         0x80000001 0x9E6B

                 Summary ASB Link States (Area 1)
Link ID          ADV Router       Age          Seq#        Checksum
192.168.3.1      192.168.112.1    387          0x80000003 0x7F71

                 Type-5 AS External Link States
Link ID          ADV Router       Age          Seq#        Checksum Tag
192.168.240.0    192.168.3.1      383          0x80000001 0x5A35    0
192.168.244.0    192.168.3.1      383          0x80000001 0x4048    0
192.168.248.0    192.168.3.1      383          0x80000001 0x1470    0
192.168.252.0    192.168.3.1      384          0x80000001 0xE798    0
```

7.   Does SanJose1's database include link IDs that use Type 7 LSAs?

No

8.   Does SanJose1's database include link IDs that use Type 5 LSAs?

yes

Because SanJose3 converts Type 7 LSAs to Type 5, SanJose1 is unaware of the NSSA configuration of Area 51:

```
SanJose1#show ip route
<output omitted>
Gateway of last resort is not set
     192.168.224.0/30 is subnetted, 1 subnets
O IA    192.168.224.0 [110/782] via 192.168.1.3, 00:06:38, FastEthernet0/0
     192.168.240.0/30 is subnetted, 1 subnets
O E2    192.168.240.0 [110/20] via 192.168.1.3, 00:06:32, FastEthernet0/0
O E2 192.168.244.0/24 [110/20] via 192.168.1.3, 00:06:32, FastEthernet0/0
     192.168.64.0/30 is subnetted, 1 subnets
C       192.168.64.0 is directly connected, Loopback0
     192.168.80.0/30 is subnetted, 1 subnets
C       192.168.80.0 is directly connected, Loopback1
     192.168.96.0/30 is subnetted, 1 subnets
C       192.168.96.0 is directly connected, Loopback2
O E2 192.168.248.0/24 [110/20] via 192.168.1.3, 00:06:33, FastEthernet0/0
     192.168.112.0/30 is subnetted, 1 subnets
C       192.168.112.0 is directly connected, Loopback3
C    192.168.1.0/24 is directly connected, FastEthernet0/0
O E2 192.168.252.0/24 [110/20] via 192.168.1.3, 00:06:35, FastEthernet0/0
     192.168.3.0/32 is subnetted, 1 subnets
O       192.168.3.1 [110/2] via 192.168.1.3, 00:06:41, FastEthernet0/0
```

Save the configuration files on each router.

Lab 6.9.6: Configuring Virtual Links

Estimated Time: 30 Minutes

Objective

In this lab, you configure an OSPF virtual link so that a disconnected area, shown in Figure 6-8, can reach the backbone, as required by OSPF.

Figure 6-8   Configuring Virtual Links

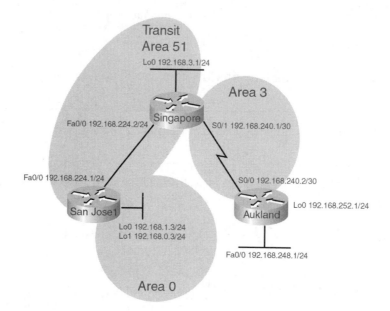

Equipment Requirements

To complete this lab, you need the following Cisco equipment:

- Three Cisco 2600 series routers

- One serial cable

- One Ethernet cable

Scenario

The network administrator in Phoenix, Arizona, receives a call. The caller says that the connectivity to Auckland and Singapore has been intermittent for several hours. Logging on to the corporate network from home and running some diagnostics, you determine that Auckland cannot be reached. Also, you notice that the shortest path first algorithm is being recalculated often on the core routers. The instability seems to be associated with the Asian region on the network. Singapore local time is approximately 4:30 p.m. You call the technical support lead in Singapore and ask if he is experiencing network connectivity issues. Technical support is disappointed that you noticed this already but indicates that OSPF Area 3 in Auckland has already been added. He says that you do not need to redistribute external routes. You agree that it would be best to include Auckland in the OSPF AS. However, you disagree that another area should be created. A teleconference is set for the next day to discuss the situation, while engaging in restoring connectivity and stability. A proper OSPF design has all areas adjacent to Area 0, but Area 3 is disconnected from the backbone. You will configure a virtual link through Area 51, connecting Area 3 to the backbone, Area 0.

Step 1

Build and configure the network according to Figure 6-8. Also configure multiarea OSPF according to Figure 6-8. However, do not configure the virtual link yet. Configure each router with the loopback address indicated in Figure 6-8. You can use the configuration files from the previous lab if they are available. Make adjustments as necessary. However, it is easiest to just remove and reapply the OSPF process.

Use **ping** to test connectivity between all directly connected interfaces. Each router should be able to ping its serial link partner.

Step 2

After you configure the network according to Figure 6-8, check Auckland's routing table, as follows:

```
Auckland#show ip route
<output omitted>
Gateway of last resort is not set

     192.168.240.0/30 is subnetted, 1 subnets
C        192.168.240.0 is directly connected, Serial0/0
C     192.168.248.0/24 is directly connected, FastEthernet0/0
C     192.168.252.0/24 is directly connected, Loopback0
```

1.   The routing table should be devoid of OSPF routes. Why?

No conexion to area 0

Interarea traffic must transit the backbone area. Even though Area 51 and Area 3 are adjacent, they do not share OSPF routing updates.

Verify that Auckland has established a neighbor relationship with Singapore by using the **show ip ospf neighbor** command:

```
Auckland#show ip ospf neighbor

Neighbor ID     Pri   State      Dead Time   Address         Interface
192.168.240.1     1   FULL/        00:00:33   192.168.240.1 Serial0/0
```

2.   What state exists between Singapore and Auckland?

Full

Singapore and Auckland should have successfully established adjacencies, shown as the "FULL" neighbor state.

Step 3

Because Area 3 is not connected to the backbone, OSPF routing is broken in this network. Configure a virtual link, or drastically redesign the network, to make routing work. To quickly restore connectivity, configure a virtual link between Singapore and SanJose1. Singapore is the

ABR for Area 3, and SanJose1 is the ABR for Area 0. Therefore, the transit area between Area 3 and Area 0 will be Area 51. Enter the following commands on Singapore:

```
Singapore(config)#router ospf 1
Singapore(config-router)#area 51 virtual-link 192.168.1.3
```

Note: You must specify SanJose1 by its router ID.

For the virtual link to function, configure both ends of the link. On SanJose1, issue the following commands:

```
SanJose1 (config)#router ospf 1
SanJose1(config-router)#area 51 virtual-link 192.168.3.1
```

Verify the creation of the virtual link by checking Auckland's routing table, as follows:

```
Auckland#show ip route
<output omitted>
Gateway of last resort is not set
O IA 192.168.224.0/24 [110/845] via 192.168.240.1, 00:01:25, Serial0/0
     192.168.240.0/30 is subnetted, 1 subnets
C       192.168.240.0 is directly connected, Serial0/0
O IA 192.168.3.0/24 [110/65] via 192.168.240.1, 00:01:25, Serial0/0
C    192.168.248.0/24 is directly connected, FastEthernet0/0
     192.168.0.0/32 is subnetted, 1 subnets
O IA    192.168.0.3 [110/846] via 192.168.240.1, 00:00:35, Serial0/0
     192.168.1.0/32 is subnetted, 1 subnets
O IA    192.168.1.3 [110/846] via 192.168.240.1, 00:00:35, Serial0/0
C    192.168.252.0/24 is directly connected, Loopback0
```

If the virtual link receives OSPF routes, it is operational.

Alternatively, you can issue the command **show ip ospf virtual-links** on Singapore:

```
Singapore#show ip ospf virtual-links
Virtual Link OSPF_VL0 to router 192.168.1.3 is up
  Run as demand circuit
  DoNotAge LSA allowed.
  Transit area 51, via interface Serial0/0, Cost of using 781
  Transmit Delay is 1 sec, State POINT_TO_POINT,
  Timer intervals configured, Hello 10, Dead 40, Wait 40,
Retransmit 5
    Hello due in 00:00:00
    Adjacency State FULL (Hello suppressed)
    Index 1/3, retransmission queue length 0, number of retransmission 1
    First 0x0(0)/0x0(0) Next 0x0(0)/0x0(0)
    Last retransmission scan length is 1, maximum is 1
    Last retransmission scan time is 0 msec, maximum is 0 msec
```

1. According to the output of this command, what is the state of the virtual link?

OSPF VL0 to router 192.168.

Lab 6.10.1: OSPF Challenge Lab

Estimated Time: 60 Minutes

Objective

In this lab, create a multiarea OSPF AS, shown in Figure 6-9, that includes a totally stubby area, an injection of external routes, and a persistent default route toward the ISP.

Figure 6-9   OSPF Autonomous System Scenario

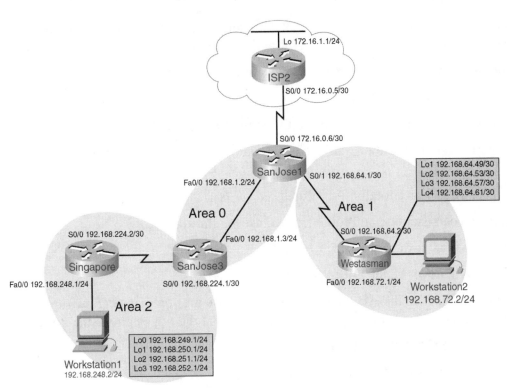

Equipment Requirements

To complete this lab, you need the following Cisco equipment:

- Three Cisco 2600 series routers

- One serial cables

- One Ethernet cable

- Two workstations

Scenario

As the enterprise network administrator for the International Travel Agency, your responsibilities include—but are not limited to—designing and implementing internetwork connectivity. To ensure success by reducing complexity, start scaling the network by connecting only the Asia region and one local site, Westasman, to the San Jose corporate headquarters and ISP2. When you are satisfied with the results, implement all other regions and sites.

Design Considerations

At this point, Westasman is in stub Area 1 with one exit point and there is no need to redistribute external routes. The router at Westasman has been in service for several years and might not be able to keep up with a large OSPF internetwork. The AS also has only one exit point to the Internet. Therefore, it is preferred that you create a totally stubby.

Instead of the administrative burden of many static routes, use a stable default route advertised through OSPF. There is concern about route flapping if the WAN link to ISP2 is unstable. A persistent default route to ISP2 is required.

When you were provisioning the network, the memory and processor were upgraded on SanJose2, which is intended to be the ASBR and the DR for any area that requires one.

Advertise only summarized or unique networks through Area 0.

Implementation Requirements

The following configurations are required for completion of this lab:

* Configure NAT overload on SanJose2 S0/0 interface. Therefore, no routing is necessary on ISP2.

* Configure Area 1 as a totally stubby area.

* Advertise a persistent default route from SanJose2 through OSPF.

* SanJose2 will always be the DR in Area 0.

* SanJose3 will never be the DR in Area 0.

* Summarize routes at the ABR and ASBR. When you are summarizing interarea routes, you need to configure the summary routes on a router that did not originate the routes.

Implementation Completion Tests

Ensure the following for completion of this lab:

* Successful pings to ISP2 from workstation1 and workstation2.

* Successful pings between workstation1 and workstation2.

* Only a default route in the Westasman route table, injected from SanJose2.

* The **show ip ospf neighbor detail** command verifies that SanJose2 is DR.

* The **show ip route** command shows summary addresses for all loopback networks.

* All loopback addresses can be reached from anywhere in the network.

* Two minutes after a WAN link failure, by disconnecting the serial cable from ISP2, an E2 default route is still present in Singapore.

Chapter 7

IS-IS

Lab 7.7.1: Configuring Basic Integrated IS-IS

Estimated Time: 90 Minutes

Objective

In this lab, you configure basic Integrated IS-IS. You also implement IS-IS authentication for security purposes. Figure 7-1 shows the sample topology for this lab.

Figure 7-1   Sample Topology for Lab 7.7.1

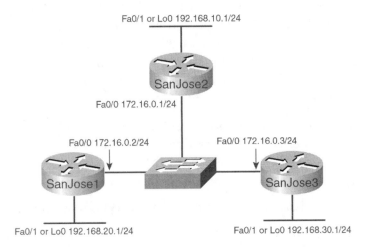

Equipment Requirements

You need the following equipment for this lab:

- Three Cisco 2600 series routers
- One Ethernet cable
- One Cisco Catalyst switch

You can use three Cisco 2620, 2621, 2620XM, or 2621XM routers or a combination for this lab. You will use Cisco IOS Release 12.2(12) with the Enterprise Plus or Enterprise Plus IPSec 56 feature set. The Enterprise Plus feature set is the minimum requirement for IS-IS support.

Cisco IOS Release 12.2(12) with the Enterprise Plus feature set requires a minimum of 16 MB of Flash and 48 MB of RAM. The Enterprise Plus IPSec 56 feature set requires a minimum of 16 MB of Flash and 64 MB of RAM.

The image names for the Cisco IOS Release 12.2(12) with the Enterprise Plus and Plus IPSec 56 feature sets are c2600-js-mz.122-12.bin and c2600-jk8s-mz.122-12.bin, respectively. The "j" indicates "Enterprise," and the "s" indicates "Plus." If a more current release of this Cisco IOS software is available, such as 12.2(12a) or 12.2(12b), you should use it instead.

Scenario

The IS-IS routing protocol has become increasingly popular with widespread usage among service providers. The International Travel Agency (ITA) is thinking about implementing IS-IS because it is a link-state protocol that enables fast convergence with large scalability and flexibility. However, before management makes a final decision, it wants a nonproduction network set up to test the IS-IS routing protocol.

The backbone of the production ITA WAN consists of three routers connected by way of an Ethernet core. Because the core routers also connect to the Internet, authentication needs to be configured to prevent unauthorized routers from participating in the IS-IS process.

Step 1

Build and configure the network according to Figure 7-1, but do not configure IS-IS yet. You can use loopback addresses to simulate the Fast Ethernet 0/1 interfaces. When you use the Fast Ethernet 0/1 interfaces, you have the option of configuring **no keepalive** on these interfaces to bring them to the up/up state without physically cabling the interfaces. This is opposed to actually connecting the Fast Ethernet 0/1 interfaces to switch ports. You must ensure that each switch port resides in a different VLAN from the switch ports that connect to the Fast Ethernet 0/0 interfaces and the other Fast Ethernet 0/1 interfaces.

Note: You cannot enable IS-IS routing on an interface until you have configured an IP address on the interface. Configure interface Loopback 0 in place of interface Fast Ethernet 0/1 on each router for the remainder of the lab. If you use Fast Ethernet 0/1 interfaces on these routers, the lab will work the same, but the interface output will vary accordingly.

Use **ping** to test connectivity between the directly connected Fast Ethernet interfaces.

Optional: To allow a smooth transition between routers through Telnet, apply the following script on each router in global configuration mode:

```
ip host r1 172.16.0.1
ip host r2 172.16.0.2
ip host r3 172.16.0.3
!
line vty 0 4
 privilege level 15
 no login
```

After you apply this script to each router, type **r1** on any router. This moves the user immediately to the privileged mode of SanJose1 without being prompted for a password. It is much faster to type r1 than SanJose1, so we use r1 as an abbreviated representation of SanJose1. You also use this process for SanJose2 and SanJose3 by typing either **r2** or **r3**, respectively. You can use this in a lab setting to move quickly between routers.

Step 2

IS-IS (ISO/IEC 10589) is implemented with network service access point (NSAP) addresses consisting of three fields: area address, system ID, and N-selector byte: service identifier (NSEL). The area address field can be from 1 to 13 octets; the system ID field is normally 6 octets (must be 6 for Cisco IOS software); and the NSEL identifies a process on the device. The NSEL is a loose equivalent to a port or socket in IP; it is not used in routing decisions.

When the NSEL is set to 00, the NSAP is referred to as the network entity title (NET). NETs and NSAPs are represented in hexadecimal and must start and end on a byte boundary, such as 49.0001.1111.1111.1111.00. In this example, the area address is 49.0001, the system ID is 1111.1111.1111, and the NSEL is 00.

Level 1, or L1, IS-IS routing is based on system ID. Therefore, each router must have a unique system ID within the area. L1 IS-IS routing equates to intra-area routing. It is customary to use either a MAC address from the router or, for Integrated IS-IS, to code the IP address (of a Loopback address, for example) into the system ID. However, numbering 1, 2, 3, 4, and so on is also acceptable.

Area addresses that start with a value of 48, 49, 50, or 51 specify private addresses. Do not advertise this group of addresses to other Connectionless Network Service (CLNS) networks. The area address must be the same for all routers in an area.

On a LAN, one of the routers is elected the designated intermediate system (DIS) based on interface priority. The default is 64. If all interface priorities are the same, the router with the highest subnetwork point of attachment (SNPA) address is selected. The (Ethernet) MAC addresses serves as the SNPA addresses for Ethernet LANs. The DIS serves the same purpose for IS-IS as the designated router (DR) does for OSPF. You decide that SanJose1 will be the DIS, so you must set its priority higher than the default setting on the SanJose2 and SanJose3 routers.

Configure Integrated IS-IS on each router and set a priority of 100 on the Fast Ethernet 0/0 interface of SanJose1, as shown in the following:

```
SanJose1(config)#router isis
SanJose1(config-router)#net 49.0001.1111.1111.1111.00
SanJose1(config-router)#interface fa0/0
SanJose1(config-if)#ip router isis
SanJose1(config-if)#isis priority 100
SanJose1(config-if)#interface lo0
SanJose1(config-if)#ip router isis

SanJose2(config)#router isis
SanJose2(config-router)#net 49.0001.2222.2222.2222.00
SanJose2(config-router)#interface fa0/0
SanJose2(config-if)#ip router isis
SanJose2(config-if)#interface lo0
SanJose2(config-if)#ip router isis

SanJose3(config)#router isis
SanJose3(config-router)#net 49.0001.3333.3333.3333.00
SanJose3(config-router)#interface fa0/0
SanJose3(config-if)#ip router isis
SanJose3(config-if)#interface lo0
SanJose3(config-if)#ip router isis
```

1.   Identify parts of the NSAP/NET addresses.

a. Area address: _____

b. SanJose1 system ID: _____

c. SanJose2 system ID: _____

d. SanJose3 system ID: _____

e. NSEL: _____

Step 3

Verify IS-IS operation using various **show** commands on any of the three routers.
The commands and sample output for SanJose1 are shown here:

```
SanJose1#show ip protocols
Routing Protocol is "isis"
  Invalid after 0 seconds, hold down 0, flushed after 0
  Outgoing update filter list for all interfaces is not set
  Incoming update filter list for all interfaces is not set
  Redistributing: isis
  Address Summarization:
    None
  Maximum path: 4
  Routing for Networks:
    FastEthernet0/0
    FastEthernet0/1
  Routing Information Sources:
    Gateway         Distance      Last Update
    192.168.30.1         115      00:00:36
    192.168.20.1         115      00:00:36
  Distance: (default is 115)
```

Notice that the update timers are set to 0. Updates are not sent at regular intervals because they
are driven by events. The Last Update field indicates how long it has been since the last update
as hours:minutes:seconds.

Issue the **show clns neighbors** command to view adjacencies:

```
SanJose1#show clns neighbors

System Id    Interface  SNPA            State  Holdtime  Type  Protocol
SanJose2     Fa0/0      0004.9ad2.d0c0  Up     9         L1L2  IS-IS
SanJose3     Fa0/0      0002.16f4.1ba0  Up     29        L1L2  IS-IS
```

Neighbor ISs and neighbor ESs are shown, if applicable. You can use the optional keyword
detail to display comprehensive neighbor information, as follows:

```
SanJose1#show clns neighbors detail

System Id    Interface  SNPA            State  Holdtime  Type  Protocol
SanJose2     Fa0/0      0004.9ad2.d0c0  Up     24        L1L2  IS-IS
  Area Address(es): 49.0001
  IP Address(es):  172.16.0.2*
  Uptime: 00:07:30
SanJose3     Fa0/0      0002.16f4.1ba0  Up     27        L1L2  IS-IS
  Area Address(es): 49.0001
  IP Address(es):  172.16.0.3*
  Uptime: 00:07:00
```

Notice that the system IDs of the IS neighbors are the host names of the respective neighbor
routers. Cisco routers support dynamic host name mapping, starting with IOS Release 12.0(5),
and the feature is enabled by default. As you can see in the sample output, the configured system
ID of 2222.2222.2222 has been replaced by the host name SanJose2. Similarly, SanJose3
replaces 3333.3333.3333.

Also notice that the adjacency type for both neighbors is L1L2. By default, Cisco IOS enables
both L1 and L2 adjacency negotiation on IS-IS routers. You can use the router configuration
mode command, **is-type**, or the interface configuration command, **isis circuit-type**, to prescribe
how the router operates in terms of L1 and L2 routing.

You can use the **show isis database** and the **show clns interface fa0/0** commands to obtain DIS
and related information. First, type the **clear isis *** command on all routers to force IS-IS to

refresh its link-state databases and recalculate all routes. It might take a minute or two for all routers to update their respective IS-IS databases:

```
All_Router#clear isis *
```

Issue the **show isis database** command to view the content of the IS-IS database:

```
SanJose1#show isis database

IS-IS Level-1 Link State Database:
LSPID              LSP Seq Num   LSP Checksum   LSP Holdtime   ATT/P/OL
SanJose1.00-00   * 0x00000008    0x088F         1191           0/0/0
SanJose1.01-00   * 0x00000002    0x9B60         1192           0/0/0
SanJose2.00-00     0x00000001    0x8736         1190           0/0/0
SanJose3.00-00     0x00000002    0x39A1         1195           0/0/0
IS-IS Level-2 Link State Database:
LSPID              LSP Seq Num   LSP Checksum   LSP Holdtime   ATT/P/OL
SanJose1.00-00   * 0x00000017    0x4E1B         1195           0/0/0
SanJose1.01-00   * 0x00000002    0x4D37         1192           0/0/0
SanJose2.00-00     0x00000010    0xF4B9         1191           0/0/0
SanJose3.00-00     0x00000002    0xD703         1195           0/0/0
```

IS-IS retains a separate database for L1 and L2 routing. Because IS-IS is a link-state protocol, the link-state database should be the same for the three San Jose routers.

As discussed earlier, if the **isis priority 100** command had not been placed on the Fast Ethernet 0/0 interface of SanJose1, the DIS would have been elected on the basis of the highest SNPA. DIS election is preemptive, unlike the behavior with OSPF. The **isis priority 100** command ensures that SanJose1 is elected the DIS, regardless of router boot order. However, how can you determine from the **show isis database** output that SanJose1 is indeed the DIS?

Look at the entries under the link-state protocol data unit ID (LSPID) column. The first six octets form the system ID. As addressed earlier, because of the dynamic host mapping feature, the respective router names are listed instead of the numerical system ID. Following the system ID are two octets.

The first octet is the pseudonode ID, representing a LAN. The pseudonode ID distinguishes between LAN IDs on the same DIS. When this value is not 0, the associated LSP is a pseudonode LSP originating from the DIS. The DIS is the only system that originates pseudonode LSPs. The DIS creates one pseudonode LSP for L1 and one for L2, as shown in the previous output.

The pseudonode ID varies upon reboot of the router as a function of the creation or deletion of virtual interfaces, such as loopback interfaces. The system ID and pseudonode ID together are referred to as the circuit ID. An example is SanJose1.01.

A nonpseudonode LSP represents a router and is distinguished by the fact that the two-byte value in the circuit ID is 00.

The last octet forms the LSP fragmentation number; 00 indicates that all data fits into a single link-state packet (LSP). If there had been more information that did not fit into the first LSP, IS-IS would have created additional LSPs with increasing LSP numbers, such as 01, 02, and so on. The asterisk (*) indicates that the local system originated the LSP.

Issue the **show clns interface fa0/0** command:

```
SanJose1#show clns interface fa0/0
FastEthernet0/0 is up, line protocol is up
  Checksums enabled, MTU 1497, Encapsulation SAP
  ERPDUs enabled, min. interval 10 msec.
```

```
CLNS fast switching enabled
CLNS SSE switching disabled
DEC compatibility mode OFF for this interface
Next ESH/ISH in 8 seconds
Routing Protocol: IS-IS
    Circuit Type: level-1-2
    Interface number 0x0, local circuit ID 0x1
    Level-1 Metric: 10, Priority: 100, Circuit ID: SanJose1.01
    Number of active level-1 adjacencies: 2
    Level-2 Metric: 10, Priority: 100, Circuit ID: SanJose1.01
    Number of active level-2 adjacencies: 2
    Next IS-IS LAN Level-1 Hello in 803 milliseconds
    Next IS-IS LAN Level-2 Hello in 2 seconds
```

The circuit ID, SanJose1.01, is made up of the system ID and pseudonode ID. It identifies the DIS. Circuit types, levels, metric, and priority information are also displayed.

You can obtain additional information about a specific LSP ID by appending the LSP ID and **detail** keyword to the **show isis database** command, as shown in the output. The host name is case-sensitive. You can also use this command to view the IS-IS database of a neighbor router by referencing its host name in the command:

```
SanJose1#show isis database SanJose1.00-00 detail


IS-IS Level-1 LSP SanJose1.00-00
LSPID                   LSP Seq Num   LSP Checksum   LSP Holdtime       ATT/P/OL
SanJose1.00-00        * 0x0000000B    0x0292         831                0/0/0
  Area Address: 49.0001
  NLPID:        0xCC
  Hostname: SanJose1
  IP Address:    192.168.10.1
  Metric: 10        IP 172.16.0.0 255.255.255.0
  Metric: 10        IP 192.168.10.0 255.255.255.0
  Metric: 10        IS SanJose1.02
  Metric: 10        IS SanJose1.01

IS-IS Level-2 LSP SanJose1.00-00
LSPID                   LSP Seq Num   LSP Checksum   LSP Holdtime       ATT/P/OL
SanJose1.00-00        * 0x0000000D    0x4703         709                0/0/0
  Area Address: 49.0001
  NLPID:        0xCC
  Hostname: SanJose1
  IP Address:    192.168.10.1
  Metric: 10        IS SanJose1.02
  Metric: 10        IS SanJose1.01
  Metric: 20        IP 192.168.30.0 255.255.255.0
  Metric: 10        IP 192.168.10.0 255.255.255.0
  Metric: 10        IP 172.16.0.0 255.255.255.0
  Metric: 20        IP 192.168.20.0 255.255.255.0
```

The default IS-IS metric for every link is 10, but notice that the metric for both the 192.168.20.0 and 192.168.30.0 networks is 20. This is because the networks do not connect directly but connect directly to neighbor routers.

Issue the **show isis topology** command as follows to display the paths to the other intermediate systems:

```
SanJose1#show isis topology

IS-IS paths to level-1 routers
System Id         Metric  Next-Hop        Interface   SNPA
SanJose1          --
SanJose2          10      SanJose2        Fa0/0       0004.9ad2.d0c0
SanJose3          10      SanJose3        Fa0/0       0002.16f4.1ba0

IS-IS paths to level-2 routers
```

```
System Id          Metric  Next-Hop        Interface  SNPA
SanJose1           --
SanJose2           10      SanJose2        Fa0/0      0004.9ad2.d0c0
SanJose3           10      SanJose3        Fa0/0      0002.16f4.1ba0
```

The highlighted entries in the SNPA column are the MAC addresses of the SanJose2 and SanJose3 Fast Ethernet 0/0 interfaces.

Issue the **show isis route** command as follows to view the IS-IS L1 routing table:

```
SanJose1#show isis route
```

IS-IS not running in OSI mode (*) (only calculating IP routes)

This command has no useful output because the command is specific to OSI routing. Remember: IP IS-IS was enabled on each router. If CLNP were configured in the network, more interesting output would appear.

Issue the **show clns route** command as follows to view the IS-IS L2 routing table:

```
SanJose1#show clns route
Codes: C - connected, S - static, d - DecnetIV
       I - ISO-IGRP,  i - IS-IS,  e - ES-IS

C  49.0001.1111.1111.1111.00 [1/0], Local IS-IS NET
C  49.0001 [2/0], Local IS-IS Area
```

Again, there is no useful output here because this command applies to OSI routing and not IP routing.

Issue the **show ip route** command to view the IP routing table:

```
SanJose1#show ip route
Codes: C - connected, S - static, I - IGRP, R - RIP, M - mobile, B - BGP
       D - EIGRP, EX - EIGRP external, O - OSPF, IA - OSPF inter area
       N1 - OSPF NSSA external type 1, N2 - OSPF NSSA external type 2
       E1 - OSPF external type 1, E2 - OSPF external type 2, E - EGP
       i - IS-IS, L1 - IS-IS level-1, L2 - IS-IS level-2, ia - IS-IS inter area
       * - candidate default, U - per-user static route, o - ODR
       P - periodic downloaded static route

Gateway of last resort is not set

i L1 192.168.30.0/24 [115/20] via 172.16.0.3, FastEthernet0/0
C    192.168.10.0/24 is directly connected, Loopback0
     172.16.0.0/24 is subnetted, 1 subnets
C       172.16.0.0 is directly connected, FastEthernet0/0
i L1 192.168.20.0/24 [115/20] via 172.16.0.2, FastEthernet0/0
```

Notice how the routes to the 192.168.30.0 and 192.168.20.0 networks were learned.

The **show clns neighbors**, **show isis database**, **show clns interface**, **show isis topology**, **show isis route**, and **show clns route** commands illustrate the somewhat confusing nature of IS-IS verification and troubleshooting. There is no clear pattern as to whether incorporation of the keyword **isis** or **clns** in a **show** command applies to IP routing or to OSI routing.

Step 4

L1 routers communicate with other L1 routers in the same area while L2 routers route between L1 areas, forming an interdomain routing backbone. This lab scenario does not illustrate the typical multiarea composition of the set of L2 routers in an IS-IS domain, because the San Jose routers all reside in Area 49.0001. Because the San Jose routers' main function is simply to route between areas in the ITA internetwork, you should configure them as L2-only routers. Configure each San Jose router as an L2-only router like this:

```
SanJose1(config)#router isis
SanJose1(config-router)#is-type level-2-only

SanJose2(config)#router isis
SanJose2(config-router)#is-type level-2-only

SanJose3(config)#router isis
SanJose3(config-router)#is-type level-2-only
```

Note: You can use the **isis circuit-type** interface command to selectively override the router configuration **is-type**, which is now L2-only.

To see the effect of the **is-type** command, re-enter the various **show** commands previously issued: **show ip protocols**, **show clns neighbors**, **show isis database**, **show clns interface fa0/0**, **show isis database SanJose1.00-00 detail**, **show isis topology**, and **show ip route**. Following is sample output:

```
SanJose1#show ip protocols
Routing Protocol is "isis"
  Invalid after 0 seconds, hold down 0, flushed after 0
  Outgoing update filter list for all interfaces is not set
  Incoming update filter list for all interfaces is not set
  Redistributing: isis
  Address Summarization:
    None
  Maximum path: 4
  Routing for Networks:
    FastEthernet0/0
    FastEthernet0/1
  Routing Information Sources:
    Gateway         Distance      Last Update
    192.168.30.1         115      00:08:48
    192.168.20.1         115      00:00:09
  Distance: (default is 115)


SanJose1#show clns neighbors

System Id      Interface    SNPA              State  Holdtime  Type  Protocol
SanJose2       Fa0/0        0004.9ad2.d0c0    Up     26        L2    IS-IS
SanJose3       Fa0/0        0002.16f4.1ba0    Up     22        L2    IS-IS


SanJose1#show isis database

IS-IS Level-2 Link State Database:
LSPID               LSP Seq Num   LSP Checksum  LSP Holdtime   ATT/P/OL
SanJose1.00-00    * 0x00000001    0x623C        1086           0/0/0
SanJose1.01-00    * 0x0000000F    0x3344        1092           0/0/0
SanJose2.00-00      0x00000001    0x13AA        1091           0/0/0
SanJose3.00-00      0x00000002    0xD703        1096           0/0/0
```

If the LSP ID is seen with an LSP Holdtime of 0 followed by a parenthetical value, you can purge that rogue entry by invoking the **clear isis *** command:

```
SanJose1#show clns interface fa0/0
FastEthernet0/0 is up, line protocol is up
  Checksums enabled, MTU 1497, Encapsulation SAP
  ERPDUs enabled, min. interval 10 msec.
  CLNS fast switching enabled
  CLNS SSE switching disabled
  DEC compatibility mode OFF for this interface
  Next ESH/ISH in 16 seconds
  Routing Protocol: IS-IS
```

```
Circuit Type: level-1-2
Interface number 0x0, local circuit ID 0x1
Level-2 Metric: 10, Priority: 100, Circuit ID: SanJose1.01
Number of active level-2 adjacencies: 2
Next IS-IS LAN Level-2 Hello in 2 seconds
```

Despite the fact that the circuit type is level-1-2, the entries following the circuit type show that only L2 operations are taking place:

SanJose1#**show isis database SanJose1.00-00 detail**

```
IS-IS Level-2 LSP SanJose1.00-00
LSPID                  LSP Seq Num  LSP Checksum  LSP Holdtime    ATT/P/OL
SanJose1.00-00       * 0x00000001   0x623C        892             0/0/0
  Area Address: 49.0001
  NLPID:        0xCC
  Hostname: SanJose1
  IP Address:   192.168.10.1
  Metric: 10        IS SanJose1.02
  Metric: 10        IS SanJose1.01
  Metric: 10        IP 192.168.10.0 255.255.255.0
  Metric: 10        IP 172.16.0.0 255.255.255.0
```

The output shows that the IDs SanJose1.02 and SanJose.01 on the circuits number the router interfaces that participate in IS-IS. This is also seen in the **show clns interface** output.

Issue the **show isis topology** and **show ip route** commands:

SanJose1#**show isis topology**

```
IS-IS paths to level-2 routers
System Id           Metric  Next-Hop         Interface   SNPA
SanJose1            --
SanJose2            10      SanJose2         Fa0/0       0004.9ad2.d0c0
SanJose3            10      SanJose3         Fa0/0       0002.16f4.1ba0
```

SanJose1#**show ip route**
```
Codes: C - connected, S - static, I - IGRP, R - RIP, M - mobile, B - BGP
       D - EIGRP, EX - EIGRP external, O - OSPF, IA - OSPF inter area
       N1 - OSPF NSSA external type 1, N2 - OSPF NSSA external type 2
       E1 - OSPF external type 1, E2 - OSPF external type 2, E - EGP
       i - IS-IS, L1 - IS-IS level-1, L2 - IS-IS level-2, ia - IS-IS inter area
       * - candidate default, U - per-user static route, o - ODR
       P - periodic downloaded static route

Gateway of last resort is not set

i L2 192.168.30.0/24 [115/20] via 172.16.0.3, FastEthernet0/0
C    192.168.10.0/24 is directly connected, Loopback0
     172.16.0.0/24 is subnetted, 1 subnets
C       172.16.0.0 is directly connected, FastEthernet0/0
i L2 192.168.20.0/24 [115/20] via 172.16.0.2, FastEthernet0/0
```

1.   What types of routes are being placed into the routing table?

_____

Step 5

The default value of the hello interval is 10 seconds, and the default value of the hello multiplier is 3. The hello multiplier specifies the number of IS-IS hello PDUs that a neighbor must miss before the router declares the adjacency as down. So, with the default hello interval of 10 seconds, it takes 30 seconds for an adjacency to be declared down due to missed hello PDUs.

The analogous settings with OSPF are governed by the **ip ospf hello-interval** and **ip ospf dead-interval** interface commands.

You make a decision to adjust the IS-IS timers so that the core routers detect network failures in less time. This increases traffic, but that is much less of a concern on the high-speed core Ethernet segment than on a busy WAN link. You determine that the need for quick convergence on the core outweighs the negative effect of extra control traffic. Change the hello interval to 5 on all Fa0/0 interfaces, as shown here for the SanJose1 router:

```
SanJose1(config)#interface fastethernet 0/0
SanJose1(config-if)#isis hello-interval 5
```

1. How long will it take for an adjacency to be declared down with the new hello interval of 5?

Step 6

There should be no unauthorized routers forming adjacencies within the IS-IS core. Adding authentication to each IS-IS–enabled interface can help to ensure this.

Configure interface authentication on SanJose1, as shown here:

```
SanJose1(config)#interface FastEthernet 0/0
SanJose1(config-if)#isis password cisco level-2
```

This command prevents unauthorized routers from forming level-2 adjacencies with this router.

Be sure to add the keyword **level-2**, which refers to the level-2 database, not an encryption level. If no keyword is specified, the default is level-1. Keep in mind that the passwords are exchanged in clear text and provide only limited security.

Wait 20 seconds, and then issue the **show clns neighbors** command on SanJose1.

1. Does SanJose1 still show that it has IS-IS neighbors? Why or why not?

Issue the **debug isis adj-packets** command to verify that SanJose1 does not recognize its neighbors because it requires authentication that has not been configured on SanJose 2 or SanJose3 yet:

```
SanJose1#debug isis adj-packets
IS-IS Adjacency related packets debugging is on
SanJose1#
03:22:28: ISIS-Adj: Sending L2 LAN IIH on FastEthernet0/0, length 1497
03:22:29: ISIS-Adj: Sending L2 LAN IIH on Loopback0, length 1514
03:22:30: ISIS-Adj: Sending L2 LAN IIH on FastEthernet0/0, length 1497
03:22:31: ISIS-Adj: Rec L2 IIH from 0004.9ad2.d0c0 (FastEthernet0/0), cir type L2, cir
id 1111.1111.1111.01, length 1497
03:22:31: ISIS-Adj: Authentication failed
```

IS-IS routers do not communicate unless the authentication parameters match. However, many other interface-specific IS-IS parameters can vary on a given segment without disrupting communication, such as those set by the commands **isis hello-interval**, **isis hello-multiplier**, **isis retransmit-interval**, **isis retransmit-throttle-interval**, and **isis csnp-interval**. Of course, it makes sense for these parameters to coincide on a given segment.

Correct the authentication mismatch by configuring interface authentication on SanJose2 and SanJose3. When configurations are complete, verify that the routers can communicate by using the **show clns neighbors** command on SanJose1:

```
SanJose2(config)#interface FastEthernet 0/0
SanJose2(config-if)#isis password cisco level-2

SanJose3(config)#interface FastEthernet 0/0
SanJose3(config-if)#isis password cisco level-2

SanJose1#show clns neighbors

System Id   Interface   SNPA             State   Holdtime   Type  Protocol
SanJose2    Fa0/0       0004.9ad2.d0c0   Up      23         L2    IS-IS
SanJose3    Fa0/0       0002.16f4.1ba0   Up      26         L2    IS-IS
```

The system IDs will resolve, in time, to the router names. This is done through the dynamic host name mapping feature that is enabled automatically on Cisco routers. In the interim, the output might appear with the actual numerical ID for that system.

Step 7

IS-IS provides two additional layers of authentication to prevent unauthorized adjacencies between routers. These are area passwords for L1 and domain passwords for L2. The interface, area, and domain password options for IS-IS use plaintext authentication and are of limited use. However, beginning with Cisco IOS Release 12.2(13)T MD5, authentication is available for IS-IS.

The command for L1 password authentication is **area-password** *password*. Using the **area-password** command on all routers in an area prevents unauthorized routers from injecting false routing information into the L1 database.

The command for L2 password authentication is **domain-password** *password*. Using the **domain-password** command on all L2 routers in a domain prevents unauthorized routers from injecting false routing information into the L2 database. Because the core routers are operating at L2, implement domain password authentication as follows:

```
SanJose1(config)#router isis
SanJose1(config-router)#domain-password sanjose
```

Note that the password is case-sensitive. It is worth configuring mismatched passwords in each case, such as interface, area, and domain. You should do this at least once to see the effect on IS-IS functionality.

Force IS-IS to refresh its link-state database and recalculate all routes by issuing the **clear isis *** command on all routers. It might take a minute or two for all routers to update their respective IS-IS databases:

```
All_Router#clear isis *
```

View the SanJose1 link state database to see the following change:

```
SanJose1#show isis database

IS-IS Level-2 Link State Database:
LSPID              LSP Seq Num   LSP Checksum   LSP Holdtime   ATT/P/OL
SanJose1.00-00   * 0x00000004    0xDCB5         1155           0/0/0
SanJose1.01-00   * 0x00000007    0xB4C1         1156           0/0/0
```

Change the other routers to reflect the new authentication policy:

```
SanJose2(config)#router isis
SanJose2(config-router)#domain-password sanjose

SanJose3(config)#router isis
SanJose3(config-router)#domain-password sanjose
```

View the SanJose1 link-state database to verify propagation of LSPs:

```
SanJose1#show isis database

IS-IS Level-2 Link State Database:
LSPID              LSP Seq Num  LSP Checksum  LSP Holdtime    ATT/P/OL
SanJose1.00-00   * 0x00000001   0xE2B2        1189            0/0/0
SanJose1.01-00   * 0x00000002   0xBEBC        1195            0/0/0
SanJose2.00-00     0x00000002   0x5A59        1190            0/0/0
SanJose3.00-00     0x00000002   0xF3DD        1185            0/0/0
```

The configuration of the basic Integrated IS-IS routing protocol is now complete. In addition to enabling Integrated IS-IS, you enabled L2-specific routing and changed the hello-interval to enable IS-IS to detect network failures more quickly. You enabled two types of password authentication—interface and domain—to prevent unauthorized routers from forming adjacencies with the SanJose core routers.

Save the SanJose1 and SanJose2 configurations for use with the next lab.

Lab 7.7.2: Configuring Multiarea Integrated IS-IS

Estimated Time: 60 Minutes

Objective

In this lab, you configure multiarea Integrated IS-IS and level-specific routers in the topology shown in Figure 7-2.

Figure 7-2   Sample Topology for Lab 7.7.2

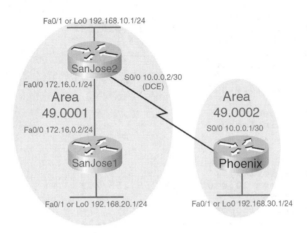

Equipment Requirements

You need the following equipment and hardware for this lab:

- Three Cisco 2600 series routers

- One Ethernet cable

- One serial cable

You can use three Cisco 2620, 2621, 2620XM, or 2621XM routers or a combination for this lab. Cisco IOS Release 12.2(12) with the Enterprise Plus or Enterprise Plus IPSec 56 feature set is used. The Enterprise Plus feature set is the minimum requirement for IS-IS support.

Cisco Release IOS 12.2(12) with the Enterprise Plus feature set requires a minimum of 16 MB of Flash and 48 MB of RAM. The Enterprise Plus IPSec 56 feature set requires a minimum of 16 MB of Flash and 64 MB of RAM.

The image names for the Cisco IOS Release 12.2(12) with the Enterprise Plus and Plus IPSec 56 feature sets are c2600-js-mz.122-12.bin and c2600-jk8s-mz.122-12.bin, respectively. The "j" indicates "Enterprise" and the "s" indicates "Plus." If a more current release of this IOS—such as 12.2(12a) or 12.2(12b)—is available, use it.

Scenario

Previous tests demonstrated that Integrated IS-IS worked well with Level-2 routers in the ITA Ethernet core. Management now wants to establish a point-to-point connection between a new Phoenix office and SanJose1. Phoenix will be in a different area from the core, so SanJose2 will now be configured as an L1 router, SanJose1 as an L1L2 router, and Phoenix as an L2 router.

Step 1

Load the SanJose1 and SanJose2 configurations from the previous lab. Clear and reload the router to be used as Phoenix.

Configure the IP address and clock rate on the serial interface of SanJose1. Use loopback interfaces in place of Fast Ethernet 0/1 interfaces on SanJose2 and Phoenix. Configure the Telnet shortcut to Phoenix on SanJose1 and SanJose2. Configure the host name, turn off DNS lookup, add the Telnet shortcuts, configure the IP address on the serial interface, and configure the loopback IP address on Phoenix:

```
SanJose1(config)#interface serial 0/0
SanJose1(config-if)#ip address 10.0.0.2 255.255.255.252
SanJose1(config-if)#clockrate 128000
SanJose1(config-if)#no shutdown
SanJose1(config-if)#ip host r3 10.0.0.1

SanJose2(config)#ip host r3 10.0.0.1

Router(config)#hostname Phoenix
Phoenix(config)#no ip domain-lookup
Phoenix(config)#ip host r1 10.0.0.2
Phoenix(config)#ip host r2 172.16.0.2

Phoenix(config)#interface serial 0/0
Phoenix(config-if)#ip address 10.0.0.1 255.255.255.252
Phoenix(config-if)#no shutdown
Phoenix(config-if)#interface loopback 0
Phoenix(config-if)#ip address 192.168.30.1 255.255.255.0
```

Use **ping** to verify connectivity between directly connected interfaces. SanJose1 should also be able to reach the loopback address of SanJose2 and vice versa.

Step 2

Recall from "Lab 7.7.1: Configuring Basic Integrated IS-IS" that SanJose1 was configured to be the DIS by setting the **isis priority** to 100 on the Fast Ethernet 0/0 interface. SanJose1 and SanJose2 were also configured to be Level-2 only routers. Verify the configuration by issuing the **show clns neighbors** and **show isis database** commands on either router. Sample output is shown, as follows:

```
SanJose1#show clns neighbors

System Id      Interface   SNPA              State  Holdtime  Type Protocol
SanJose2       Fa0/0       0004.9ad2.d0c0    Up     12        L2   IS-IS
```

```
SanJose1#show isis database

IS-IS Level-2 Link State Database:
LSPID                 LSP Seq Num    LSP Checksum  LSP Holdtime    ATT/P/OL
SanJose1.00-00      * 0x00000014     0xBCC5        409             0/0/0
SanJose1.01-00      * 0x00000015     0x1B0D        819             0/0/0
SanJose2.00-00        0x00000016     0x326D        698             0/0/0
```

Note: Although it is not absolutely necessary, it might be a good idea to issue a **clear isis *** command first to force IS-IS to update its database.

Notice that the neighbor Type is still L2. There is only one L2 link-state database, SanJose1 is still the DIS, and LSPID SanJose1.01-00 has a nonzero pseudonode ID. The LSPID might appear as SanJose1.02-00, depending on whether a loopback was used on SanJose1 in place of interface Fa0/0 and what the timing was of the configuration of the loopback interface.

Step 3

Configure IS-IS on Phoenix, Area 2, and on the Serial 0/0 interface of SanJose1, as shown in the following:

```
Phoenix(config)#router isis
Phoenix(config-router)#net 49.0002.3333.3333.3333.00
Phoenix(config-router)#interface serial 0/0
Phoenix(config-if)#ip router isis
Phoenix(config-if)#interface loopback 0
Phoenix(config-if)#ip router isis

SanJose1(config)#interface serial 0/0
SanJose1(config-if)#ip router isis
```

Step 4

Verify IS-IS operation between SanJose1 and Phoenix. A ping from Phoenix to loopback addresses on SanJose1 and SanJose2 should be successful. Issue various **show** commands on Phoenix, as the following will show. Resulting output should be similar to the samples shown:

```
Phoenix#show clns neighbor

System Id    Interface   SNPA        State  Holdtime  Type  Protocol
SanJose1     Se0/0       *HDLC*      Up     28        L2    IS-IS
```

Recall that serial interfaces do not have a MAC address, so the encapsulation type for the serial link is listed in the SNPA column:

```
Phoenix#show isis database

IS-IS Level-1 Link State Database:
LSPID                 LSP Seq Num   LSP Checksum  LSP Holdtime  ATT/P/OL
Phoenix.00-00       * 0x00000009    0x8FFA        1180          1/0/0
IS-IS Level-2 Link State Database:
LSPID                 LSP Seq Num   LSP Checksum  LSP Holdtime  ATT/P/OL
SanJose1.00-00        0x0000001C    0x25EC        1174          0/0/0
SanJose1.01-00        0x00000017    0x170F        965           0/0/0
SanJose2.00-00        0x00000018    0x2E6F        794           0/0/0
Phoenix.00-00       * 0x00000008    0x4551        1176          0/0/0
```

By default, Phoenix is an L1L2 router, so it retains a separate link-state database for each level. Note, too, that SanJose1 is identified as the DIS. SanJose1 and SanJose2 are not listed in the IS-IS Level-1 link-state database because both were previously configured as L2-only routers. Issue the **show clns interface serial 0/0** command to see both L1 and L2 entries and verify the Phoenix circuit ID:

```
Phoenix#show clns interface serial 0/0
Serial0/0 is up, line protocol is up
  Checksums enabled, MTU 1500, Encapsulation HDLC
  ERPDUs enabled, min. interval 10 msec.
  CLNS fast switching enabled
  CLNS SSE switching disabled
  DEC compatibility mode OFF for this interface
  Next ESH/ISH in 26 seconds
  Routing Protocol: IS-IS
    Circuit Type: level-1-2
    Interface number 0x0, local circuit ID 0x100
    Neighbor System-ID: SanJose1
    Level-1 Metric: 10, Priority: 64, Circuit ID: Phoenix.00
    Number of active level-1 adjacencies: 0
    Level-2 Metric: 10, Priority: 64, Circuit ID: Phoenix.00
    Number of active level-2 adjacencies: 1
    Next IS-IS Hello in 7 seconds
```

Note that the circuit ID is Phoenix.00.

From SanJose1, ping 192.168.30.1 on Phoenix. The ping should not be successful.

Check the IP routing table of SanJose1.

```
SanJose1#show ip route
Codes: C - connected, S - static, I - IGRP, R - RIP, M - mobile, B - BGP
       D - EIGRP, EX - EIGRP external, O - OSPF, IA - OSPF inter area
       N1 - OSPF NSSA external type 1, N2 - OSPF NSSA external type 2
       E1 - OSPF external type 1, E2 - OSPF external type 2, E - EGP
       i - IS-IS, L1 - IS-IS level-1, L2 - IS-IS level-2, ia - IS-IS inter area
       * - candidate default, U - per-user static route, o - ODR
       P - periodic downloaded static route

Gateway of last resort is not set

C    192.168.10.0/24 is directly connected, FastEthernet0/1
     172.16.0.0/24 is subnetted, 1 subnets
C       172.16.0.0 is directly connected, FastEthernet0/0
i L2 192.168.20.0/24 [115/20] via 172.16.0.2, FastEthernet0/0
     10.0.0.0/30 is subnetted, 1 subnets
C       10.0.0.0 is directly connected, Serial0/0
```

All prior checks indicated that IS-IS was working properly between SanJose1 and Phoenix. However, there is no entry in the routing table for the 192.168.30.0 network.

Step 5

Recall that domain password authentication was configured on both SanJose1 and SanJose2. If domain authentication is to be retained, you need to configure Phoenix appropriately, as follows:

```
Phoenix(config)#router isis
Phoenix(config-router)#domain-password sanjose
```

Now, examine the routing table of either SanJose1 or SanJose2. A sample for SanJose1 is shown here:

```
SanJose1#show ip route
Codes: C - connected, S - static, I - IGRP, R - RIP, M - mobile, B - BGP
       D - EIGRP, EX - EIGRP external, O - OSPF, IA - OSPF inter area
       N1 - OSPF NSSA external type 1, N2 - OSPF NSSA external type 2
       E1 - OSPF external type 1, E2 - OSPF external type 2, E - EGP
       i - IS-IS, L1 - IS-IS level-1, L2 - IS-IS level-2, ia - IS-IS inter area
       * - candidate default, U - per-user static route, o - ODR
       P - periodic downloaded static route

Gateway of last resort is not set

i L2 192.168.30.0/24 [115/20] via 10.0.0.1, Serial0/0
C    192.168.10.0/24 is directly connected, FastEthernet0/1
     172.16.0.0/24 is subnetted, 1 subnets
C       172.16.0.0 is directly connected, FastEthernet0/0
i L2 192.168.20.0/24 [115/20] via 172.16.0.2, FastEthernet0/0
     10.0.0.0/30 is subnetted, 1 subnets
C       10.0.0.0 is directly connected, Serial0/0
```

The route to 192.168.30.0 now appears, and a ping from SanJose1 or SanJose2 to 192.168.30.1 should be successful.

Step 6

In this topology, SanJose1 is an L1L2 router. However, SanJose1 was previously configured as an L2-only router. Reconfigure SanJose1 to be an L1L2 router:

```
SanJose1(config)#router isis
SanJose1(config-router)#no is-type or is-type level-1-2
```

In this topology, SanJose2 is a Level-1 only router. However, SanJose2 was also configured as a Level-2 only router. Reconfigure SanJose2 to be a Level-1 only router:

```
SanJose2(config)#router isis
SanJose2(config-router)#is-type level-1
```

Note that -**only** is not part of the level-1 command as is required for the **is-type level-2-only** command.

Recall that an interface password authentication for L2 was also configured on SanJose1 and SanJose2. Because SanJose2 is now an L1-only router, making the link with SanJose1 an L1 connection, you should change the interface password authentication to L1, as the following shows:

```
SanJose1(config)#interface fastethernet0/0
SanJose1(config-if)#isis password cisco level-1

SanJose2(config)#interface fastethernet0/0
SanJose2(config-if)#isis password cisco level-1
```

Verify authentication with a ping from SanJose1 to 192.168.20.1. The ping should be successful, indicating that authentication is working properly.

Issue the **clear isis *** command on all routers to force IS-IS to recalculate the route and to refresh its link-state databases. Wait a minute or two after issuing the **clear** command before continuing to issue the respective **show** commands on SanJose1 so that you can verify the changes made:

```
All_Routers#clear isis *


SanJose1#show clns neighbors

System Id    Interface   SNPA            State   Holdtime   Type   Protocol
SanJose2     Fa0/0       0004.9ad2.d0c0  Up      14         L1     IS-IS
Phoenix      Se0/0       *HDLC*          Up      23         L2     IS-IS
```

SanJose2 is shown as an L1 type of router. Although Phoenix is an L1L2 router, Phoenix shows up as type L2 because of the interarea connection between Phoenix and SanJose1:

```
SanJose1#show isis database

IS-IS Level-1 Link State Database:
LSPID               LSP Seq Num    LSP Checksum   LSP Holdtime   ATT/P/OL
SanJose1.00-00    * 0x00000002     0xDC22         1187           0/0/0
SanJose1.01-00    * 0x00000002     0xBDFD         1188           0/0/0
SanJose2.00-00      0x00000002     0x833B         1187           0/0/0
IS-IS Level-2 Link State Database:
LSPID               LSP Seq Num    LSP Checksum   LSP Holdtime   ATT/P/OL
SanJose1.00-00    * 0x00000005     0xD732         1198           0/0/0
SanJose1.01-00    * 0x00000001     0x890C         1183           0/0/0
Phoenix.00-00       0x00000004     0xD7B9         1193           0/0/0
```

The presence of L1 and L2 link-state databases confirm that SanJose1 is now an L1L2 router:

```
SanJose1#show clns interface fa0/0
FastEthernet0/0 is up, line protocol is up
  Checksums enabled, MTU 1497, Encapsulation SAP
  ERPDUs enabled, min. interval 10 msec.
  CLNS fast switching enabled
  CLNS SSE switching disabled
  DEC compatibility mode OFF for this interface
  Next ESH/ISH in 36 seconds
  Routing Protocol: IS-IS
    Circuit Type: level-1-2
    Interface number 0x0, local circuit ID 0x1
    Level-1 Metric: 10, Priority: 100, Circuit ID: SanJose1.01
```

```
    Number of active level-1 adjacencies: 1
    Level-2 Metric: 10, Priority: 100, Circuit ID: SanJose1.01
    Number of active level-2 adjacencies: 0
    Next IS-IS LAN Level-1 Hello in 938 milliseconds
    Next IS-IS LAN Level-2 Hello in 74 milliseconds
```

In addition to confirming that SanJose1 is an L1L2 router, the priority of 100 and the SanJose1.01 circuit ID indicate that SanJose1 is the DIS. This would be the same for SanJose1.02, as noted in Step 2.

Issue the following to obtain neighbor adjacency information for SanJose2:

```
SanJose2#show clns neighbors

System Id    Interface    SNPA            State   Holdtime   Type  Protocol
SanJose1     Fa0/0        0002.16de.3440  Up      4          L1    IS-IS
```

Although SanJose1 is an L1L2 router, the adjacency is an L1 connection.

```
SanJose2#show isis database

IS-IS Level-1 Link State Database:
LSPID                   LSP Seq Num    LSP Checksum   LSP Holdtime    ATT/P/OL
SanJose1.00-00          0x0000001C     0xB02C         1024            1/0/0
SanJose1.01-00          0x0000001C     0x8918         1112            0/0/0
SanJose2.00-00        * 0x0000001B     0x5154         554             0/0/0
```

Only an L1 link-state database is maintained, confirming that SanJose2 is now an L1-only router:

```
SanJose2#show clns interface fa0/0
FastEthernet0/0 is up, line protocol is up
  Checksums enabled, MTU 1497, Encapsulation SAP
  ERPDUs enabled, min. interval 10 msec.
  CLNS fast switching enabled
  CLNS SSE switching disabled
  DEC compatibility mode OFF for this interface
  Next ESH/ISH in 41 seconds
  Routing Protocol: IS-IS
    Circuit Type: level-1-2
    Interface number 0x1, local circuit ID 0x2
    Level-1 Metric: 10, Priority: 64, Circuit ID: SanJose1.01
    Number of active level-1 adjacencies: 1
    Next IS-IS LAN Level-1 Hello in 2 seconds
```

In addition to confirming that SanJose2 is an L1-only router, the circuit ID shows that SanJose1 is the DIS.

Step 7

Issue the **show clns interface serial0/0** command on the Phoenix router, as follows:

```
Phoenix#show clns interface serial 0/0
Serial0/0 is up, line protocol is up
  Checksums enabled, MTU 1500, Encapsulation HDLC
  ERPDUs enabled, min. interval 10 msec.
  CLNS fast switching enabled
  CLNS SSE switching disabled
  DEC compatibility mode OFF for this interface
  Next ESH/ISH in 22 seconds
  Routing Protocol: IS-IS
    Circuit Type: level-1-2
    Interface number 0x0, local circuit ID 0x100
    Neighbor System-ID: SanJose1
    Level-1 Metric: 10, Priority: 64, Circuit ID: Phoenix.00
    Number of active level-1 adjacencies: 0
    Level-2 Metric: 10, Priority: 64, Circuit ID: Phoenix.00
    Number of active level-2 adjacencies: 1
    Next IS-IS Hello in 1 seconds
```

Because Phoenix is presently an L1L2 router, it maintains information for both levels. This is unnecessary because Phoenix should be an L2-only router. Configure Phoenix for L2-only routing, as follows:

```
Phoenix(config)#router isis
Phoenix(config-router)#is-type level-2-only
```

Verify the configuration with the **show clns interface serial0/0** or **show isis database** command:

```
Phoenix#show clns interface serial0/0
Serial0/0 is up, line protocol is up
  Checksums enabled, MTU 1500, Encapsulation HDLC
  ERPDUs enabled, min. interval 10 msec.
  CLNS fast switching enabled
  CLNS SSE switching disabled
  DEC compatibility mode OFF for this interface
  Next ESH/ISH in 28 seconds
  Routing Protocol: IS-IS
    Circuit Type: level-1-2
    Interface number 0x0, local circuit ID 0x100
    Level-2 Metric: 10, Priority: 64, Circuit ID: Phoenix.00
    Number of active level-2 adjacencies: 1
    Next IS-IS Hello in 1 seconds


Phoenix#show isis database

IS-IS Level-2 Link State Database:
LSPID             LSP Seq Num    LSP Checksum  LSP Holdtime    ATT/P/OL
SanJose1.00-00    0x00000021     0x9F4E        1117            0/0/0
SanJose1.01-00    0x0000001B     0x5526        741             0/0/0
Phoenix.00-00   * 0x00000021     0x9DD6        1119            0/0/0
```

Both outputs show only L2 information, confirming that Phoenix is now an L2-only router.

A successful ping throughout the network indicates that multiarea Integrated IS-IS with authentication has been configured properly.

Step 8

Issue the **show ip route** command on SanJose2:

```
SanJose2#show ip route
Codes: C - connected, S - static, I - IGRP, R - RIP, M - mobile, B - BGP
       D - EIGRP, EX - EIGRP external, O - OSPF, IA - OSPF inter area
       N1 - OSPF NSSA external type 1, N2 - OSPF NSSA external type 2
       E1 - OSPF external type 1, E2 - OSPF external type 2, E - EGP
       i - IS-IS, L1 - IS-IS level-1, L2 - IS-IS level-2, ia - IS-IS inter area
       * - candidate default, U - per-user static route, o - ODR
       P - periodic downloaded static route

Gateway of last resort is 172.16.0.1 to network 0.0.0.0

i L1 192.168.10.0/24 [115/20] via 172.16.0.1, FastEthernet0/0
     172.16.0.0/24 is subnetted, 1 subnets
C        172.16.0.0 is directly connected, FastEthernet0/0
C    192.168.20.0/24 is directly connected, Loopback0
     10.0.0.0/30 is subnetted, 1 subnets
i L1     10.0.0.0 [115/20] via 172.16.0.1, FastEthernet0/0
i*L1 0.0.0.0/0 [115/10] via 172.16.0.1, FastEthernet0/0
```

The SanJose2 routing table shown would have included an entry for 192.168.30.0 as an L2 route if SanJose2 had been left as an L2-only router. However, because SanJose2 was changed to an L1-only router, it no longer has L2 routes.

Note that the gateway of last resort has been set in the SanJose2 routing table. L1-only routers, such as SanJose2, always learn a default route from a neighboring L1L2 router. In this case, it was SanJose1. This is standard operating procedure for Integrated IS-IS. SanJose2 learns to exit area 49.0001 by way of SanJose1 as a result of the attached bit (ATT) being set in the L1 nonpseudonode LSP sent by SanJose1.

Issue the **show isis database** command on SanJose2:

```
SanJose2#show isis database

IS-IS Level-1 Link State Database:
LSPID                LSP Seq Num  LSP Checksum  LSP Holdtime    ATT/P/OL
SanJose1.00-00       0x0000001F   0xAA2F        690             1/0/0
SanJose1.01-00       0x0000001E   0x851A        900             0/0/0
SanJose2.00-00     * 0x0000001E   0x4B57        934             0/0/0
```

The attached bit (ATT) indicates that SanJose1 is also an L2 router and can reach other areas.

You can also see the attached bit in the SanJose1 L1 link-state database:

```
SanJose1#show isis database

IS-IS Level-1 Link State Database:
LSPID                LSP Seq Num  LSP Checksum  LSP Holdtime    ATT/P/OL
SanJose1.00-00     * 0x0000001F   0xAA2F        640             1/0/0
SanJose1.01-00     * 0x0000001E   0x851A        849             0/0/0
SanJose2.00-00       0x0000001E   0x4B57        879             0/0/0
IS-IS Level-2 Link State Database:
LSPID                LSP Seq Num  LSP Checksum  LSP Holdtime    ATT/P/OL
SanJose1.00-00     * 0x00000022   0x9D4F        583             0/0/0
SanJose1.01-00     * 0x0000001D   0x5128        890             0/0/0
Phoenix.00-00        0x00000022   0x9BD7        584             0/0/0
```

Save all configurations for future reference.

Reflection

Although SanJose2 and Phoenix were configured as L1-only and L2-only routers, respectively, they could have been left with the default setting of L1L2. The result would have been each forming adjacencies for both levels, but unnecessarily. Why should unnecessary IS-IS adjacencies be eliminated?

Lab 7.7.3: Configuring IS-IS over Frame Relay

Estimated Time: 50 Minutes

Objective

In this lab, you configure IS-IS over a hub-and-spoke Frame Relay topology using point-to-point (p2p) subinterfaces on the topology shown in either Figure 7-3 or Figure 7-4. Multipoint configurations are not used with IS-IS as they are in OSPF.

Figure 7-3   Sample Topology for Using the Adtran Atlas 550

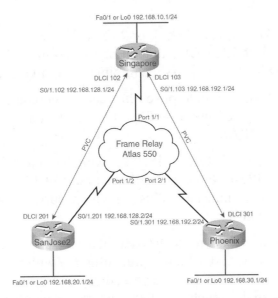

Figure 7-4   Sample Topology for Using the Frame Relay Switch

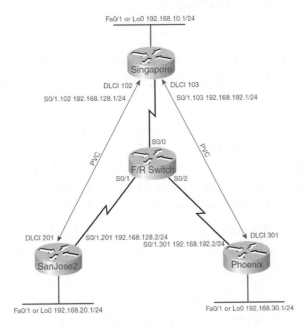

Equipment Requirements

You need the following equipment to complete this lab using the Adtran Atlas 550:

- Three Cisco 2600 series routers
- One Adtran Atlas 550 Frame Relay simulator
- Three serial cables

You need the following equipment to complete this lab using the Frame Relay switch:

- Four Cisco 2600 series routers (One of which must have at least three serial connections.)
- Three serial cables

You can use three Cisco 2620, 2621, 2620XM, or 2621XM routers or a combination for this lab. You will use Cisco IOS Release 12.2(12) with the Enterprise Plus or Enterprise Plus IPSec 56 feature set. The Enterprise Plus feature set is the minimum requirement for IS-IS support.

Cisco IOS Release 12.2(12) with the Enterprise Plus feature set requires a minimum of 16 MB of Flash and 48 MB of RAM, and the Enterprise Plus IPSec 56 feature set requires a minimum of 16 MB of Flash and 64 MB of RAM.

The image names for the Cisco IOS Release 12.2(12) with the Enterprise Plus and Plus IPSec 56 feature sets are c2600-js-mz.122-12.bin and c2600-jk8s-mz.122-12.bin, respectively. The "j" indicates "Enterprise" and the "s" indicates "Plus." If a more current release of this IOS— such as 12.2(12a) or 12.2(12b)—is available, use it instead.

This lab requires another router or device to act as a Frame Relay switch. Figure 7-3 assumes that you will use an Adtran Atlas 550, which is preconfigured with the CCNP Version 3.0 Adtran configuration file. Figure 7-4 assumes that you will configure a router with at least three serial interfaces as a Frame Relay switch (such as a 2600 router with two WIC-2A/S installed). See the configuration at the end of this lab for an example of how to configure a router as a Frame Relay switch. If desired, you can copy the configuration to a 2600 router for use in this lab.

Scenario

The International Travel Agency has just connected two regional headquarters to Singapore using Frame Relay in a hub-and-spoke topology. You are asked to configure IS-IS routing over this network.

Step 1

Cable the network according to Figures 7-1 and 7-2. Configure the host names according to Figures 7-1 and 7-2. Configure the host name, turn off DNS lookup, add the Telnet shortcuts as was done in "Lab 7.7.1: Configuring Basic Integrated IS-IS," and configure the IP address on the Fast Ethernet or Loopback interfaces, whichever option was selected.

Configure each router's Fast Ethernet interface or Loopback interface as shown, but leave the serial interfaces and IS-IS routing unconfigured for now. Until you configure Frame Relay, you cannot use **ping** to test connectivity.

Step 2

Singapore acts as the hub in this hub-and-spoke network. It reaches SanJose2 and Phoenix via two separate PVCs.

IS-IS can work only over NBMA clouds (such as Frame Relay) configured with a full mesh. Anything less than a full mesh can cause serious connectivity and routing issues. Even if a full mesh is configured, it might not exist at all times. A failure in the underlying switched WAN network, or a misconfiguration on one or more routers, could break the full mesh either temporarily or permanently. Avoid NBMA multipoint configurations for IS-IS networks. Use point-to-point subinterfaces.

Configure Frame Relay on Singapore's serial interface, as shown here:

```
Singapore(config)#interface serial 0/1
Singapore(config-if)#encapsulation frame-relay
Singapore(config-if)#no shutdown
Singapore(config-if)#interface s0/1.102 point-to-point
Singapore(config-subif)#ip address 192.168.128.1 255.255.255.0
Singapore(config-subif)#frame-relay interface-dlci 102
Singapore(config-subif)#interface s0/1.103 point-to-point
Singapore(config-subif)#ip address 192.168.192.1 255.255.255.0
Singapore(config-subif)#frame-relay interface-dlci 103
```

Configure SanJose2's serial interface:

```
SanJose2(config)#interface serial 0/1
SanJose2(config-if)#encapsulation frame-relay
SanJose2(config-if)#no shutdown
SanJose2(config-if)#interface s0/1.201 point-to-point
SanJose2(config-subif)#ip address 192.168.128.2 255.255.255.0
SanJose2(config-subif)#frame-relay interface-dlci 201
```

Finally, configure Phoenix's serial interface:

```
Phoenix(config)#interface serial 0/1
Phoenix(config-if)#encapsulation frame-relay
Phoenix(config-if)#no shutdown
Phoenix(config-if)#interface s0/1.301 point-to-point
Phoenix(config-subif)#ip address 192.168.192.2 255.255.255.0
Phoenix(config-subif)#frame-relay interface-dlci 301
```

Verify Frame Relay operation with a ping from Singapore to SanJose2 and Phoenix.

1.   Are you able to ping all the interfaces?

Issue **show frame-relay pvc** and **show frame-relay map** to troubleshoot connectivity problems:

```
Singapore#show frame-relay pvc

PVC Statistics for interface Serial0/1 (Frame Relay DTE)

                Active      Inactive      Deleted       Static
Local             2            0             0             0
Switched          0            0             0             0
Unused            0            1             0             0

DLCI = 102, DLCI USAGE = LOCAL, PVC STATUS = ACTIVE, INTERFACE = Serial0/1.102

  input pkts 51          output pkts 55        in bytes 14032
  out bytes 15488        dropped pkts 0        in pkts dropped 0
  out pkts dropped 0        out bytes dropped 0
  in FECN pkts 0         in BECN pkts 0        out FECN pkts 0
  out BECN pkts 0        in DE pkts 0          out DE pkts 0
  out bcast pkts 50      out bcast bytes 14968
  pvc create time 00:50:57, last time pvc status changed 00:31:03

DLCI = 103, DLCI USAGE = LOCAL, PVC STATUS = ACTIVE, INTERFACE = Serial0/1.103
```

```
input pkts 48           output pkts 49          in bytes 13093
out bytes 13811         dropped pkts 0          in pkts dropped 0
out pkts dropped 0             out bytes dropped 0
in FECN pkts 0          in BECN pkts 0          out FECN pkts 0
out BECN pkts 0         in DE pkts 0            out DE pkts 0
out bcast pkts 44       out bcast bytes 13291
pvc create time 00:51:00, last time pvc status changed 00:31:07
```

```
DLCI = 104, DLCI USAGE = UNUSED, PVC STATUS = INACTIVE, INTERFACE = Serial0/1
```

```
input pkts 0            output pkts 0           in bytes 0
out bytes 0             dropped pkts 0          in pkts dropped 0
out pkts dropped 0             out bytes dropped 0
in FECN pkts 0          in BECN pkts 0          out FECN pkts 0
out BECN pkts 0         in DE pkts 0            out DE pkts 0
out bcast pkts 0        out bcast bytes 0
switched pkts 0
Detailed packet drop counters:
no out intf 0           out intf down 0         no out PVC 0
in PVC down 0           out PVC down 0          pkt too big 0
shaping Q full 0        pkt above DE 0          policing drop 0
pvc create time 00:28:02, last time pvc status changed 00:28:02
```

```
Singapore#show frame-relay map
Serial0/1.103 (up): point-to-point dlci, dlci 103(0x67,0x1870), broadcast
        status defined, active
Serial0/1.102 (up): point-to-point dlci, dlci 102(0x66,0x1860), broadcast
        status defined, active
```

You can disregard the DLCI 104 information in the show frame-relay pvc output—it is discovered via LMI exchanges with the switch. (The Adtran Atlas 550 is configured to advertise DLCIs 102, 103, and 104 out port 1/1.) DLCI 104 is inactive because no device is connected to port 2/2. The 550 is configured to support a 4-node full mesh.

Step 3

Like OSPF, you configure IS-IS by enabling an IS-IS process and specifying which interfaces are to participate in the IS-IS process. Configure IS-IS to run over this point-to-point network with the following commands:

```
Singapore(config)#router isis
Singapore(config-router)#net 49.0001.1111.1111.1111.00
Singapore(config-router)#int serial 0/1.102
Singapore(config-if)#ip router isis
Singapore(config-if)#int serial 0/1.103
Singapore(config-if)#ip router isis
Singapore(config-if)#int lo0
Singapore(config-if)#ip router isis

SanJose2(config)#router isis
SanJose2(config-router)#net 49.0001.2222.2222.2222.00
SanJose2(config-router)#int serial 0/1.201
SanJose2(config-if)#ip router isis
SanJose2(config-if)#int lo0
SanJose2(config-if)#ip router isis

Phoenix(config)#router isis
Phoenix(config-router)#net 49.0001.3333.3333.3333.00
Phoenix(config-router)# int serial 0/1.301
Phoenix(config-if)#ip router isis
Phoenix(config-if)#int lo0
Phoenix(config-if)#ip router isis
```

Verify your IS-IS configuration by issuing the **show ip route** command on each of the routers:

```
Phoenix#show ip route
Codes: C - connected, S - static, I - IGRP, R - RIP, M - mobile, B - BGP
       D - EIGRP, EX - EIGRP external, O - OSPF, IA - OSPF inter area
       N1 - OSPF NSSA external type 1, N2 - OSPF NSSA external type 2
```

```
    E1 - OSPF external type 1, E2 - OSPF external type 2, E - EGP
    i - IS-IS, L1 - IS-IS level-1, L2 - IS-IS level-2, ia - IS-IS inter area
    * - candidate default, U - per-user static route, o - ODR
    P - periodic downloaded static route

Gateway of last resort is not set

C    192.168.192.0/24 is directly connected, Serial0/1.301
C    192.168.30.0/24 is directly connected, Loopback0
i L1 192.168.128.0/24 [115/20] via 192.168.192.1, Serial0/1.301
i L1 192.168.10.0/24 [115/20] via 192.168.192.1, Serial0/1.301
i L1 192.168.20.0/24 [115/30] via 192.168.192.1, Serial0/1.301
```

If each router has a complete table, including routes to 192.168.10.0/24, 192.168.20.0/24, and 192.168.30.0/24, you have successfully configured IS-IS to operate over Frame Relay.

Test these routes by pinging the Fast Ethernet/Loopback interfaces of each router from Phoenix's console.

1.   Can you ping all the Fast Ethernet/Loopback interfaces?

_____

Finally, issue the **show isis database** and **show isis topology** commands:

```
Singapore#show isis database

IS-IS Level-1 Link State Database:
LSPID              LSP Seq Num   LSP Checksum   LSP Holdtime   ATT/P/OL
Singapore.00-00  * 0x00000007    0x3B7A         737            0/0/0
SanJose2.00-00     0x00000004    0xA0ED         736            0/0/0
Phoenix.00-00      0x00000003    0x7603         666            0/0/0
IS-IS Level-2 Link State Database:
LSPID              LSP Seq Num   LSP Checksum   LSP Holdtime   ATT/P/OL
Singapore.00-00  * 0x00000009    0x2F3C         744            0/0/0
SanJose2.00-00     0x00000006    0x90E7         747            0/0/0
Phoenix.00-00      0x00000004    0x5B53         742            0/0/0


SanJose2#show isis topology

IS-IS paths to level-1 routers
System Id      Metric   Next-Hop       Interface    SNPA
Singapore      10       Singapore      Se0/1.201    DLCI 201
SanJose2       --
Phoenix        20       Singapore      Se0/1.201    DLCI 201

IS-IS paths to level-2 routers
System Id      Metric   Next-Hop       Interface    SNPA
Singapore      10       Singapore      Se0/1.201    DLCI 201
SanJose2       --
Phoenix        20       Singapore      Se0/1.201    DLCI 201
```

Note that no pseudonode LSPs (with nonzero circuit IDs) appear in the **show isis database** output because you are using p2p links to connect the routers.

2.   How is the subnetwork point of attachment (SNPA) expressed in a Frame Relay network?

_____

Step 4

A common error with IS-IS configuration is mismatched interface types in an NBMA environment (normally Frame Relay or ATM). To illustrate this, switch SanJose2's point-to-point interface to a multipoint interface:

```
SanJose2(config)#interface s0/1.201
SanJose2(config-subif)#no ip address
SanJose2(config-subif)#no ip router isis
SanJose2(config-subif)#no frame-relay interface-dlci 201
SanJose2(config-subif)#interface s0/1.2001 multipoint
SanJose2(config-subif)#ip address 192.168.128.2 255.255.255.0
SanJose2(config-subif)#ip router isis
SanJose2(config-subif)#frame-relay interface-dlci 201
```

Allow the Frame Relay PVC to become active. Then view the output of the **show clns neighbors** command on Singapore and SanJose2:

```
Singapore#show clns neighbors

System Id    Interface   SNPA            State   Holdtime   Type Protocol
Phoenix      Se0/1.103   DLCI 103        Up      27         L1L2 IS-IS

SanJose2#show clns neighbors

System Id    Interface   SNPA            State   Holdtime   Type Protocol
Singapore    Se0/1.2001  DLCI 201        Up      258        IS   ES-IS
```

The output indicates mismatched interface types! Recall from the curriculum that, since IOS Release 12.1(1)T, an Integrated IS-IS mismatch is indicated in this case:

- SanJose2 (multipoint) receives a point-to-point hello PDU, realizes it is the wrong hello type, and installs the neighbor as an ES. SanJose shows Singapore in the **show clns neighbors** with protocol ES-IS.

- Singapore (point-to-point) receives the LAN hello PDU, recognizes the mismatch, and ignores the neighbor. SanJose2 never appears in Singapore's **show clns neighbors** output. **debug isis adj-packets** output shows the incoming LAN IIH PDU and R2 declaring the mismatch:

```
SanJose2#debug isis adj-packets
IS-IS Adjacency related packets debugging is on
00:31:58: ISIS-Adj: Sending L1 LAN IIH on Loopback0, length 1514
00:31:58: ISIS-Adj: Sending L2 LAN IIH on Loopback0, length 1514
00:31:59: ISIS-Adj: Encapsulation failed for L2 LAN IIH on Serial0/1.2001
00:31:59: ISIS-Adj: Encapsulation failed for L1 LAN IIH on Serial0/1.2001
00:32:01: ISIS-Adj: Sending L1 LAN IIH on Loopback0, length 1514
00:32:01: ISIS-Adj: Sending L2 LAN IIH on Loopback0, length 1514
00:32:02: ISIS-Adj: Encapsulation failed for L2 LAN IIH on Serial0/1.2001
00:32:03: ISIS-Adj: Encapsulation failed for L1 LAN IIH on Serial0/1.2001
00:32:04: ISIS-Adj: Sending L2 LAN IIH on Loopback0, length 1514
00:32:04: ISIS-Adj: Sending L1 LAN IIH on Loopback0, length 1514
00:32:04: ISIS-Adj: Rec serial IIH from DLCI 201 (Serial0/1.2001), cir type L1L2, cir
id 00, length 1499
00:32:04: ISIS-Adj: Point-to-point IIH received on multi-point interface: ignored IIH
00:32:05: ISIS-Adj: Encapsulation failed for L2 LAN IIH on Serial0/1.2001
00:32:06: ISIS-Adj: Encapsulation failed for L1 LAN IIH on Serial0/1.2001
```

This completes the IS-IS over Frame Relay lab. You easily can configure Integrated IS-IS over a Frame Relay cloud. The only caveat is that IS-IS NBMA configurations, unlike OSPF, are essentially limited to point-to-point implementations. Mismatched interface types in an NBMA environment are a common problem. The symptoms are reflected in the output of the **show clns neighbors** command and the **debug isis adj-packets** command.

Router as Frame Relay Switch Configuration

The following configuration enables a 2600 router with two WIC-2A/S to act as a Frame Relay switch for this lab:

```
Frame-Switch#show run
version 12.2
service timestamps debug uptime
service timestamps log uptime
service password-encryption
!
hostname Frame-Switch
!
ip subnet-zero
no ip domain-lookup
!
ip audit notify log
ip audit po max-events 100
frame-relay switching
!
process-max-time 200
!
interface Serial0/0
 no ip address
 no ip directed-broadcast
 encapsulation frame-relay
 clockrate 128000
 frame-relay intf-type dce
 frame-relay route 102 interface Serial0/1 201
 frame-relay route 103 interface Serial0/2 301
!
interface Serial0/1
 no ip address
 no ip directed-broadcast
 encapsulation frame-relay
 clockrate 128000
 frame-relay intf-type dce
 frame-relay route 201 interface Serial0/0 102
!
interface Serial0/2
 no ip address
 no ip directed-broadcast
 encapsulation frame-relay
 clockrate 128000
 frame-relay intf-type dce
 frame-relay route 301 interface Serial0/0 103
!
interface Serial0/3
 no ip address
 no ip directed-broadcast
 shutdown
!
ip classless
no ip http server
!
line con 0
 password cisco
 login
 transport input none
line aux 0
line vty 0 4
 password cisco
 login
!
no scheduler allocate
end
```

Chapter 8

Route Optimization

Lab 8.5.1: Configuring Distribute Lists and Passive Interfaces

Estimated Time: 45 Minutes

Objective

In this lab, you use a combination of advanced routing features to optimize routing for the routers shown in the sample topology in Figure 8-1. These features include distribute lists, passive interfaces, default routes, and route redistribution.

Figure 8-1   Sample Topology for Lab 8.5.1

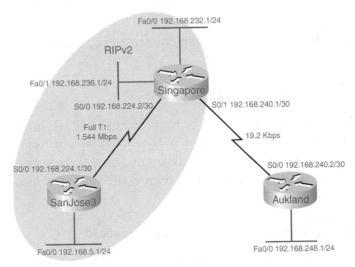

Equipment Requirements

You need the following equipment for this exercise:

* Three 2600 series Cisco routers

* Two serial cables

Scenario

The International Travel Agency (ITA) uses RIP v2 for dynamic routing. Perform an analysis to determine whether RIP v2 is optimized.

A slow 19.2 kbps link is used to connect Singapore and Auckland until a faster link can be provisioned. To reduce traffic, try to avoid dynamic routing on this link.

The LAN connects to SanJose3 is a stub network that is near saturation. To reduce traffic, filter RIP v2 updates from entering the Ethernet LAN 192.168.5.0/24 of router SanJose3; the updates serve no purpose.

ITA has a large research and development division in Singapore. The R&D engineers are on LAN 192.168.232.0/24. The R&D managers on the 192.168.236.0/24 LAN need access to this experimental network; however, this LAN needs to be invisible to the rest of the company—that is, subnets not attached to the Singapore site. Also, the two R&D LANs have many UNIX hosts that need to exchange RIP v2 updates with the Singapore router.

Step 1

Build and configure the network according to the diagram, but do not configure RIP v2 yet.

Use Cisco Discovery Protocol (CDP) to verify Layer 2 connectivity with directly connected neighbors. Use **ping** to verify the work and test connectivity between the serial interfaces. Ping only the other side of the link that is the directly connected neighbor IP address.

Note: Auckland should not be able to ping SanJose3 until additional configurations have been made.

Step 2

On SanJose3, configure RIP v2 to advertise both connected networks, as shown in the following:

```
SanJose3(config)#router rip
SanJose3(config-router)#version 2
SanJose3(config-router)#network 192.168.224.0
SanJose3(config-router)#network 192.168.5.0
```

On the Ethernet LAN of SanJose3, no routers or hosts require RIP v2; however, if the 192.168.5.0 network in the RIP v2 configuration is not included, SanJose3 will not advertise the network to Singapore. Fast Ethernet 0/0 can be configured as a passive interface, keeping the router from sending RIP v2 updates out the Fast Ethernet 0/0 interface. Use the following commands:

```
SanJose3(config)#router rip
SanJose3(config-router)#passive-interface fastethernet0/0
```

RIP v2 updates will no longer be sent through Fast Ethernet 0/0.

Step 3

Configure RIP v2 on Singapore. At this point, issue the following commands to enable RIP v2 only on the 192.168.224.0/30 network so that Singapore can exchange routing information with SanJose3:

```
Singapore(config)#router rip
Singapore(config-router)#version 2
Singapore(config-router)#network 192.168.224.0
```

After you enter this RIP v2 configuration on Singapore, check the routing table on SanJose3 with the **show ip route** command, as follows:

Note: SanJose3 has not learned routes through RIP v2.

```
SanJose3#show ip route
<output omitted>
C    192.168.5.0/24 is directly connected, FastEthernet0/0
C    192.168.224.0/24 is directly connected, Serial0/0
```

1.   SanJose3 has not learned about 192.168.232.0/24 and 192.168.236.0/24. Why not? Issue the **debug ip rip** command on SanJose3 to validate this assumption. Are RIP updates seen coming in through the Serial 0/0 interface?

RIP has not been configured on Singapore to advertise the Ethernet networks. Also, RIP will not advertise a route for 192.168.224.0/30 out interface serial 0/0, where the network resides.

Step 4

Review the network requirements. Then, issue the following to enable RIP v2 on the Ethernet interfaces of Singapore so that UNIX hosts on these LANs can receive routing information:

```
Singapore(config)#router rip
Singapore(config-router)#Version 2
Singapore(config-router)#network 192.168.232.0
Singapore(config-router)#network 192.168.236.0
```

RIP v2 is now sending updates to these networks, as required for the UNIX hosts. Reissue the **show ip route** command to recheck the routing table of SanJose3:

Note: Turn off **debug ip rip** before continuing.

```
SanJose3#show ip route

Gateway of last resort is not set

     192.168.224.0/30 is subnetted, 1 subnets
C       192.168.224.0 is directly connected, Serial0/0
C    192.168.5.0/24 is directly connected, FastEthernet0/0
R    192.168.232.0/24 [120/1] via 192.168.224.1, 00:00:13, Serial0/0
R    192.168.236.0/24 [120/1] via 192.168.224.1, 00:00:09, Serial0/0
```

The **network** command enables RIP updates on interfaces within that major network and advertises those networks out all other RIP-enabled interfaces. SanJose3 now has routes to 192.168.232.0/24 and 192.168.236.0/24. Having route 192.168.232.0/24 is intended. However, having route 192.168.236.0/24 is a potential problem. Remember that this network is to be kept invisible to the rest of the company.

Step 5

You can omit RIP advertisements regarding the 192.168.236.0/24 network from updates in one of two ways. If you issue the **no network 192.168.236.0** command on the Singapore router, advertisements about this network cease; however, by using this method, network 192.168.236.0 is no longer visible to the UNIX hosts that are on this network. The preferred method of filtering this network advertisement from reaching the SanJose3 router is to filter routing protocol updates with the **distribute-list** command.

Distribution lists define which networks are permitted or denied when receiving or sending routing updates. Distribution lists require an access list to define which networks are permitted and which networks are denied.

Because 192.168.236.0/24 is to be filtered from outgoing updates to the SanJose3 router, use the following commands:

```
Singapore(config)#access-list 1 deny 192.168.236.0
Singapore(config)#access-list 1 permit any
Singapore(config)#router rip
Singapore(config-router)#distribute-list 1 out serial 0/0
```

It is critical to include the interface at the end of the **distribute-list** command so that this filter is applied only to routing updates sent out to SanJose3. Without the reference to the particular interface, the router filters out all advertisement of the 192.168.236.0/24 network to all interfaces, including the UNIX hosts that are connected to the 192.168.232.0 LAN on Singapore. The [*interface-name*] argument is optional and specifies the interface on which the update is expected. It is possible to define one inbound interface-specific distribute list per interface, and one globally defined distribute list.

Verify that this filter has been applied by issuing the **show ip protocols** command on Singapore:

```
Singapore#show ip protocols
Routing Protocol is "rip"
  Sending updates every 30 seconds, next due in 4 seconds
  Invalid after 180 seconds, hold down 180, flushed after 240
  Outgoing update filter list for all interfaces is not set
    Serial0/0 filtered by 1 (per-user), default is 1
  Incoming update filter list for all interfaces is
  Redistributing: rip
  Default version control: send version 2, receive version 2
    Interface        Send  Recv  Triggered RIP  Key-chain
    FastEthernet0/0  2     2
    Serial0/0        2     2
    FastEthernet0/1  2     2
  Routing for Networks:
    192.168.224.0
    192.168.232.0
    192.168.236.0
  Passive Interface(s):
    Serial0/1
  Routing Information Sources:
    Gateway          Distance      Last Update
    192.168.224.2         120       00:00:03
  Distance: (default is 120)
```

1. According to the output of this command, to which interface is the outgoing update filter list applied?

Do not set the list that is applied to all RIP-enabled interfaces. Instead, notice that the Serial 0/0 interface is being filtered by list 1, which happens to be the access list number that was configured in the previous example.

With the distribute list configured on Singapore, return to SanJose3 and flush the routing table with the **clear ip route *** command. Wait at least five seconds, and then use the **show ip route** command as follows to check the routing table of SanJose3:

```
SanJose3#show ip route

Gateway of last resort is not set

     192.168.224.0/30 is subnetted, 1 subnets
C       192.168.224.0 is directly connected, Serial0/0
C     192.168.5.0/24 is directly connected, FastEthernet0/0
R     192.168.232.0/24 [120/1] via 192.168.224.1, 00:00:01,
Serial0/0
```

2.   Looking at the routing table of SanJose3, is 192.168.236.0/24 present?

The distribute list should have removed 192.168.236.0/24 from further RIP updates. 192.168.232.0/24 should be the only RIP route in the SanJose3 routing table at this point.

Step 6

The SanJose3 routing table is almost complete, but it does not include a route to 192.168.240.0/30, which is connected directly to Singapore. You can use two methods to advertise the link between Singapore and Auckland by way of RIP. The first method is similar to what you did previously with the other routers and the advertisement of their directly connected networks. The process involves entering a network command in the RIP v2 configuration of router Singapore so that it will advertise the 192.168.240.0/30 network. Of course, you should not send RIP v2 updates out the 19.2 kbps link. Therefore, you would need to place S0/1 of Singapore into passive mode. You do this with the **passive-interface serial 0/1** command while you are at the Singapore RIP router configuration prompt. You must advertise this network using a different approach. The alternative method is to configure the Singapore router to redistribute connected networks into RIP v2. Enter the following commands on Singapore:

```
Singapore(config)#router rip
Singapore(config-router)#redistribute connected
Singapore(config-router)#no auto-summary
```

When issuing these commands, Singapore imports all directly connected routes into the RIP process. Therefore, 192.168.240.0/30 is redistributed into RIP v2 and sent to SanJose3 as part of each RIP v2 update. Verify the configuration by issuing the following command on Singapore:

```
Singapore #show ip route 192.168.240.1
Routing entry for 192.168.240.0/30
  Known via 'connected', distance 0, metric 0 (connected, via interface)
  Redistributing via rip
  Advertised by rip
  Routing Descriptor Blocks:
  * directly connected, via Serial0/1
      Route metric is 0, traffic share count is 1
```

The output of this command should confirm that this connected route is being redistributed and advertised by RIP v2.

Check the routing table of SanJose3 with the **show ip route** command, as follows:

```
SanJose3#show ip route
Gateway of last resort is not set
     192.168.224.0/30 is subnetted, 1 subnets
C       192.168.224.0 is directly connected, Serial0/0
     192.168.240.0/30 is subnetted, 1 subnets
R       192.168.240.0 [120/1] via 192.168.224.1, 00:00:02, Serial0/0
R    192.168.240.0/24 [120/1] via 192.168.224.1 00:01:17 Serial 0/0
C    192.168.5.0/24 is directly connected, FastEthernet0/0
R    192.168.232.0/24 [120/1] via 192.168.224.1, 00:00:02, Serial0/0
```

SanJose3 should now have RIP v2 routes to both 192.168.240.0/30 and 192.168.232.0/24.

Step 7

With routing between Singapore and SanJose3 almost complete, view Auckland. Avoid dynamic routing on the WAN link of router Auckland, and use a static route.

Try to ping Auckland serial interface 192.168.240.2 from SanJose3. Is this successful?

Auckland is a stub network. It has only one exit point to the rest of the world. In this situation, configure a static default route that will work for all nonlocal traffic by using the following command:

```
Auckland(config)#ip route 0.0.0.0 0.0.0.0 192.168.240.1 210
```

The administrative distance of 210 was added so that the static route would not default to 1. A distance of 1 prohibits an administrator from overriding the route if the topology changes in the future. Although adding an administrative distance of 210 is not required, it is a best practice to avoid routes that end up with an administrative distance equal to 1.

Verify that Auckland is using a default route. From the console of SanJose3, enter the **debug ip packet** command, as follows:

```
SanJose3#debug ip packet
```

Leave the SanJose3 router console session open and then return to Auckland. From the Auckland router console, ping the SanJose3 FastEthernet 0/0 at 192.168.5.1.

You can see debug output on the SanJose3 router:

```
IP packet debugging is on
00:53:31: IP: s=192.168.240.2 (Serial0/0), d=192.168.5.1, len 100,
rcvd 4
00:53:31: IP: s=192.168.5.1 (local), d=192.168.240.2 (Serial0/0),
len 100, sending
```

These pings should be successful.

Note: The debug output of SanJose3 reports that the pings have been received and replied to.

Next, ping SanJose3 using **extended ping** commands. Invoke an extended ping by typing **ping** and pressing **Enter** in privileged mode. Use the extended commands and source the ping from the Fast Ethernet 0/0 address of Auckland, 192.168.248.1, as follows:

```
Auckland#ping
Protocol [ip]: ip
Target IP address: 192.168.5.1
Repeat count [5]: 5
Datagram size [100]: 100
Timeout in seconds [2]: 2
Extended commands [n]: y
Source address or interface: 192.168.248.1
Type of service [0]: 0
Set DF bit in IP header? [no]: no
Validate reply data? [no]: no
Data pattern [0xABCD]: 0xABCD
Loose, Strict, Record, Timestamp, Verbose[none]: none
Sweep range of sizes [n]: n
```

1.   Were these pings successful?

Check the **debug ip packet** output on SanJose3.

The following shows the **debug** output as seen on the SanJose3 router:

```
IP packet debugging is on
00:56:53: IP: s=192.168.248.1 (Serial0/0), d=192.168.5.1, len 100,
rcvd 4
00:56:53: IP: s=192.168.5.1 (local), d=192.168.248.1, len 100, unroutable
```

2.   You should see the arrival of the ICMP echo requests, or pings. SanJose3 did not respond. Why not?

_____

3.   Check the routing table of SanJose3. Does SanJose3 have a route to the 192.168.248.0/24 network?

_____

At this point, SanJose3 does not have a route to network 192.168.248.0/24 or a default route for unknown destinations.

Step 8

For Singapore and SanJose3 to route to 192.168.248.0/24, you must configure it as a static route. You decide to configure the static route on Singapore and let Singapore propagate this route to other routers, such as SanJose3, dynamically. This saves the task of entering a static route on every router. Enter the following command on Singapore:

```
Singapore(config)#ip route 192.168.248.0 255.255.255.0 192.168.240.2 210
```

This command configures a static route for the 192.168.248.0/24 network using the S0/0 of Auckland as the next hop with an administrative distance of 210.

For Singapore to dynamically update SanJose3 with this information, you must configure RIP v2 to redistribute static routes on Singapore. Issue the following commands:

```
Singapore(config)#router rip
Singapore(config-router)#redistribute static metric 2
```

Although a metric is not required when you are redistributing a static route into RIP, it is a good idea to include one. The value of 2 indicates to the SanJose3 router that the 192.168.248.0/24 network exists one hop beyond the advertising Singapore router.

Check the routing table on SanJose3, as follows:

```
SanJose3#show ip route
Gateway of last resort is not set
     192.168.224.0/30 is subnetted, 1 subnets
C       192.168.224.0 is directly connected, Serial0/0
     192.168.240.0/30 is subnetted, 1 subnets
R       192.168.240.0 [120/1] via 192.168.224.1, 00:00:01, Serial0/0
C     192.168.5.0/24 is directly connected, FastEthernet0/0
R     192.168.232.0/24 [120/1] via 192.168.224.1, 00:00:02, Serial0/0
R     192.168.248.0/24 [120/2] via 192.168.224.1, 00:00:02, Serial0/0
```

This should now be complete. Verify connectivity with an extended ping from the Fast Ethernet 0/0 of SanJose3 to the Fast Ethernet 0/0 of Auckland.

Lab 8.5.2a: Configuring Route Maps

Estimated Time: 50 Minutes

Objective

In this lab, you apply a routing policy by configuring a route map on the routers shown in the topology in Figure 8-2.

Figure 8-2   Sample Topology for Lab 8.5.2a

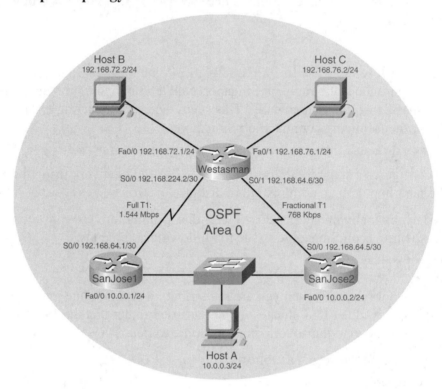

Equipment Requirements

You need the following equipment for this exercise:

*   Three 2600 series Cisco routers

*   Cisco Catalyst switch

*   Three workstations

Scenario

The International Travel Agency maintains two WAN links from the West Tasman site to its core network 10.0.0.0/24. West Tasman is also referred to as Westasman. One link is full T1 or 1.544 Mbps. The other link is a fractional T1 with a capacity of 768 kbps. Under OSPF, West Tasman prefers the full T1 link by virtue of its higher bandwidth and lower cost. All traffic that originates from the 192.168.72.0/24 network that is destined for the 10.0.0.0/24 network needs to be routed through the fractional T1 link. This T1 link has a crypto box allowing encryption and improved security. Apply this policy by configuring a route map on the Westasman router.

Step 1

Build and configure the network according to the diagram. Ensure that the bandwidth for each serial interface listed is set to 1544 kbps. Do not configure the link between Westasman and SanJose2 as a fractional T1 yet. WIC 2T and standard serial interfaces will default to 1544k. Serial interfaces that are Sync/Async will default to 128k. If you use a WIC 2A/S in one of the lab routers, be sure to adjust the bandwidth to 1544 initially. Configure all interfaces for OSPF Area 0. Configure Host A and Host B with IP addresses and default gateways as indicated in the diagram. Initially, configure the serial links for equal cost share. That is, do not configure the serial link bandwidth statements at this time.

Note: Use SanJose1 as the gateway of Host A.

Use **ping** and **show ip route** to verify the work and test connectivity between all interfaces and hosts.

Step 2

Check the routing table on Westasman, as follows:

```
Westasman#show ip route

Gateway of last resort is not set

C    192.168.72.0/24 is directly connected, FastEthernet0/0
C    192.168.76.0/24 is directly connected, FastEthernet0/1
     192.168.64.0/30 is subnetted, 2 subnets
C    192.168.64.0 is directly connected, Serial0/0
C    192.168.64.4 is directly connected, Serial0/1
     10.0.0.0/24 is subnetted, 1 subnets
O    10.0.0.0 [110/65] via 192.168.64.1, 00:00:17, Serial0/0
               [110/65] via 192.168.64.5, 00:00:17, Serial0/1
```

1. How many routes does Westasman have to 10.0.0.0/24?

_____

Two equal cost routes are in the routing table.

Configure S0/1 and S0/0 on Westasman to accurately reflect the bandwidth of the WAN links to SanJose2 and SanJose1, as follows:

```
Westasman(config)#interface serial0/1
Westasman(config-if)#bandwidth 768
Westasman(config)#interface serial0/0
Westasman(config-if)#bandwidth 1544
```

After you set the bandwidth, check the routing table on Westasman, as follows:

```
Westasman#show ip route
Gateway of last resort is not set
C    192.168.72.0/24 is directly connected, FastEthernet0/0
C    192.168.76.0/24 is directly connected, FastEthernet0/1
     192.168.64.0/30 is subnetted, 2 subnets
C       192.168.64.0 is directly connected, Serial0/0
C       192.168.64.4 is directly connected, Serial0/1
     10.0.0.0/24 is subnetted, 1 subnets
O       10.0.0.0 [110/65] via 192.168.64.1, 00:00:01, Serial0/0
```

2. How many routes are there to 10.0.0.0/24?

_____

3.   Which interface is OSPF using to route to 10.0.0.0/24?

Westasman should have one route to the core Fast Ethernet network using S0/0. OSPF uses bandwidth to derive cost for each route. With unequal costs, only the preferred lower cost route is placed in the routing table.

Step 3

Configure a route map to force Westasman to use S0/1 to route traffic from 192.168.72.0/24 bound for 10.0.0.0/24. Before you configure the route map, create an access list that matches the traffic that needs to be policy routed. Because traffic that is sourced from 192.168.72.0/24 will be affected, create the following access list on Westasman:

```
Westasman (config)#access-list 101 permit ip 192.168.72.0 0.0.0.255 10.0.0.0 0.0.0.255
```

Next, create the route map, which will be called CRYPTO. The route map will reference access list 101, which was just created. Use the following commands:

```
Westasman(config)#route-map CRYPTO permit 10
Westasman(config-route-map)#match ip address 101
Westasman(config-route-map)#set interface serial 0/1
```

You will apply this policy to the Fast Ethernet 0/0 of Westasman, because this is the interface that will accept the traffic that is to be policy routed. On Fast Ethernet 0/0, enter the following commands:

```
Westasman(config)#interface fastethernet 0/0
Westasman(config-if)#no ip route-cache
Westasman(config-if)#ip policy route-map CRYPTO
```

Route map CRYPTO is now applied to Fast Ethernet 0/0. To verify this, issue the **show ip interface fastethernet 0/0** command, as follows:

```
Westasman#show ip interface fastethernet 0/0
FastEthernet0/0 is up, line protocol is up
  Internet address is 192.168.72.1/24
  Broadcast address is 255.255.255.255
  Address determined by setup command
  MTU is 1500 bytes
  Helper address is not set
  Directed broadcast forwarding is disabled
  Multicast reserved groups joined: 224.0.0.5 224.0.0.6
  Outgoing access list is not set
  Inbound access list is not set
  Proxy ARP is enabled
  Security level is default
  Split horizon is enabled
  ICMP redirects are always sent
  ICMP unreachables are always sent
  ICMP mask replies are never sent
  IP fast switching is disabled
  IP fast switching on the same interface is disabled
  IP Flow switching is disabled
  IP Feature Fast switching turbo vector
  IP multicast fast switching is enabled
  IP multicast distributed fast switching is disabled
  IP route-cache flags are Fast
  Router Discovery is disabled
  IP output packet accounting is disabled
  IP access violation accounting is disabled
  TCP/IP header compression is disabled
  RTP/IP header compression is disabled
  Probe proxy name replies are disabled
```

```
Policy routing is enabled, using route map CRYPTO
Network address translation is disabled
WCCP Redirect outbound is disabled
WCCP Redirect inbound is disabled
WCCP Redirect exclude is disabled
BGP Policy Mapping is disabled
```

Another simple way to verify that the route map is properly applied to the interface is to issue the **show ip policy** command. The output is displayed, as follows:

```
Westasman#show ip policy
Interface       Route map
Fa0/0           CRYPTO
```

After this configuration is completed, use **show ip route** to verify that S0/0 is still the exit interface for router Westasman to network 10.0.0.0/24.

Step 4

Verify that the policy has taken effect. Issue the **debug ip policy** command at the Westasman console. Leave this window open or issue the **logging buffered** command:

```
Westasman#debug ip policy
Westasman#config t
Westasman(config)#logging buffered
```

From Host B, use a trace route program, such as **tracert**, to trace the route to 10.0.0.1.

During the trace, you should see the output from the **debug ip policy** command, indicating that packets are being policy routed. If the output from the Westasman router is not visible, issue **show logging** to see the output. Using either approach should display output that is similar to the following:

```
01:02:06: IP: s=192.168.72.2 (FastEthernet0/0), d=10.0.0.1, len
78, policy match 01:02:06: IP: route map CRYPTO, item 10, permit

01:02:06: IP: s=192.168.72.2 (FastEthernet0/0), d=10.0.0.1
(Serial0/1), len 78, policy routed
```

Examine the output from the trace route of Host B.

1.   Did this trace hop through 192.168.64.5?

```
Microsoft(R) Windows 95
   (C)Copyright Microsoft Corp  1981-1996.

C:\WINDOWS>tracert 10.0.0.1

Tracing route to 10.0.0.1 over a maximum of 30 hops

  1     1 ms     2 ms     2 ms   192.168.72.1
  2    29 ms    28 ms    36 ms   192.168.64.5
  3    35 ms    34 ms    34 ms   10.0.0.1

Trace complete.

C:\WINDOWS>
```

The next hop should have been 192.168.64.5.

2.   From which of the interfaces of Westasman did this packet exit?

The exit interface should have been S0/1.

From Host C, use a trace route program to trace the route to 10.0.0.2 and examine the output from the trace route:

```
C:\WINDOWS>tracert 10.0.0.2

Tracing route to 10.0.0.2 over a maximum of 30 hops

  1      2 ms      1 ms      2 ms   192.168.76.1
  2     26 ms     26 ms     25 ms   192.168.64.1
  3     31 ms     31 ms     31 ms   10.0.0.2

Trace complete.

C:\WINDOWS>
```

3.   Did this trace hop through 192.168.64.1?

_____

4.   From which of the interfaces of Westasman did this packet exit?

_____

The ICMP packets of Host C took a different route to network 10.0.0.0/24. The access list that was associated with the route map denied the Host C IP address. It was not permitted to be policy routed.

Issue the **show route-map** command on Westasman, as follows:

```
Westasman#show route-map CRYPTO
route-map CRYPTO, permit, sequence 10
  Match clauses:
    ip address (access-lists): 101
  Set clauses:
    interface Serial0/1
  Policy routing matches: 33 packets, 4149 bytes
```

5.   How many packets have been matched for policy routing?

_____

Step 5

1.   Is the network configuration finished?

_____

You can compromise security if you do not return traffic to the 192.168.72.0/24 network through the link with the crypto box. The following commands will complete the scenario.

On router SanJose1, create a route map named RETURN_TRAFFIC that will route all traffic coming from the 10.0.0.0/24 network to the SanJose2 next hop IP address 10.0.0.2:

```
SanJose1(config)#route-map RETURN_TRAFFIC permit 10
SanJose1(config-route-map)#match ip address 101
SanJose1(config-route-map)#set interface fastethernet 0/0
SanJose1(config-route-map)#set ip next-hop 10.0.0.2
```

Create the access list that is referenced in the preceding route map:

```
SanJose1(config)#access-list 101 permit ip 10.0.0.0 0.0.0.255 192.168.72.0 0.0.0.255
```

Activate this route map by issuing the following commands:

```
SanJose1(config)#interface fastethernet 0/0
SanJose1(config-if)#no ip route-cache
SanJose1(config-if)#ip policy route-map RETURN_TRAFFIC
```

Verify that the route map is active with the **show ip policy** or **show ip interface fastethernet 0/0** command, as follows:

```
SanJose1#show ip policy
Interface       Route map
Fa0/0           RETURN_TRAFFIC

SanJose1#show ip interface fastethernet 0/0
FastEthernet0/0 is up, line protocol is up
  Internet address is 10.0.0.1/24
  Broadcast address is 255.255.255.255
  Address determined by setup command
  MTU is 1500 bytes
  Helper address is not set
  Directed broadcast forwarding is disabled
  Multicast reserved groups joined: 224.0.0.5 224.0.0.6
  Outgoing access list is not set
  Inbound  access list is not set
  Proxy ARP is enabled
  Security level is default
  Split horizon is enabled
  ICMP redirects are always sent
  ICMP unreachables are always sent
  ICMP mask replies are never sent
  IP fast switching is disabled
  IP fast switching on the same interface is disabled
  IP Flow switching is disabled
  IP Feature Fast switching turbo vector
  IP multicast fast switching is enabled
  IP multicast distributed fast switching is disabled
  IP route-cache flags are Fast
  Router Discovery is disabled
  IP output packet accounting is disabled
  IP access violation accounting is disabled
  TCP/IP header compression is disabled
  RTP/IP header compression is disabled
  Probe proxy name replies are disabled
  Policy routing is enabled, using route map RETURN_TRAFFIC
  Network address translation is disabled
  WCCP Redirect outbound is disabled
  WCCP Redirect inbound is disabled
  WCCP Redirect exclude is disabled
  BGP Policy Mapping is disabled
```

Step 6

Ensure that the SanJose2 router does not send the route request back to the SanJose1 router. To do so, create a policy that will override the routing table on SanJose2. To complete this requirement, issue the following commands:

```
SanJose2(config)#route-map RETURN_TRAFFIC permit 10
SanJose2(config-route-map)#match ip address 101
SanJose2(config-route-map)#set interface serial 0/0
```

Create the access list that is referenced in the preceding route map.

```
SanJose2(config)#access-list 101 permit ip 10.0.0.0 0.0.0.255 192.168.72.0 0.0.0.255
```

Activate this route map by issuing the following commands:

```
SanJose2(config)#interface fastethernet 0/0
SanJose2(config-if)#no ip route-cache
SanJose2(config-if)#ip policy route-map RETURN_TRAFFIC
```

Verify that the route map is active with the **show ip policy** or **show ip interface fastethernet 0/0** command, as follows:

```
SanJose2#show ip policy
Interface       Route map
Fa0/0           RETURN_TRAFFIC

SanJose2#show ip interface fastethernet 0/0
FastEthernet0/0 is up, line protocol is up
  Internet address is 10.0.0.2/24
  Broadcast address is 255.255.255.255
  Address determined by setup command
  MTU is 1500 bytes
  Helper address is not set
  Directed broadcast forwarding is disabled
  Multicast reserved groups joined: 224.0.0.5 224.0.0.6
  Outgoing access list is not set
  Inbound  access list is not set
  Proxy ARP is enabled
  Security level is default
  Split horizon is enabled
  ICMP redirects are always sent
  ICMP unreachables are always sent
  ICMP mask replies are never sent
  IP fast switching is enabled
  IP fast switching on the same interface is disabled
  IP Flow switching is disabled
  IP Feature Fast switching turbo vector
  IP multicast fast switching is enabled
  IP multicast distributed fast switching is disabled
  IP route-cache flags are Fast
  Router Discovery is disabled
  IP output packet accounting is disabled
  IP access violation accounting is disabled
  TCP/IP header compression is disabled
  RTP/IP header compression is disabled
  Probe proxy name replies are disabled
  Policy routing is enabled, using route map RETURN_TRAFFIC
  Network address translation is disabled
  WCCP Redirect outbound is disabled
  WCCP Redirect inbound is disabled
  WCCP Redirect exclude is disabled
  BGP Policy Mapping is disabled
```

Step 7

Verify that the router maps are active. Does each router enforce the policy when a ping originates from host 192.168.72.2 that is destined for host 10.0.0.3?

The following output was collected from router SanJose2:

```
02:34:27: IP: s=10.0.0.3 (FastEthernet0/0), d=192.168.72.2, len 100, policy match
02:34:27: IP: route map RETURN_TRAFFIC, item 10, permit
02:34:27: IP: s=10.0.0.3 (FastEthernet0/0), d=192.168.72.2 (Serial0/0), len 100,
policy routed
```

Lab 8.5.2b: NAT: Dynamic Translation with Multiple Pools Using Route Maps

Estimated Time: 45 Minutes

Objective

In this lab, you configure dynamic Network Address Translation (NAT) with multiple pools using route maps on the routers shown in the topology in Figure 8-3.

Figure 8-3   Sample Topology for Lab 8.5.2b

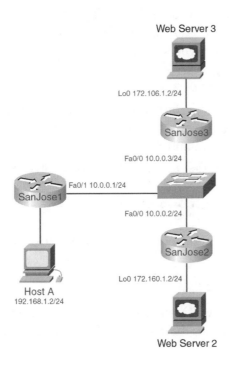

Equipment Requirements

You need the following equipment for this exercise:

* Three 2600 series Cisco routers

* One Cisco Catalyst switch

* Three workstations

* Six Ethernet cables

Scenario

The single Class C address used on the SanJose1 LAN is insufficient for the users and devices. That is why NAT is being used to represent all inside local addresses, 192.168.1.x. However, all users on the SanJose1 LAN require HTTP access to the web servers on the SanJose2 and

SanJose3 LANs. This is represented by the respective loopback addresses. Therefore, you must use a multiple pool of addresses and translate all the hosts on the 192.168.1.0 network as follows:

- 172.106.2.0 when accessing web server 3 on the 172.106.1.0 network

- 172.160.2.0 when accessing web server 2 on the 172.160.1.0 network

As the network administrator, configure the SanJose1 router according to the requirements described using dynamic NAT translation with multiple pools and route maps.

Step 1

Build and configure the network according to the diagram. Also, if you are running an IOS version below 12.0, enable the SanJose2 and SanJose3 routers for HTTP access, as shown in the following, to simulate the attached web servers:

```
SanJose2(config)#ip http server
SanJose3(config)#ip http server
```

Because you are not using a routing protocol, you must configure static routes on SanJose1 to the respective web servers on the SanJose2 and SanJose3 LANs. Configure default routes to the 192.168.1.0 network from SanJose2 and SanJose3:

```
SanJose1(config)#ip route 172.106.1.0 255.255.255.0 10.0.0.3
SanJose1(config)#ip route 172.160.1.0 255.255.255.0 10.0.0.2

SanJose2(config)#ip route 0.0.0.0 0.0.0.0 10.0.0.1
SanJose3(config)#ip route 0.0.0.0 0.0.0.0 10.0.0.1
```

Test connectivity between the routers and between the SanJose1 Host A and its gateway with a ping.

Step 2

Create the pool of addresses that will translate hosts on the 192.168.1.0 network. Create the access control lists to allow hosts on the 192.168.1.0 network to access the 172.106.1.0 and 172.160.1.0 networks:

```
SanJose1(config)#ip nat pool pool106 172.106.2.1 172.106.2.254 prefix-length 24
SanJose1(config)#ip nat pool pool160 172.160.2.1 172.160.2.254 prefix-length 24

SanJose1(config)#access-list 106 permit ip 192.168.1.0 0.0.0.255 172.106.1.0 0.0.0.255
SanJose1(config)#access-list 160 permit ip 192.168.1.0 0.0.0.255 172.160.1.0 0.0.0.255
```

Step 3

Designate at least one inside NAT interface and one outside NAT interface on the NAT router, SanJose1:

```
SanJose1(config)#interface fastethernet 0/0
SanJose1(config-if)#ip nat inside

SanJose1(config-if)#interface fastethernet 0/1
SanJose1(config-if)#ip nat outside
```

Step 4

So far, every task completed is the same as if you were using the access control lists with no overload approach.

Recall that NAT uses access lists and route maps only when it needs to create a translation entry. If a translation entry already exists that matches the traffic that will be used and any access lists or route maps will not be consulted. The difference between using an access list or route map is the type of translation entry that will be created.

When NAT uses a route map to create a translation entry, it always creates a "fully extended" translation entry. This translation entry contains both the inside and outside, local and global addresses and any TCP or UDP port information.

When NAT uses an access list, it creates a simple translation entry. This simple entry only contains local and global IP address entries for the inside or outside. This also depends on whether the **ip nat inside** or **ip nat outside** command is configured. In addition, it will not include TCP or UDP port information.

Test the access list approach to see exactly why it does not provide the ideal solution for NAT in this situation.

Configure the inside source access lists and address pools:

```
SanJose1(config)#ip nat inside source list 106 pool pool106
SanJose1(config)#ip nat inside source list 160 pool pool160
```

Enable **debug ip packet** on the SanJose1 and SanJose3 routers.

Open a browser window from the SanJose1 Host A to access web server 3 on the SanJose3 LAN, loopback address 172.106.1.2. Observe the **debug** output on SanJose1 and SanJose3. Sample output is shown here:

```
SanJose1#debug ip packet
IP packet debugging is on
SanJose1#
00:35:10: IP: s=172.106.2.1 (FastEthernet0/0), d=172.106.1.2 (FastEthernet0/1),
g=10.0.0.3, len 44, forward
00:35:10: IP: s=172.106.1.2 (FastEthernet0/1), d=192.168.1.2 (FastEthernet0/0),
g=192.168.1.2, len 44, forward
00:35:10: IP: s=172.106.1.2 (FastEthernet0/1), d=192.168.1.2 (FastEthernet0/0),
g=192.168.1.2, len 40, forward
00:35:10: IP: s=172.106.2.1 (FastEthernet0/0), d=172.106.1.2 (FastEthernet0/1),
g=10.0.0.3, len 40, forward
--output omitted--
SanJose1#

SanJose3#debug ip packet
IP packet debugging is on
SanJose3#
SanJose3#
00:35:37: IP: s=172.106.2.1 (FastEthernet0/0), d=172.106.1.2, len 44, rcvd 4
00:35:37: IP: s=172.106.1.2 (local), d=172.106.2.1 (FastEthernet0/0), len 44,
    sending
00:35:37: IP: s=172.106.2.1 (FastEthernet0/0), d=172.106.1.2, len 40, rcvd 4
00:35:37: IP: s=172.106.2.1 (FastEthernet0/0), d=172.106.1.2, len 364, rcvd 4
00:35:37: IP: s=172.106.1.2 (local), d=172.106.2.1 (FastEthernet0/0), len 596,
    sending
00:35:37: IP: s=172.106.1.2 (local), d=172.106.2.1 (FastEthernet0/0), len 596,
    sending
--output omitted--
SanJose3#
```

Issue the **show ip nat translations verbose** command on the SanJose1 router. Sample output is shown here:

```
SanJose1#show ip nat translations verbose
Pro Inside global      Inside local      Outside local      Outside global
--- 172.106.2.1        192.168.1.2       ---                ---
    create 00:01:37, use 00:00:31, left 23:59:28,
    flags:
none, use_count: 0
```

1.   Why are only the inside global and local address translations shown and no protocol or port information?

Enable **debug ip packet** on the SanJose2 router and SanJose1 if necessary.

From SanJose1 Host A, use a browser to access web server 2 on the SanJose2 LAN, loopback address 172.160.1.2. Observe the **debug** output on SanJose1 and SanJose2. Sample output is shown here:

```
SanJose1#debug ip packet
IP packet debugging is on
SanJose1#
00:55:22: IP: s=172.106.2.1 (FastEthernet0/0), d=172.160.1.2 (FastEthernet0/1),
    g=10.0.0.2, len 44, forward
00:55:22: IP: s=172.160.1.2 (FastEthernet0/1), d=192.168.1.2 (FastEthernet0/0),
    g=192.168.1.2, len 44, forward
00:55:22: IP: s=172.160.1.2 (FastEthernet0/1), d=192.168.1.2 (FastEthernet0/0),
    g=192.168.1.2, len 40, forward
00:55:22: IP: s=172.106.2.1 (FastEthernet0/0), d=172.160.1.2 (FastEthernet0/1),
    g=10.0.0.2, len 40, forward
SanJose1#

SanJose2#debug ip packet
IP packet debugging is on
SanJose2#
00:55:56: IP: s=172.106.2.1 (FastEthernet0/0), d=172.160.1.2, len 44, rcvd 4
00:55:56: IP: s=172.160.1.2 (local), d=172.106.2.1 (FastEthernet0/0), len 44,
    sending
00:55:56: IP: s=172.106.2.1 (FastEthernet0/0), d=172.160.1.2, len 40, rcvd 4
00:55:56: IP: s=172.106.2.1 (FastEthernet0/0), d=172.160.1.2, len 364, rcvd 4
00:55:56: IP: s=172.160.1.2 (local), d=172.106.2.1 (FastEthernet0/0), len 596,
    sending
00:55:56: IP: s=172.160.1.2 (local), d=172.106.2.1 (FastEthernet0/0), len 596,
    sending
--output omitted--
SanJose2#
```

Issue the **show ip nat translations verbose** command on the SanJose1 router. Sample output is shown here:

```
SanJose1#show ip nat translations verbose
Pro Inside global      Inside local      Outside local      Outside global
--- 172.106.2.1        192.168.1.2       ---                ---
    create 00:21:44, use 00:00:26, left 23:59:33,
    flags:
none, use_count: 0
SanJose1#
```

2.   After you analyze the data output, document the problem.

Step 5

Before you configure the route maps, disable the **debug ip packet** command by using the **undebug ip packet** command on SanJose1. Then, remove the previously configured inside source access lists and address pools:

```
SanJose1#undebug ip packet
SanJose1#clear ip nat translation *
SanJose1#configure terminal
SanJose1(config)#no ip nat inside source list 106 pool pool106
SanJose1(config)#no ip nat inside source list 160 pool pool160
```

Now, configure route maps to resolve the problems you encountered when using the access lists.

Create the inside source route maps and address pools, as follows:

```
SanJose1(config)#ip nat inside source route-map MAP-106 pool pool106
SanJose1(config)#ip nat inside source route-map MAP-160 pool pool160
```

Create the route maps, as follows:

```
SanJose1(config)#route-map MAP-106 permit 10
SanJose1(config-route-map)#match ip address 106

SanJose1(config-route-map)#route-map MAP-160 permit 10
SanJose1(config-route-map)#match ip address 160
```

Step 6

Enable **debug ip packet** on the SanJose1 router.

Open a browser window from the SanJose1 Host A to access web server 3 on the SanJose3 LAN, loopback address 172.106.1.2. Observe the **debug** output on SanJose1 and SanJose3. Samples from both routers are shown here:

```
SanJose1#debug ip packet
IP packet debugging is on
SanJose1#
01:13:52: IP: s=172.106.2.1 (FastEthernet0/0), d=172.106.1.2 (FastEthernet0/1),
g=10.0.0.3, len 44, forward
01:13:52: IP: s=172.106.1.2 (FastEthernet0/1), d=192.168.1.2 (FastEthernet0/0),
g=192.168.1.2, len 44, forward
01:13:52: IP: s=172.106.1.2 (FastEthernet0/1), d=192.168.1.2 (FastEthernet0/0),
g=192.168.1.2, len 40, forward
01:13:52: IP: s=172.106.2.1 (FastEthernet0/0), d=172.106.1.2 (FastEthernet0/1),
g=10.0.0.3, len 40, forward
SanJose1#

SanJose3#debug ip packet
IP packet debugging is on
SanJose3#
01:14:19: IP: s=172.106.2.1 (FastEthernet0/0), d=172.106.1.2, len 44, rcvd 4
01:14:19: IP: s=172.106.1.2 (local), d=172.106.2.1 (FastEthernet0/0), len 44,
    sending
01:14:19: IP: s=172.106.2.1 (FastEthernet0/0), d=172.106.1.2, len 40, rcvd 4
01:14:19: IP: s=172.106.2.1 (FastEthernet0/0), d=172.106.1.2, len 234, rcvd 4
01:14:19: IP: s=172.106.1.2 (local), d=172.106.2.1 (FastEthernet0/0), len 596,
    sending
01:14:19: IP: s=172.106.1.2 (local), d=172.106.2.1 (FastEthernet0/0), len 596,
    sending
--output omitted--
SanJose3#
```

Issue the **show ip nat translations verbose** command on the SanJose1 router. Sample output is shown here:

```
SanJose1#show ip nat translations verbose
Pro Inside global      Inside local      Outside local      Outside global
tcp 172.106.2.1:1118   192.168.1.2:1118  172.106.1.2:80     172.106.1.2:80
    create 00:00:08, use 00:00:07, left 00:00:52,
    flags:
extended, timing-out, use_count: 0
SanJose1#
```

Notice that although there are no differences in the **debug ip packet** output generated previously, the output of the **show ip nat translations verbose** command *is* different.

1.   What additional information is now available, and why?

Open a browser window from the SanJose1 Host A to access web server 2 on the SanJose2 LAN, loopback address 172.160.1.2. Observe the debug output on SanJose1 and SanJose2. Sample output is shown here:

```
SanJose1#debug ip packet
IP packet debugging is on
SanJose1#
01:35:28: IP: s=172.160.2.1 (FastEthernet0/0), d=172.160.1.2 (FastEthernet0/1),
g=10.0.0.2, len 44, forward
01:35:28: IP: s=172.160.1.2 (FastEthernet0/1), d=192.168.1.2 (FastEthernet0/0),
g=192.168.1.2, len 44, forward
01:35:29: IP: s=172.160.1.2 (FastEthernet0/1), d=192.168.1.2 (FastEthernet0/0),
g=192.168.1.2, len 40, forward
01:35:29: IP: s=172.160.2.1 (FastEthernet0/0), d=172.160.1.2 (FastEthernet0/1),
g=10.0.0.2, len 40, forward
SanJose1#

SanJose2#debug ip packet
IP packet debugging is on
SanJose2#
01:35:54: IP: s=172.160.2.1 (FastEthernet0/0), d=172.160.1.2, len 44, rcvd 4
01:35:54: IP: s=172.160.1.2 (local), d=172.160.2.1 (FastEthernet0/0), len 44,
    sending
01:35:54: IP: s=172.160.2.1 (FastEthernet0/0), d=172.160.1.2, len 40, rcvd 4
01:35:54: IP: s=172.160.2.1 (FastEthernet0/0), d=172.160.1.2, len 234, rcvd 4
01:35:54: IP: s=172.160.1.2 (local), d=172.160.2.1 (FastEthernet0/0), len 596,
    sending
01:35:54: IP: s=172.160.1.2 (local), d=172.160.2.1 (FastEthernet0/0), len 596,
    sending
--output omitted--
SanJose2#
```

Issue the **show ip nat translations verbose** command on the SanJose1 router. Sample output is shown here:

```
SanJose1#show ip nat translations verbose
Pro Inside global     Inside local      Outside local      Outside global
tcp 172.160.2.1:1122   192.168.1.2:1122    172.160.1.2:80     172.160.1.2:80
    create 00:00:34, use 00:00:34, left 00:00:25,
    flags:
extended, timing-out, use_count: 0
SanJose1#
```

Dynamic NAT with multiple pools using route maps is configured successfully now.

2.   Why does the translation from the SanJose1 Host A to the web server 2 on the SanJose2 LAN now work correctly with route maps?

```
SanJose1#show ip nat translations verbose
Pro Inside global     Inside local      Outside local      Outside global
tcp 172.106.2.1:1126   192.168.1.2:1126    172.106.1.2:80     172.106.1.2:80
    create 00:00:04, use 00:00:04, left 00:00:55,
    flags:
extended, timing-out, use_count: 0
tcp 172.160.2.1:1125   192.168.1.2:1125    172.160.1.2:80     172.160.1.2:80
    create 00:00:24, use 00:00:24, left 00:00:35,
    flags:
extended, timing-out, use_count: 0
SanJose1#
```

Note: NAT's ability to use route maps with static translations was introduced with Cisco IOS Version 12.2(4)T and 12.2(4)T2 for the Cisco 7500 series routers.

NAT with access list and overload will create a "fully extended" translation and is the same as the route map.

Lab 8.5.3: Redistributing RIP and OSPF with Distribution Lists

Estimated Time: 45 Minutes

Objective

In this lab, you configure mutual redistribution between RIP v1 and OSPF on the routers in the topology shown in Figure 8-4.

Figure 8-4   Sample Topology for Figure 8-4

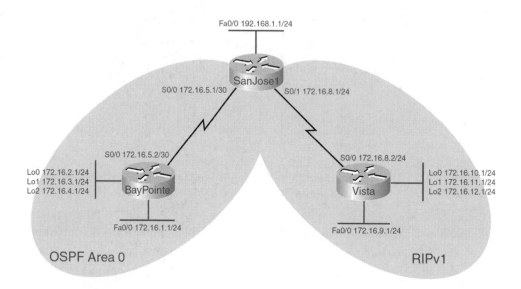

Equipment Requirements

You need the following equipment for this exercise:

- Three Cisco 2600 series routers

- Two serial cables

Scenario

The International Travel Agency is adding two new sites to the San Jose campus. BayPointe uses OSPF, and Vista supports only RIP v1 until the hardware is upgraded. You are to configure the mutual redistribution between the two protocols on the ASBR, SanJose1. Routers in the RIP v1 domain should learn about OSPF networks, and routers in the OSPF domain should learn about RIP v1 networks. Advertise network 172.16.4.0/24 on BayPointe within the OSPF Area. However, do not pass it into the RIP region. Likewise, redistribute each of the RIP subnets into the OSPF region, with the exception of network 172.16.12.0/24, which is located on Vista.

Step 1

Build and configure the network according to the diagram. First, erase all existing configurations on the routers or install a fresh IOS image. Configure the loopback interfaces with the IP addresses according to the diagram. The loopbacks will simulate networks within each routing domain. Configure OSPF on BayPointe for all connected networks, and RIP v1 on Vista for all connected networks. Do not configure routing on SanJose1 at this time.

Use **show running-config** to verify the work.

Step 2

Configure routing on the serial interfaces for SanJose1. Use the following commands to configure SanJose1 routing processes:

```
SanJose1(config)#router rip
SanJose1(config-router)#network 172.16.0.0
SanJose1(config-router)#passive-interface serial0/0
SanJose1(config-router)#passive-interface fastethernet0/0
SanJose1(config-router)#router ospf 1
SanJose1(config-router)#network 172.16.5.0 0.0.0.3 area 0
```

1.   Why are the **passive interface** statements applied to Serial 0/0 and Fast Ethernet 0/0 in RIP?

Those networks do not have other RIP hosts. Turn off periodic RIP updates on all RIP-enabled interfaces that do not require them.

2.   It is not necessary to configure passive interfaces in the OSPF configuration. Why not?

Updates are sent and acknowledged between OSPF neighbors. OSPF does not begin to send multicast Hello packets out an interface until a network statement is added to the OSPF configuration that includes or overlaps with the interface IP address.

After the routing is configured, check the routing table of SanJose1, as follows:

```
SanJose1#show ip route
Gateway of last resort is not set
     172.16.0.0/16 is variably subnetted, 10 subnets, 3 masks
R       172.16.12.0/24 [120/1] via 172.16.8.2, 00:00:02, Serial0/1
C       172.16.8.0/24 is directly connected, Serial0/1
R       172.16.9.0/24 [120/1] via 172.16.8.2, 00:00:02, Serial0/1
R       172.16.10.0/24 [120/1] via 172.16.8.2, 00:00:02, Serial0/1
R       172.16.11.0/24 [120/1] via 172.16.8.2, 00:00:02, Serial0/1
O       172.16.4.1/32 [110/782] via 172.16.5.2, 00:09:07, Serial0/0
C       172.16.5.0/30 is directly connected, Serial0/0
O       172.16.1.0/24 [110/782] via 172.16.5.2, 00:09:08, Serial0/0
O       172.16.3.1/32 [110/782] via 172.16.5.2, 00:09:08, Serial0/0
O       172.16.2.1/32 [110/782] via 172.16.5.2, 00:09:08, Serial0/0
C       192.168.1.0/24 is directly connected, FastEthernet0/0
```

SanJose1 should learn about the connected networks of BayPointe by way of OSPF, and the connected networks of Vista by way of RIP v1. Troubleshoot if necessary. SanJose1 and Vista will see the loopbacks that are advertised on the BayPointe router as /32 networks regardless of the subnetmask that is assigned to the loopback interface. This is the standard method by which OSPF treats advertised loopback interfaces. Although this occurs regularly in this lab environment, it is not customary to create and advertise loopback networks on a production network.

Issue the **show ip route** command to check the routing table of BayPointe, as follows:

```
BayPointe#show ip route
Gateway of last resort is not set
     172.16.0.0/16 is variably subnetted, 5 subnets, 2 masks
C       172.16.4.0/24 is directly connected, Loopback2
C       172.16.5.0/30 is directly connected, Serial0/0
```

```
C        172.16.1.0/24 is directly connected, FastEthernet0/0
C        172.16.2.0/24 is directly connected, Loopback0
C        172.16.3.0/24 is directly connected, Loopback1
```

No dynamically learned routes should be present. Issue the **show ip route** command to check the routing table of Vista, as follows:

```
Vista#show ip route
Gateway of last resort is not set
     172.16.0.0/24 is subnetted, 5 subnets
C        172.16.12.0 is directly connected, Loopback2
C        172.16.8.0 is directly connected, Serial0/0
C        172.16.9.0 is directly connected, FastEthernet0/0
C        172.16.10.0 is directly connected, Loopback0
C        172.16.11.0 is directly connected, Loopback1
```

3.   Has Vista learned about routes by way of RIP v1? Why?

_____

_____

Vista is connected directly to all RIP v1 networks, and redistribution has not been configured.

Step 3

Configure redistribution on SanJose1 so that all the OSPF routes except 172.16.4.0/24 are injected into the RIP v1 process. Use the following commands to configure redistribution on SanJose1:

```
SanJose1(config)#router rip
SanJose1(config-router)#redistribute ospf 1
SanJose1(config-router)#default-metric 2
```

1.   What is the **default-metric** command used for? Does it have to be used?

_____

2.   Does this accomplish the network design goal? Does this allow for the redistribution of the unintended subnet as well?

_____

_____

Consider a route filter policy that is similar to the previous lab and will allow for filtering out of the 172.16.4.0 route. Issue the following commands to complete this route filter requirement:

```
SanJose1(config)#access-list 10 deny 172.16.4.0 0.0.0.255
SanJose1(config)#access-list 10 permit any
SanJose1(config)#router rip
SanJose1(config-router)#distribute-list 10 out s0/1
```

This completes the filtering. Now, the previous commands in Step 3 will redistribute only the desired networks.

Check the routing table of Vista in the RIP v1 domain, as follows:

Note: Use the **clear ip route *** command first.

```
Vista#show ip route
Gateway of last resort is not set
         172.16.0.0/16 is variably subnetted, 8 subnets, 2 masks
C        172.16.12.0/24 is directly connected, Loopback2
C        172.16.8.0/24 is directly connected, Serial0/0
C        172.16.9.0/24 is directly connected, FastEthernet0/0
```

```
C        172.16.10.0/24 is directly connected, Loopback0
C        172.16.11.0/24 is directly connected, Loopback1
R        172.16.1.0/24 [120/2] via 172.16.8.1, 00:00:05, Serial0/0
R        172.16.3.1/32 [120/2] via 172.16.8.1, 00:00:05, Serial0/0
R        172.16.2.1/32 [120/2] via 172.16.8.1, 00:00:06, Serial0/0
```

3.   Has Vista learned about any of the networks from the OSPF side?

Creating a seed metric can minimize routing loops or black holes in the network. RIP cannot differentiate between internal and external redistributed routes. When a route on a network is redistributed without a default metric, the network appears to be adjacent to the autonomous system. Elevating the external default metric above any internal routes is a crude but effective way of differentiating between internal and external routes.

In summary, ensure that a metric statement is included at the end of the redistribute command or identify a default metric value on a separate line. Failure to do so causes a route to be redistributed with an unreachable value.

4.   What is the metric for each of these routes?

The metric should be 2.

Step 4

Configure redistribution on SanJose1 so that RIP v1 routes are injected into the OSPF process. Use the following commands to configure mutual redistribution on SanJose1:

```
SanJose1(config)#router ospf 1
SanJose1(config-router)#redistribute rip
SanJose1(config-router)#default-metric 10
```

Now, include the following necessary commands to filter out the 172.16.12.0/24 network from being advertised:

```
SanJose1(config)#access-list 20 deny 172.16.12.0 0.0.0.255
SanJose1(config)#access-list 20 permit any
SanJose1(config)#router ospf 1
SanJose1(config-router)#distribute-list 20 out
```

Notice when you are applying the distribution list within OSPF that the interface option has been omitted. OSPF will not allow a distribute list to be applied in the outbound direction for one particular interface. It must be configured as a global distribute list. RIP does not have this same restriction, so the interface and direction were specified in the command syntax in Step 3.

Check the routing table of BayPointe in the OSPF domain. BayPointe has not learned about any of the networks from the RIP v1 side.

1.   Why has BayPointe not learned about any of the networks from the RIP v1 side?

BayPointe should not have new routes in its routing table. That is because OSPF will not redistribute RIP subnets unless they are explicitly configured with the **subnets** keyword. Return to SanJose1 and enter the following configuration:

```
SanJose1(config)#router ospf 1
SanJose1(config-router)#redistribute rip subnets
```

After you enter these commands, check the routing table of BayPointe again, as follows:

```
BayPointe#show ip route
Gateway of last resort is not set
     172.16.0.0/16 is variably subnetted, 9 subnets, 2 masks
O E2    172.16.8.0/24 [110/10] via 172.16.5.1, 00:00:10, Serial0/0
O E2    172.16.9.0/24 [110/10] via 172.16.5.1, 00:00:10, Serial0/0
O E2    172.16.10.0/24 [110/10] via 172.16.5.1, 00:00:10, Serial0/0
O E2    172.16.11.0/24 [110/10] via 172.16.5.1, 00:00:10, Serial0/0
C       172.16.4.0/24 is directly connected, Loopback2
C       172.16.5.0/30 is directly connected, Serial0/0
C       172.16.1.0/24 is directly connected, FastEthernet0/0
C       172.16.2.0/24 is directly connected, Loopback0
C       172.16.3.0/24 is directly connected, Loopback1
```

2. Has BayPointe learned about the routes from the RIP v1 domain? What is the metric for these routes?

_____

_____

The metric should be 10.

In the routing table, you see the redistributed routes tagged with E2.

3. What does E2 mean?

_____

_____

Recall that Type 2 (E2) routes originated outside the OSPF AS and were redistributed into OSPF using Type 5 LSA.

Step 5

Look carefully at the routing table of BayPointe.

1. Is there a route to 192.168.1.0/24?

_____

2. Does Vista have a route to 192.168.1.0/24?

_____

3. Why is this route missing from the routing tables of BayPointe and Vista?

_____

Interface Fast Ethernet0/0 on SanJose1 is not enabled for either OSPF or RIP v1.

Complete the routing table of BayPointe by configuring SanJose1 to redistribute connected routes into OSPF as a type 1 external route with a metric of 5000:

```
SanJose1(config)#router ospf 1
SanJose1(config-router)#redistribute connected subnets metric-type 1 metric 5000
```

4. What will the metric be for redistributed connected routes? Will they use the 5000 issued or the default metric of 10, configured previously?

_____

Issue the following to configure the RIP v1 process of SanJose1 to redistribute the connected route:

```
SanJose1(config)#router rip
SanJose1(config-router)#redistribute connected
```

Check the routing tables one more time. BayPointe and SanJose1 should contain all routes.

```
BayPoint#show ip route
Gateway of last resort is not set
     172.16.0.0/16 is variably subnetted, 9 subnets, 2 masks
O E1    172.16.8.0/24 [110/5781] via 172.16.5.1, 00:01:52, Serial0/0
O E2    172.16.9.0/24 [110/10] via 172.16.5.1, 00:01:52, Serial0/0
O E2    172.16.10.0/24 [110/10] via 172.16.5.1, 00:01:52, Serial0/0
O E2    172.16.11.0/24 [110/10] via 172.16.5.1, 00:01:52, Serial0/0
C       172.16.4.0/24 is directly connected, Loopback2
C       172.16.5.0/30 is directly connected, Serial0/0
C       172.16.1.0/24 is directly connected, FastEthernet0/0
C       172.16.2.0/24 is directly connected, Loopback0
C       172.16.3.0/24 is directly connected, Loopback1
O E1 192.168.1.0/24 [110/5781] via 172.16.5.1, 00:01:53, Serial0/0

SanJose1#show ip route
Gateway of last resort is not set
     172.16.0.0/16 is variably subnetted, 10 subnets, 3 masks
R       172.16.12.0/24 [120/1] via 172.16.8.2, 00:00:03, Serial0/1
C       172.16.8.0/24 is directly connected, Serial0/1
R       172.16.9.0/24 [120/1] via 172.16.8.2, 00:00:03, Serial0/1
R       172.16.10.0/24 [120/1] via 172.16.8.2, 00:00:03, Serial0/1
R       172.16.11.0/24 [120/1] via 172.16.8.2, 00:00:03, Serial0/1
O       172.16.4.1/32 [110/65] via 172.16.5.2, 00:03:23, Serial0/0
C       172.16.5.0/30 is directly connected, Serial0/0
O       172.16.1.0/24 [110/65] via 172.16.5.2, 00:03:24, Serial0/0
O       172.16.3.1/32 [110/65] via 172.16.5.2, 00:03:24, Serial0/0
O       172.16.2.1/32 [110/65] via 172.16.5.2, 00:03:24, Serial0/0
C    192.168.1.0/24 is directly connected, FastEthernet0/0

Vista#show ip route
Gateway of last resort is not set
     172.16.0.0/16 is variably subnetted, 8 subnets, 2 masks
C       172.16.12.0/24 is directly connected, Loopback2
C       172.16.8.0/24 is directly connected, Serial0/0
C       172.16.9.0/24 is directly connected, FastEthernet0/0
C       172.16.10.0/24 is directly connected, Loopback0
C       172.16.11.0/24 is directly connected, Loopback1
R       172.16.1.0/24 [120/2] via 172.16.8.1, 00:00:07, Serial0/0
R       172.16.3.1/32 [120/2] via 172.16.8.1, 00:00:07, Serial0/0
R       172.16.2.1/32 [120/2] via 172.16.8.1, 00:00:08, Serial0/0
R    192.168.1.0/24 [120/1] via 172.16.8.1, 00:00:08, Serial0/0
```

Vista will not have a route to 172.16.5.0/30 because 172.16.0.0 is variably subnetted, and RIP v1 does not support VLSM. The **ip classless** command allows the 32-bit networks listed to support default networks in RIP and IGRP.

Summarize the RIP routes that are being sent to the BayPointe router. To do this, issue the following command on the SanJose1 router:

```
SanJose1(config)#router ospf 1
SanJose1(config-router)#summary-address 172.16.8.0 255.255.252.0
```

Verify that the summary statement was effective by viewing the routing table of the BayPointe router:

```
Gateway of last resort is not set
     172.16.0.0/16 is variably subnetted, 6 subnets, 3 masks
O E2    172.16.8.0/22 [110/10] via 172.16.5.1, 00:01:33, Serial0/0
C       172.16.4.0/24 is directly connected, Loopback2
C       172.16.5.0/30 is directly connected, Serial0/0
```

```
C        172.16.1.0/24 is directly connected, FastEthernet0/0
C        172.16.2.0/24 is directly connected, Loopback0
C        172.16.3.0/24 is directly connected, Loopback1
O E1 192.168.1.0/24 [110/5781] via 172.16.5.1, 00:13:14, Serial0/0
```

Lab 8.6.1: Route Optimization Challenge Lab

Estimated Time: 60 Minutes

Objective

Create and optimize a network using RIP v2 and OSPF on the routers in the topology shown in Figure 8-5. The network must connect to the Internet.

Figure 8-5   Sample Topology for Lab 8.6.1

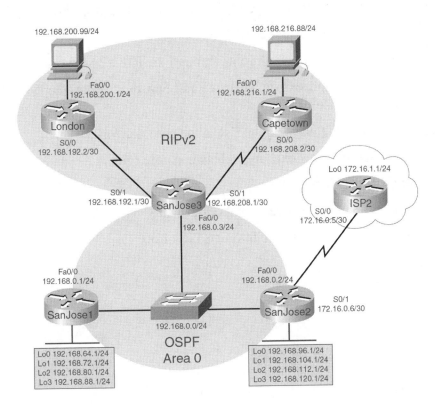

Equipment Requirements

You need the following equipment for this exercise:

- Six Cisco 2600 series routers

- One Catalyst switch

- Two workstations

Scenario

The International Travel Agency is finally connecting its disparate networks. Working as the network engineer, you need to ensure that all locations can communicate by the end of the month per the agencies' request. The only monies available for the project are for provisioning WAN links.

Design Considerations

Work with the existing routers in London and Capetown that support only RIP v2. For simplicity, propagate a default route from SanJose2 to as many routers as possible. Redistribute the connected loopbacks on SanJose1 and SanJose2, simulating sections of the internetwork. Summarize if appropriate.

Implementation Requirements

The implementation requirements are as follows:

- Redistribute all RIP v2 networks into OSPF. Summarize if appropriate.
- Use default routes between SanJose2 and ISP2.
- Allow SanJose3 to advertise a default route through the RIP v2 network.
- Redistribute connected loopbacks on SanJose1 and SanJose2. Filter the ISP2 WAN link from being advertised by SanJose2.
- Ensure that SanJose1 will always be the DR in the core network.
- Minimize the number of routes exchanged between core routers.

Implementation Completion Tests

The implementation completion tests require the following:

- Successful pings from all hosts to the Internet, ISP2 Lo0.
- SanJose1 is the DR.

Chapter 9

BGP

Lab 9.11.1: Configuring BGP with Default Routing

Estimated Time: 50 Minutes

Objective

In this lab, you configure BGP to exchange routing information with two Internet service providers (ISPs), as shown in Figure 9-1. You configure route filtering to control which BGP routes are advertised. Finally, you configure default routing to control which ISP is the primary and which is the backup using floating static routes and within BGP.

Figure 9-1   Sample Topology for Lab 9.11.1

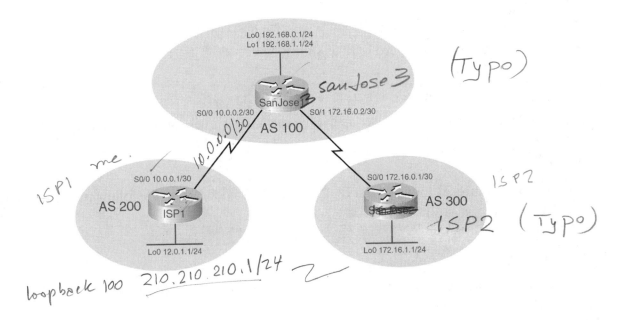

Equipment Requirements

You need the following equipment for this exercise:

- Three Cisco 2600 series routers

- Two serial cables

Scenario

The International Travel Agency relies extensively on the Internet for sales. The company has contracted with two ISPs for Internet connectivity with fault tolerance. You need to configure the BGP that runs between the SanJose3 boundary router and the two ISP routers.

Step 1

Build and configure the network according to the diagram, but do not configure a routing protocol. First, erase all configurations on the routers or load a new IOS prior to starting this lab. Configure a loopback interface with an IP address for each ISP router, as shown in the figure. These loopbacks simulate real networks that you can reach through the ISP. Configure two loopback interfaces with the IP addresses for the SanJose3 router. These loopbacks simulate the connections between the core routers.

Use **ping** to test connectivity between the directly connected routers.

Note: The ISP1 router cannot reach the ISP2 router.

Step 2

Configure the ISP routers. In this lab, configure the providers' equipment and the International Travel Agency's boundary router, SanJose3. On the ISP1 router, enter the following configuration:

```
ISP1(config)#router bgp 200
ISP1(config-router)#neighbor 10.0.0.2 remote-as 100
ISP1(config-router)#network 12.0.1.0 mask 255.255.255.0
```

On the router for ISP2, configure BGP as shown here:

```
ISP2(config)#router bgp 300
ISP2(config-router)#neighbor 172.16.0.2 remote-as 100
ISP2(config-router)#network 172.16.1.0 mask 255.255.255.0
```

With the ISP routers configured, set up the International Travel Agency's boundary router, SanJose3.

Step 3

Configure the SanJose3 router to run BGP with both providers. Use the following configuration:

```
SanJose3(config)#router bgp 100
SanJose3(config-router)#neighbor 10.0.0.1 remote-as 200
SanJose3(config-router)#neighbor 172.16.0.1 remote-as 300
SanJose3(config-router)#network 192.168.0.0
SanJose3(config-router)#network 192.168.1.0
```

This completes the BGP configuration. Check the routing table for SanJose3 with the **show ip route** command, as follows:

```
SanJose3#show ip route

Gateway of last resort is not set

     172.16.0.0/16 is variably subnetted, 2 subnets, 2 masks
C       172.16.0.0/30 is directly connected, Serial0/1
B       172.16.1.0/24 [20/0] via 172.16.0.1, 00:00:03
     10.0.0.0/30 is subnetted, 1 subnets
C       10.0.0.0 is directly connected, Serial0/0
C    192.168.0.0/24 is directly connected, Loopback0
     12.0.0.0/24 is subnetted, 1 subnets
B       12.0.1.0 [20/0] via 10.0.0.1, 00:00:42
C    192.168.1.0/24 is directly connected, Loopback1
```

SanJose3 has routes to the loopback networks at each ISP router. Verify that SanJose3 has connectivity to these networks by pinging each loopback address from its console. These pings should be successful.

Step 4

Use **show** commands to verify the operation of SanJose3. On SanJose3, issue the **show ip bgp** command, as follows:

```
SanJose3#show ip bgp
BGP table version is 5, local router ID is 192.168.1.1
Status codes: s suppressed, d damped, h history, * valid, > best, i - internal
Origin codes: i - IGP, e - EGP, ? - incomplete

   Network          Next Hop         Metric LocPrf Weight Path
*> 12.0.1.0/24      10.0.0.1              0             0 200 i
*> 172.16.1.0/24    172.16.0.1            0             0 300 i
*> 192.168.0.0      0.0.0.0               0         32768 i
*> 192.168.1.0      0.0.0.0               0         32768 i
```

1.   What do the asterisks (*) next to each route indicate?

        Valid

2.   What do the brackets (>) next to each route indicate?

        Best

3.   What is the local router ID?

        _192.168.1.1_

4.   Which table version is displayed?

        5, after change it will go 6

On the ISP1 router, issue the **shutdown** command on Loopback0. Return to SanJose3 and issue the **show ip bgp** command again.

5.   Which table version is displayed?

        _6_

The version number varies, but the **shutdown** command should have caused a routing table update; therefore, the version should be one higher than the last.

Bring up the ISP1 router Loopback0 again by issuing the **no shutdown** command.

On SanJose3, issue the **show ip bgp neighbors** command. The following is partial sample output of the command:

```
BGP neighbor is 172.16.0.1, remote AS 300, external link
Index 2, Offset 0, Mask 0x4
BGP version 4, remote router ID 172.16.1.1
BGP state = Established, table version = 5, up for 00:02:24
Last read 00:00:24, hold time is 180
```

6.   Based on the output of this command, what is the BGP state between this router and ISP2?

        Establish

7.   How long has this connection been up?

        _5m 30s_

Step 5

Check the routing table from ISP2 with the **show ip route** command. ISP2 should have a route that belongs to ISP1, 12.0.1.0.

SanJose3 might advertise a route belonging to ISP1. ISP2 then installs that route in its table. ISP2 might then attempt to route transit traffic through the International Travel Agency. Configure the SanJose3 router so that it advertises only International Travel Agency networks 192.168.0.0 and 192.168.1.0 to both providers. On the SanJose3 router, configure the following access list:

```
SanJose3(config)#access-list 1 permit 192.168.0.0 0.0.1.255
```

Then, apply this access list as a route filter as follows, using the **distribute-list** keyword with the BGP **neighbor** statement:

```
SanJose3(config)#router bgp 100
SanJose3(config-router)#neighbor 10.0.0.1 distribute-list 1 out
SanJose3(config-router)#neighbor 172.16.0.1 distribute-list 1 out
```

After you configure the route filter, check the routing table for ISP2 again. The route to 12.0.1.0, ISP1, should still be in the table.

Return to SanJose3 and issue the **clear ip bgp *** command. Wait until the routers reach the Established state, which might take several seconds.

After the routers reach the Established state, recheck the ISP2 routing table. The route to ISP1 should no longer be in the routing table.

The route to 172.16.1.0, ISP2, should not be in the routing table for ISP1.

Step 6

Now that bidirectional communication has been established with each ISP by way of BGP, you must declare the primary route and backup route. You can do this with floating static routes or within BGP.

To look at the floating static route method, issue the **show ip route** command as follows on the SanJose3 router:

```
Gateway of last resort is not set

     172.16.0.0/16 is variably subnetted, 2 subnets, 2 masks
C       172.16.0.0/30 is directly connected, Serial0/1
B       172.16.1.0/24 [20/0] via 172.16.0.1, 00:07:37
     10.0.0.0/30 is subnetted, 1 subnets
C       10.0.0.0 is directly connected, Serial0/0
C     192.168.0.0/24 is directly connected, Loopback0
     12.0.0.0/24 is subnetted, 1 subnets
B       12.0.1.0 [20/0] via 10.0.0.1, 00:07:42
C     192.168.1.0/24 is directly connected, Loopback1
```

Notice that no Gateway of Last Resort is defined. This is a huge problem because SanJose3 is the border router for the corporate network. Assume that ISP1 is the primary provider and ISP2 acts as the backup provider. Configure static routes to reflect this policy:

```
SanJose3(config)#ip route 0.0.0.0 0.0.0.0 10.0.0.1 210
SanJose3(config)#ip route 0.0.0.0 0.0.0.0 172.16.0.1 220
```

Now, verify that a default route is defined. Issue the **show ip route** command, as follows:

```
Gateway of last resort is 10.0.0.1 to network 0.0.0.0

        172.16.0.0/16 is variably subnetted, 2 subnets, 2 masks
C          172.16.0.0/30 is directly connected, Serial0/1
B          172.16.1.0/24 [20/0] via 172.16.0.1, 00:16:34
        10.0.0.0/30 is subnetted, 1 subnets
C          10.0.0.0 is directly connected, Serial0/0
C       192.168.0.0/24 is directly connected, Loopback0
        12.0.0.0/24 is subnetted, 1 subnets
B          12.0.1.0 [20/0] via 10.0.0.1, 00:16:39
C       192.168.1.0/24 is directly connected, Loopback1
S*      0.0.0.0/0 [210/0] via 10.0.0.1
```

Test this default route by creating an unadvertised loopback on the router for ISP1, as follows:

```
ISP1#config t
ISP1(config)#int loopback 100
ISP1(config-if)#ip address 210.210.210.1 255.255.255.0
```

Issue the **clear ip bgp 10.0.0.1** command on SanJose3 to re-establish a conversation with the 10.0.0.1 BGP speaker, as follows:

```
SanJose3#clear ip bgp 10.0.0.1
```

Wait until the BGP conversation is re-established with the 10.0.0.1 host.

Issue the **show ip route** command to ensure that the newly added 210.210.210.0 /24 network does not appear in the routing table:

```
SanJose3#show ip route

Gateway of last resort is 10.0.0.1 to network 0.0.0.0

        172.16.0.0/16 is variably subnetted, 2 subnets, 2 masks
C          172.16.0.0/30 is directly connected, Serial0/1
B          172.16.1.0/24 [20/0] via 172.16.0.1, 00:27:40
        10.0.0.0/30 is subnetted, 1 subnets
C          10.0.0.0 is directly connected, Serial0/0
C       192.168.0.0/24 is directly connected, Loopback0
        12.0.0.0/24 is subnetted, 1 subnets
B          12.0.1.0 [20/0] via 10.0.0.1, 00:27:45
C       192.168.1.0/24 is directly connected, Loopback1
S*      0.0.0.0/0 [210/0] via 10.0.0.1
```

Issue an extended **ping** to the 210.210.210.1 loopback interface originating from the 192.168.1.1, SanJose3, interface as follows:

```
SanJose3#ping
Protocol [ip]:
Target IP address: 210.210.210.1
Repeat count [5]:
Datagram size [100]:
Timeout in seconds [2]:
Extended commands [n]: y
Source address or interface: 192.168.1.1
Type of service [0]:
Set DF bit in IP header? [no]:
Validate reply data? [no]:
Data pattern [0xABCD]:
Loose, Strict, Record, Timestamp, Verbose [none]:
Sweep range of sizes [n]:
Type escape sequence to abort.
Sending 5, 100-byte ICMP Echos to 210.210.210.1, timeout is 2 seconds:
!!!!!
Success rate is 100 percent (5/5), round-trip min/avg/max = 32/32/36 ms
```

Step 7

Another solution uses the **default-network** command instead of a 0.0.0.0/0 route.

Remove the floating static routes issued from the previous step, as follows:

```
SanJose3(config)#no ip route 0.0.0.0 0.0.0.0 10.0.0.1 210
SanJose3(config)#no ip route 0.0.0.0 0.0.0.0 172.16.0.1 220
```

You should now advertise the network that you added in Step 6, 210.210.210.0/24, on the ISP1 router for this portion of the lab:

```
ISP1(config)#router bgp 200
ISP1(config-router)#network 210.210.210.0

ISP1# clear ip bgp 10.0.0.2
```

Now, you need to configure the SanJose3 router with a **default-network** statement to re-establish a Gateway of Last Resort. Make sure that the classful network 210.210.210.0 /24 appears in the routing table, and issue the **ip default-network** command:

```
Gateway of last resort is not set

B    210.210.210.0/24 [20/0] via 10.0.0.1, 00:04:51
     172.16.0.0/16 is variably subnetted, 2 subnets, 2 masks
C       172.16.0.0/30 is directly connected, Serial0/1
B       172.16.1.0/24 [20/0] via 172.16.0.1, 00:21:19
     10.0.0.0/30 is subnetted, 1 subnets
C       10.0.0.0 is directly connected, Serial0/0
C    192.168.0.0/24 is directly connected, Loopback0
     12.0.0.0/24 is subnetted, 1 subnets
B       12.0.1.0 [20/0] via 10.0.0.1, 00:04:51
C    192.168.1.0/24 is directly connected, Loopback1

SanJose3(config)#ip default-network 210.210.210.0
```

Wait a few seconds, and then re-examine the routing table on SanJose3, as follows:

```
Gateway of last resort is 10.0.0.1 to network 210.210.210.0

B*   210.210.210.0/24 [20/0] via 10.0.0.1, 00:04:28
     172.16.0.0/16 is variably subnetted, 2 subnets, 2 masks
C       172.16.0.0/30 is directly connected, Serial0/1
B       172.16.1.0/24 [20/0] via 172.16.0.1, 00:20:56
     10.0.0.0/30 is subnetted, 1 subnets
C       10.0.0.0 is directly connected, Serial0/0
C    192.168.0.0/24 is directly connected, Loopback0
     12.0.0.0/24 is subnetted, 1 subnets
B       12.0.1.0 [20/0] via 10.0.0.1, 00:04:28
C    192.168.1.0/24 is directly connected, Loopback1
```

This establishes ISP1 as the only default route. You can manipulate this route with policy routing. Correct this by adding a backup route to the 172.16.0.1 host on ISP2, as follows:

```
SanJose3(config)#ip route 0.0.0.0 0.0.0.0 172.16.0.1 220
```

External Border Gateway Protocol (EBGP) learned routes have an administrative distance of 20 and are preferred to any routes with administrative distances greater than 20, such as the default route defined earlier with an administrative distance of 220, which acts as a backup if the 210.210.210.0 /24 network is unavailable. This network could be unavailable because of a fault, misconfiguration, or the short period after a **clear ip bgp 10.0.0.1** command is issued.

Verify that this newly added route establishes a consistent default route while the BGP conversation between SanJose3 and ISP1 re-establishes. Notice that the routing table includes two candidate default routes (*), only one of which is used because of different administrative distances:

```
SanJose3#show ip route
Codes: C - connected, S - static, I - IGRP, R - RIP, M - mobile,
B - BGP D - EIGRP, EX - EIGRP external, O - OSPF, IA - OSPF inter area N1 - OSPF NSSA
  external type 1, N2 - OSPF NSSA external
type 2 E1 - OSPF external type 1, E2 - OSPF external type 2,
E - EGP i - IS-IS, L1 - IS-IS level-1, L2 - IS-IS level-2, ia - IS-IS inter area * -
  candidate default, U - per-user static route, o - ODR  P - periodic downloaded
  static route

Gateway of last resort is 10.0.0.1 to network 210.210.210.0

B*    210.210.210.0/24 [20/0] via 10.0.0.1, 00:19:17
      172.16.0.0/16 is variably subnetted, 2 subnets, 2 masks
C        172.16.0.0/30 is directly connected, Serial0/1
B        172.16.1.0/24 [20/0] via 172.16.0.1, 00:35:45
      10.0.0.0/30 is subnetted, 1 subnets
C        10.0.0.0 is directly connected, Serial0/0
C     192.168.0.0/24 is directly connected, Loopback0
      12.0.0.0/24 is subnetted, 1 subnets
B        12.0.1.0 [20/0] via 10.0.0.1, 00:19:17
C     192.168.1.0/24 is directly connected, Loopback1
S*    0.0.0.0/0 [220/0] via 172.16.0.1

SanJose3#clear ip bgp 10.0.0.1
SanJose3#show ip route

Gateway of last resort is 172.16.0.1 to network 0.0.0.0

      172.16.0.0/16 is variably subnetted, 2 subnets, 2 masks
C        172.16.0.0/30 is directly connected, Serial0/1
B        172.16.1.0/24 [20/0] via 172.16.0.1, 00:45:31
      10.0.0.0/30 is subnetted, 1 subnets
C        10.0.0.0 is directly connected, Serial0/0
C     192.168.0.0/24 is directly connected, Loopback0
C     192.168.1.0/24 is directly connected, Loopback1
S*    0.0.0.0/0 [220/0] via 172.16.0.1

SanJose3#show ip route
Gateway of last resort is 10.0.0.1 to network 210.210.210.0
B*    210.210.210.0/24 [20/0] via 10.0.0.1, 00:01:03
      172.16.0.0/16 is variably subnetted, 2 subnets, 2 masks
C        172.16.0.0/30 is directly connected, Serial0/1
B        172.16.1.0/24 [20/0] via 172.16.0.1, 00:46:42
      10.0.0.0/30 is subnetted, 1 subnets
C        10.0.0.0 is directly connected, Serial0/0
C     192.168.0.0/24 is directly connected, Loopback0
      12.0.0.0/24 is subnetted, 1 subnets
B        12.0.1.0 [20/0] via 10.0.0.1, 00:01:03
C     192.168.1.0/24 is directly connected, Loopback1
S*    0.0.0.0/0 [220/0] via 172.16.0.1
```

As expected, while the BGP conversation was down between SanJose3 and ISP1, the route to ISP2 was added as the Gateway of Last Resort. However, after BGP re-established the conversation between SanJose3 and ISP1, the default route of 210.210.210.0 was again set as the Gateway of Last Resort on SanJose3.

Lab 9.11.2: Configuring BGP with NAT

Estimated Time: 60 Minutes

Objective

In this lab, you configure EBGP with ISP1, as shown in Figure 9-2. You configure NAT with the S0/0 link to the ISP using the public IP address range of 66.122.33.96/27. You need to advertise this network range through BGP. Finally, you configure a default gateway for the OSPF network.

Figure 9-2   Topology for BGP with NAT Configuration

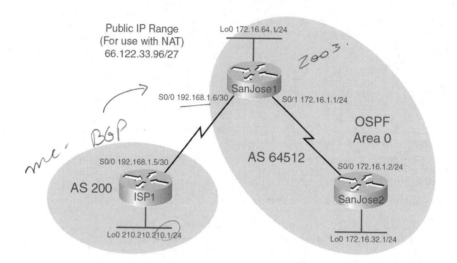

Equipment Requirements

You need the following equipment for this exercise:

* Three Cisco 2600 series routers

* Two serial cables

Scenario

The International Travel Agency runs BGP on its SanJose1 router externally with ISP1, AS 200. You use OSPF as the internal routing protocol between the SanJose1 and SanJose2 routers. You must configure EBGP between ISP1 and SanJose1, and configure NAT on the boundary router in AS 64512.

Step 1

Build and configure the network according to the diagram, but do not configure a routing protocol. Configure a loopback interface on the three routers, as shown in Figure 9-2. You use these loopbacks to give a stable router ID for OSPF and BGP, as well as to simulate an existing network segment. Make sure to erase any configurations on the routers and configure the appropriate IP addresses and subnet masks on the interfaces indicated in Figure 9-2.

Use **ping** to test connectivity between the directly connected routers.

Note: The SanJose1 router should be able to ping the neighbor addresses of 192.168.1.5 and 172.16.1.2. SanJose2 will not be able to ping the ISP1 router and visa versa.

Step 2

Configure OSPF between the SanJose1 and SanJose2 routers with the following commands:

```
SanJose1(config)#router ospf 1
SanJose1(config-router)#network 172.16.64.1 0.0.0.0 area 0
SanJose1(config-router)#network 172.16.1.1 0.0.0.0 area 0

SanJose2(config)#router ospf 1
SanJose2(config-router)#network 172.16.32.1 0.0.0.0 area 0
SanJose2(config-router)#network 172.16.1.2 0.0.0.0 area 0
```

Verify that the SanJose1 and SanJose2 routers have formed an OSPF adjacency. Troubleshoot as necessary, first with the **show ip ospf neighbor** command, and then with the **show ip ospf interface** command. You should see the following output:

```
SanJose1#show ip ospf neighbor

Neighbor ID      Pri   State           Dead Time   Address        Interface
172.16.32.1        1   FULL/ -         00:00:37    172.16.1.2     Serial0/1

SanJose1#show ip ospf interface
Loopback0 is up, line protocol is up
  Internet Address 172.16.64.1/24, Area 0
  Process ID 1, Router ID 172.16.64.1, Network Type LOOPBACK, Cost: 1
  Loopback interface is treated as a stub Host
Serial0/1 is up, line protocol is up
  Internet Address 172.16.1.1/24, Area 0
  Process ID 1, Router ID 172.16.64.1, Network Type POINT_TO_POINT, Cost:64
  Transmit Delay is 1 sec, State POINT_TO_POINT,
  Timer intervals configured, Hello 10, Dead 40, Wait 40, Retransmit 5
    Hello due in 00:00:01
  Index 2/2, flood queue length 0
  Next 0x0(0)/0x0(0)
  Last flood scan length is 1, maximum is 1
  Last flood scan time is 0 msec, maximum is 0 msec
  Neighbor Count is 1, Adjacent neighbor count is 1
    Adjacent with neighbor 172.16.32.1
  Suppress hello for 0 neighbor(s)
```

The OSPF cost on Serial 0/1 might be different from the 64 listed in the output.

Note: Remember that OSPF calculates its costs by dividing 100,000,000 by the bandwidth.

1.   What must be the bandwidth configured on the Serial 0/1 interface?

_____ 128 K bps _____

Router SanJose1 should have a route to the 172.16.32.0 /24 network that ~~is~~ OSPF. Also, SanJose2 should have a route to the 172.16.64.0 /24 networ~~k~~ OSPF.

Step 3

Configure EBGP between the ISP1 and SanJose1 routers. On ISP1 route~~r~~

```
ISP1(config)#router bgp 200
ISP1(config-router)#network 210.210.210.0
ISP1(config-router)#neighbor 192.168.1.6 remote-as 64512

SanJose1(config)#router bgp 64512
SanJose1(config-router)#neighbor 192.168.1.5 remote-as 200
SanJose1(config-router)#end
SanJose1#clear ip bgp *
```

The 172.16.0.0 /16 network has purposely not been advertised through BGP. That is because it is a private address that will not be able to route through the network. After a few minutes pass, issue the **show ip bgp summary** command on the SanJose1 router.

1.　　　Has a BGP conversation with ISP1 router been formed?

yes

Because BGP eventually advertises outside networks that are not part of the OSPF area, you must enter the following command on the SanJose1 router:

```
SanJose1(config)#router bgp 64512
SanJose1(config-router)#no synchronization
```

The **no synchronization** command permits BGP to advertise networks without caring whether the IGP—in this case, OSPF—has the route. Usually, a BGP speaker does not advertise a route to an external neighbor unless that route is local or exists in the IGP.

The routing table of SanJose1 should look similar to the output that follows:

```
Gateway of last resort is not set

B    210.210.210.0/24 [20/0] via 192.168.1.5, 00:03:24
     172.16.0.0/16 is variably subnetted, 3 subnets, 2 masks
O       172.16.32.1/32 [110/65] via 172.16.1.2, 00:41:55, Serial0/1
C       172.16.1.0/24 is directly connected, Serial1
C       172.16.64.0/24 is directly connected, Loopback0
     192.168.1.0/30 is subnetted, 1 subnets
C       192.168.1.4 is directly connected, Serial0/0
```

SanJose1 should be able to ping the 210.210.210.1 host with a standard ping because this ping is sourced from the SanJose1 S0/0 interface address 192.168.1.6.

An extended ping to the 210.210.210.1 host sourced from the Loopback 0, 172.16.64.1, should not be successful.

2.　　　Why not?　*No return route from 210.210.210.1 to 172.16.64*

Step 4

It is now time to configure Network Address Translation (NAT) to change the source IP addresses on packets from the internal private numbered network, 172.16.0.0, into public addresses that are routable on the Internet:

```
SanJose1(config)#int s0/0
SanJose1(config-if)#ip nat outside
SanJose1(config-if)#int lo 0
SanJose1(config-if)#ip nat inside
SanJose1(config-if)#int s0/1
SanJose1(config-if)#ip nat inside
```

Next, configure the NAT pool name and NAT translation policy, as follows:

```
SanJose1(config)#ip nat pool NAT_PUBLIC_SUBNET 66.122.33.98 66.122.33.126 netmask
  255.255.255.224
SanJose1(config)#access-list 10 permit 172.16.0.0 0.0.255.255
SanJose1(config)#ip nat inside source list 10 pool NAT_PUBLIC_SUBNET overload
```

Access-list 10 declares eligibility for NAT. Only those addresses that are permitted in this access-list are eligible for NAT. Any IP address that is omitted from the permit range will not be translated but will still be routed. This ACL is not intended as the only means of securing the network. Imagine that SanJose2 added a 172.20.1.0 /24 network, and access-list 10 had not been updated to reflect this additional network, perhaps for security reasons. Any packets that originate from the new 172.20.1.0 /24 network, which is destined for either network 210.210.210.0 or the Internet, will not be translated. Therefore, the ISP drops those packets as unrouteable. Although this keeps the nodes from being able to connect to the Internet, it does so at a considerable cost. Each of the packets that is dropped crosses the WAN link to the ISP but never returns.

Verify that NAT is working properly. An attempt to ping from the inside interface on SanJose1 to the ISP results in dropped packets because the ISP still does not know about the 66.122.33.96 /27 network. Issue the **debug ip nat** command and then issue an extended **ping** from an inside address to an outside address, as follows:

```
SanJose1#debug ip nat
IP NAT debugging is on

SanJose1#ping              (extended!)
Protocol [ip]:
Target IP address: 192.168.1.6
Repeat count [5]:
Datagram size [100]:
Timeout in seconds [2]:
Extended commands [n]: y
Source address or interface: 172.16.64.1
Type of service [0]:
Set DF bit in IP header? [no]:
Validate reply data? [no]:
Data pattern [0xABCD]:
Loose, Strict, Record, Timestamp, Verbose[none]:
Sweep range of sizes [n]:
Type escape sequence to abort.
Sending 5, 100-byte ICMP Echos to 192.168.1.6, timeout is 2 seconds:
!!!!!
Success rate is 100 percent (5/5), round-trip min/avg/max = 44/48/52 ms

00:22:13: NAT: s=172.16.64.1->66.122.33.98, d=192.168.1.6 [0]
00:22:13: NAT: s=192.168.1.6, d=66.122.33.98->172.16.64.1 [0]
00:22:13: NAT: s=172.16.64.1->66.122.33.98, d=192.168.1.6 [1]
00:22:13: NAT: s=192.168.1.6, d=66.122.33.98->172.16.64.1 [1]
00:22:13: NAT: s=172.16.64.1->66.122.33.98, d=192.168.1.6 [2]
00:22:13: NAT: s=192.168.1.6, d=66.122.33.98->172.16.64.1 [2]
00:22:13: NAT: s=172.16.64.1->66.122.33.98, d=192.168.1.6 [3]
00:22:13: NAT: s=192.168.1.6, d=66.122.33.98->172.16.64.1 [3]
00:22:13: NAT: s=172.16.64.1->66.122.33.98, d=192.168.1.6 [4]
00:22:13: NAT: s=192.168.1.6, d=66.122.33.98->172.16.64.1 [4]
```

This debug output shows that source 172.16.64.1 is re-encapsulated as public (external) host 66.122.33.98 destined for host 192.168.1.6. The next line shows that the return packet sources from 192.168.1.6 and is sent to destination, external host 66.122.33.98. This is actually re-encapsulated to internal host IP 172.16.64.1.

Connectivity to the ISP is sometimes lost not because of a routing issue, but because NAT is not translating properly. When in doubt, issue **debug ip nat** and look for output that is similar to the previous output. Notice that this process never left the SanJose1 router; therefore, it was not influenced by routing or BGP issues that might exist. Attempt to localize your troubleshooting.

Step 5

Configure the SanJose1 router to advertise the NAT pool via BGP. Reset the BGP conversation and test connectivity with an extended **ping** from SanJose1 to the ISP1 router, as follows:

```
SanJose1(config)#router bgp 64512
SanJose1(config-router)#network 66.122.33.96 mask 255.255.255.224

SanJose1#clear ip bgp *
```

1.   Was the extended **ping** successful from Lo0 or S0/1 on SanJose1 to either interface IP address of the ISP1 router?

       No

2.   Issue the **show ip bgp** command to investigate. What did you find? Is anything missing from this output that you expected to see here?

       nat pool   nothing was assigned to phy int.

```
SanJose1#show ip bgp
BGP table version is 4, local router ID is 172.16.64.1
Status codes: s suppressed, d damped, h history, * valid, > best, i - internal  Origin
   codes: i - IGP, e - EGP, ? - incomplete

   Network          Next Hop          Metric LocPrf Weight Path
*> 210.210.210.0    192.168.1.5            0             0 200i
```

If the user cannot see the local routes listed in the **show ip bgp** output, the ISP1 router, BGP Peer, will not see the routes either.

Note: Remember that BGP will advertise routes that are connected directly, identified by a static route. Routes that exist in the routing table by way of a dynamic routing protocol that has been redistributed into BGP might also be advertised. You have two options here. You can either create a loopback interface by using one of the IP addresses from the NAT pool, or you can create a static route referencing the NAT pool. Review the following solutions from these options:

*   Using a loopback interface results in the following:

```
SanJose1(config)#interface loopback 100
SanJose1(config-if)#ip addr 66.122.33.97 255.255.255.224
SanJose1(config-if)#ip nat outside

SanJose1#show ip bgp
BGP table version is 4, local router ID is 172.16.64.1
Status codes: s suppressed, d damped, h history, * valid, > best, i - internal
Origin codes: i - IGP, e - EGP, ? - incomplete

   Network          Next Hop          Metric LocPrf Weight Path
*> 66.122.33.96/27  0.0.0.0                0         32768 i
*> 210.210.210.0    192.168.1.5            0             0 200 I
```

*   Using a static route results in the following:

```
SanJose1(config)#ip route 66.122.33.96 255.255.255.224 null0 230
SanJose1#show ip bgp
BGP table version is 6, local router ID is 172.16.64.1
Status codes: s suppressed, d damped, h history, * valid, > best, i - internal  Origin
   codes: i - IGP, e - EGP, ? - incomplete

   Network          Next Hop          Metric LocPrf Weight Path
*> 66.122.33.96/27  0.0.0.0                0         32768 i
*> 210.210.210.0    192.168.1.5            0             0 200 i
```

Note: Using the loopback address that is assigned to IP NAT outside can be useful for testing. Imagine that the link to the ISP has not been provisioned. Using an outside loopback address allows for configuration and testing prior to this link being put into production. The downside is that it uses one of the IP addresses from the public range—in this case, a subnet of 32 hosts. The NAT pool was started at X.X.X.98 instead of X.X.X.97 in anticipation of this loopback address.

Testing connectivity to the 210.210.210.1 host off ISP1 shows that any interface, or subnet, on SanJose1 can ping successfully.

Step 6

SanJose2 cannot reach the 210.210.210.1 host when attempting communication from any of its three interfaces.

1.   Why is this the case?

NAT changes from public to private address, so no return is possible

Issue the **debug ip packet** and reattempt the **ping** from the SanJose2 router to 210.210.210.1. Notice that each attempted packet was dropped because of unroutable error messages:

```
SanJose2#ping 210.210.210.1

Sending 5, 100-byte ICMP Echos to 210.210.210.1, timeout is 2 seconds:

00:35:29: IP: s=172.16.32.1 (local), d=210.210.210.1, len 100, unroutable.
00:35:31: IP: s=172.16.32.1 (local), d=210.210.210.1, len 100, unroutable
00:35:33: IP: s=172.16.32.1 (local), d=210.210.210.1, len 100, unroutable.
00:35:35: IP: s=172.16.32.1 (local), d=210.210.210.1, len 100, unroutable.
00:35:37: IP: s=172.16.32.1 (local), d=210.210.210.1, len 100, unroutable
Success rate is 0 percent (0/5)
```

Look at the routing table on SanJose2 and check to see whether a Gateway of Last Resort has been defined. Then, check the SanJose1 router for the same information.

2.   Does either router have a default route or Gateway of Last Resort?

No.

Step 7

Establish a default route on SanJose1 and allow it to be advertised within OSPF to SanJose2:

```
SanJose1(config)#ip default-network 210.210.210.0
SanJose1(config)#router ospf 1
SanJose1(config-router)#default-information originate always metric 2500 metric-type 1
```

Use the **show ip route** command on SanJose2 to verify that SanJose1 is advertising the candidate default route by way of OSPF:

```
Gateway of last resort is 172.16.1.1 to network 0.0.0.0

     172.16.0.0/16 is variably subnetted, 3 subnets, 2 masks
C       172.16.32.0/24 is directly connected, Loopback0
C       172.16.1.0/24 is directly connected, Serial0/1
O       172.16.64.1/32 [110/65] via 172.16.1.1, 00:03:15, Serial0/1
O*E1 0.0.0.0/0 [110/2564] via 172.16.1.1, 00:02:24, Serial0/1
```

From any of the interface IP addresses on SanJose2, ping the 210.210.210.1, ISP1, address.

This should be successful now:

```
SanJose2#ping 210.210.210.1
Type escape sequence to abort.
Sending 5, 100-byte ICMP Echos to 210.210.210.1, timeout is 2 seconds:
!!!!!
Success rate is 100 percent (5/5), round-trip min/avg/max = 80/82/84 ms
```

Note that each packet being sent from SanJose2 to ISP1 is also being translated once on the way out and again on the way back, as shown next in the output from **debug ip nat** while pinging from SanJose2. This would have been an appropriate area to investigate if we had seen unsuccessful ping attempts after having established the Gateway of Last Resort on SanJose2:

```
SanJose1#
01:03:57: NAT: s=172.16.1.2->66.122.33.98, d=210.210.210.1 [20]
01:03:57: NAT: s=210.210.210.1, d=66.122.33.98->172.16.1.2 [20]
01:03:58: NAT: s=172.16.1.2->66.122.33.98, d=210.210.210.1 [21]
01:03:58: NAT: s=210.210.210.1, d=66.122.33.98->172.16.1.2 [21]
01:03:58: NAT: s=172.16.1.2->66.122.33.98, d=210.210.210.1 [22]
01:03:58: NAT: s=210.210.210.1, d=66.122.33.98->172.16.1.2 [22]
01:03:58: NAT: s=172.16.1.2->66.122.33.98, d=210.210.210.1 [23]
01:03:58: NAT: s=210.210.210.1, d=66.122.33.98->172.16.1.2 [23]
01:03:58: NAT: s=172.16.1.2->66.122.33.98, d=210.210.210.1 [24]
01:03:58: NAT: s=210.210.210.1, d=66.122.33.98->172.16.1.2 [24]
01:04:02: NAT: expiring 66.122.33.98 (172.16.1.2) icmp 4548 (4548)
01:04:03: NAT: expiring 66.122.33.98 (172.16.1.2) icmp 4549 (4549)
01:04:03: NAT: expiring 66.122.33.98 (172.16.1.2) icmp 4550 (4550)
01:04:03: NAT: expiring 66.122.33.98 (172.16.1.2) icmp 4551 (4551)
01:04:03: NAT: expiring 66.122.33.98 (172.16.1.2) icmp 4552 (4552)
```

Lab 9.11.3: Using the AS_PATH Attribute

Estimated Time: 30 Minutes

Objective

In this lab, you use BGP commands to prevent private AS numbers from being advertised to the outside world, as shown in Figure 9-3. You also use the AS_PATH attribute to filter BGP routes based on their source AS numbers.

Figure 9-3   Sample Topology for Lab 9.11.3

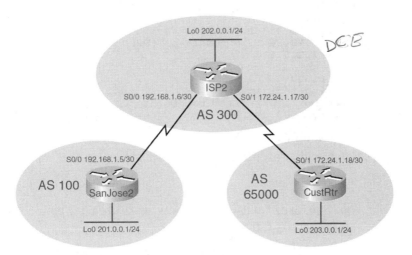

Equipment Requirements

You need the following equipment for this exercise:

* Three Cisco 2600 series routers

* Three serial cables

Scenario

The International Travel Agency's Internet service provider ISP2 has been assigned an AS number of 300. This provider uses BGP to exchange routing information with several customer networks. Each customer network is assigned an AS number from the private range, such as AS 65000. Configure ISP2 to remove the private AS numbers within the AS_Path information from the CustRtr. In addition, Provider ISP2 would like to prevent its customer networks from receiving route information from International Travel Agency's AS 100. Use the AS_PATH attribute to implement this policy.

Step 1

Build and configure the network according to the diagram, but do not configure a routing protocol. Make sure either to erase any configurations on the routers or configure the appropriate IP addresses and subnet masks on the interfaces indicated in Figure 9-3.

Use **ping** to test connectivity between the directly connected routers.

Note: SanJose2 will not be able to reach the customer network for ISP2, CustRtr, by the IP address in the link leading to the CustRtr, or the loopback interface, 202.0.0.1/24.

Step 2

Configure BGP for normal operation. Enter the appropriate BGP commands on each router so that they can identify their BGP neighbors and advertise their Ethernet networks:

```
SanJose2(config)#router bgp 100
SanJose2(config-router)#no synchronization
SanJose2(config-router)#neighbor 192.168.1.6 remote-as 300
SanJose2(config-router)#network 201.0.0.0

ISP2(config)#router bgp 300
ISP2(config-router)#no synchronization
ISP2(config-router)#neighbor 192.168.1.5 remote-as 100
ISP2(config-router)#neighbor 172.24.1.18 remote-as 65000
ISP2(config-router)#network 202.0.0.0

CustRtr(config)#router bgp 65000
CustRtr(config-router)#no synchronization
CustRtr(config-router)#neighbor 172.24.1.17 remote-as 300
CustRtr(config-router)#network 203.0.0.0
```

Verify that these routers have established the appropriate neighbor relationships by issuing the **show ip bgp neighbors** command at each router.

Step 3

Check the routing table from SanJose2 by using the **show ip route** command. SanJose2 should have a route to both 202.0.0.0 and 203.0.0.0. Troubleshoot if necessary.

1. Can the SanJose2 router ping to the 203.0.0.0 /24 network off of CustRtr?

_____

2. A ping should not be successful when you are issuing just a standard ping. Why is this the case?

_____

Try the **ping** again, this time as an extended **ping**, sourcing from the Loopback 0 interface, as follows:

```
SanJose2#ping
Protocol [ip]:
Target IP address: 203.0.0.1
Repeat count [5]:
Datagram size [100]:
Timeout in seconds [2]:
Extended commands [n]: y
Source address or interface: 201.0.0.1
Type of service [0]:
Set DF bit in IP header? [no]:
Validate reply data? [no]:
Data pattern [0xABCD]:
Loose, Strict, Record, Timestamp, Verbose[none]:
Sweep range of sizes [n]:
Type escape sequence to abort.
Sending 5, 100-byte ICMP Echos to 203.0.0.1, timeout is 2 seconds:
!!!!!
Success rate is 100 percent (5/5), round-trip min/avg/max = 64/64/68 ms
```

Check the BGP table from SanJose2 by using the **show ip bgp** command. Note the AS path for the 203.0.0.0 network. The AS 65000 should be listed in the path to 203.0.0.0. Why is this a problem?

```
BGP table version is 4, local router ID is 201.0.0.1
Status codes: s suppressed, d damped, h history, * valid, > best, i - internal
Origin codes: i - IGP, e - EGP, ? - incomplete

   Network          Next Hop           Metric LocPrf Weight Path
*> 201.0.0.0        0.0.0.0                 0          32768 i
*> 202.0.0.0        192.168.1.6             0              0 300 i
*> 203.0.0.0        192.168.1.6                            0 300 65000 I
```

Configure ISP2 to strip the private AS numbers from BGP routes exchanged with SanJose2. Use the following commands:

```
ISP2(config)#router bgp 300
ISP2(config-router)#neighbor 192.168.1.5 remove-private-as
```

After you issue these commands, use the **clear ip bgp** * command on SanJose2 to re-establish the BGP relationships between the three routers.

Wait several seconds, and then return to SanJose2 to check its routing table.

3.   Does SanJose2 still have a route to 203.0.0.0?

SanJose2 should be able to ping 203.0.0.0.

Now, check the BGP table on SanJose2. The AS_PATH to the 203.0.0.0 network should be AS 300:

```
BGP table version is 8, local router ID is 201.0.0.1
Status codes: s suppressed, d damped, h history, * valid, > best, i - internal
Origin codes: i - IGP, e - EGP, ? - incomplete

   Network          Next Hop           Metric LocPrf Weight Path
*> 201.0.0.0        0.0.0.0                 0          32768 i
*> 202.0.0.0        192.168.1.6             0              0 300 i
*> 203.0.0.0        192.168.1.6                            0 300 i
```

Step 4

As a final configuration, use the AS_PATH attribute to filter routes based on their origin. In a complex environment, you can use this attribute to enforce routing policy. In this case, you must configure the provider router, ISP2, so that it does not propagate routes that originate from AS 100 to the customer router, CustRtr.

Configure a special kind of access list to match BGP routes with an AS_PATH attribute that both begins and ends with the number 100. Enter the following commands on ISP2:

```
ISP2(config)#ip as-path access-list 1 deny ^100$
ISP2(config)#ip as-path access-list 1 permit .*
```

The first command uses the ^ character to indicate that the AS_PATH must begin with the given number, 100. The $ character indicates that the AS_PATH attribute must also end with 100. Essentially, this statement only matches paths that are sourced from AS 100. Other paths, which might include AS 100 along the way, will not match this list.

In the second statement, the . character is a wildcard, and the * symbol stands for a repetition of the wildcard. Together, .* matches any value of the AS_PATH attribute, which in effect permits any update that has not been denied by the previous **access-list** statement.

Now that the access list has been configured, apply it as follows:

```
ISP2(config)#router bgp 300
ISP2(config-router)#neighbor 172.24.1.18 filter-list 1 out
```

The **out** keyword specifies that the list should be applied to routing information sent to this neighbor.

Use the **clear ip bgp *** command to reset the routing information. Wait several seconds, and then check the routing table for ISP2. The route to 201.0.0.0 should be in the routing table.

Check the routing table for CustRtr. It should not have a route to 201.0.0.0 in its routing table.

Return to ISP2 and verify that the filter is working as intended. Issue the command **show ip bgp regexp ^100$**.

The output of this command shows all matches for the regular expressions that were used in the access list. The path to 201.0.0.0 matches the access list and is filtered out of updates to CustRtr:

```
ISP2#show ip bgp regexp ^100$
BGP table version is 4, local router ID is 202.0.0.1
Status codes: s suppressed, d damped, h history, * valid, > best, i - internal
Origin codes: i - IGP, e - EGP, ? - incomplete

   Network          Next Hop            Metric LocPrf Weight Path
*> 201.0.0.0        192.168.1.5              0             0 100 i
```

Lab 9.11.4a: Configuring IBGP and EBGP Sessions, Local Preference, and MED

Estimated Time: 90 Minutes

Objective

In this lab, you configure both Internal BGP (IBGP) and EBGP using redundant links to the ISP from separate routers in the corporate AS, as shown in Figure 9-4. For IBGP peers to correctly exchange routing information, you must use the **next-hop-self** command. You must also use **local-preference** and **med** (Multiple Exit Discriminator) attributes. This ensures that the flat rate unlimited use T1 link sends and receives data to and from the AS 200 on ISP1. Only use the metered T1 if the primary T1 link has failed. Traffic that you send across the metered T1 link offers the same bandwidth as the primary link but at a greater expense. Ensure that this link is not used unnecessarily.

Figure 9-4   Sample Topology for Lab 9.11.4a

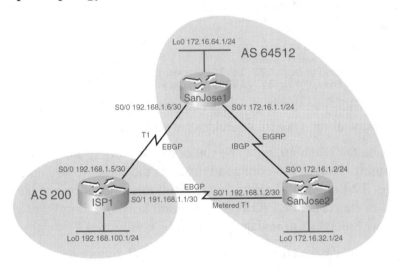

Equipment Requirements

You need the following equipment for this exercise:

*   Three Cisco 2600 series routers

*   Three serial cables

Scenario

The International Travel Agency runs BGP on its SanJose1 and SanJose2 routers externally with ISP1, AS 200. It runs IBGP internally between SanJose1 and SanJose2. Finally, it runs EIGRP on the corporate network. Your job is to configure both EBGP and IBGP for this internetwork to allow for redundancy.

Step 1

Build and configure the network according to the diagram, but do not configure a routing protocol. Configure a loopback interface on the SanJose1 and SanJose2 routers, as shown in

Figure 9-4. You use these loopbacks with BGP **neighbor** statements for increased stability. Make sure either to erase any configurations on the routers or configure the appropriate IP addresses and subnet masks on the interfaces indicated in Figure 9-4.

Use **ping** to test connectivity between the directly connected routers.

Note: The ISP1 router will not be able to reach the segment between SanJose1 and SanJose2. Both SanJose routers should be able to ping each other as well as their local ISP serial link IP address.

Step 2

Configure EIGRP between the SanJose1 and SanJose2 routers with the same commands as follows:

```
(config)#router eigrp 64512
(config-router)#network 172.16.0.0
```

Step 3

Configure IBGP between the SanJose1 and SanJose2 routers. On the SanJose1 router, enter the following configuration:

```
SanJose1(config)#router bgp 64512
SanJose1(config-router)#no auto-summary
SanJose1(config-router)#neighbor 172.16.32.1 remote-as 64512
SanJose1(config-router)#neighbor 172.16.32.1 update-source lo0
```

This topology uses variable-length subnet mask (VLSM). Therefore, you should disable automatic summarization along classful boundaries with the **no auto-summary** command.

If multiple pathways to the neighbor exist, the router can use any IP interface to communicate by way of BGP. The **update-source lo0** command instructs the router to use interface loopback 0 for TCP connections. This command offers greater fault tolerance if one of the potentially numerous links within the corporate EIGRP WAN cloud fails. For simplicity in the lab environment, only one link is illustrated and needs to be configured.

Because BGP will eventually advertise outside networks that are not part of the EIGRP cloud, you must enter the following command on SanJose1 and SanJose2:

```
SanJose1(config)#router bgp 64512
SanJose1(config-router)#no synchronization

SanJose2(config)#router bgp 64512
SanJose2(config-router)#no synchronization
```

The **no synchronization** command permits BGP to advertise networks regardless of whether EIGRP knows of the network. Usually, a BGP speaker does not advertise a route to an external neighbor unless that route is local or exists in the IGP.

Step 4

Complete the IBGP configuration on SanJose2 by entering the following commands:

```
SanJose2(config)#router bgp 64512
SanJose2(config-router)#no auto-summary
SanJose2(config-router)#neighbor 172.16.64.1 remote-as 64512
SanJose2(config-router)#neighbor 172.16.64.1 update-source lo0
```

Verify that SanJose1 and SanJose2 become BGP neighbors by issuing the **show ip bgp neighbors** command on SanJose1. View the following partial output. If the BGP state is not established, troubleshoot the connection.

The link between SanJose1 and SanJose2 should indicate an internal link, as shown here:

```
SanJose2#show ip bgp neighbors
BGP neighbor is 172.16.64.1,   remote AS 64512, internal link
             BGP version 4, remote router ID 172.16.64.1
             BGP state = Established, up for 00:00:01
```

Step 5

Configure ISP1 to run EBGP with SanJose1 and SanJose2. Enter the following commands on ISP1, as shown here:

```
ISP1(config)#router bgp 200
ISP1(config-router)#no auto-summary
ISP1(config-router)#neighbor 192.168.1.6 remote-as 64512
ISP1(config-router)#neighbor 192.168.1.2 remote-as 64512
ISP1(config-router)#network 192.168.100.0
```

Because EBGP sessions are almost always established over point-to-point links, you do not need to use the **update-source** keyword in this configuration. Only one path exists between the peers. If this path goes down, alternative paths are not available.

Step 6

Configure SanJose1 as an EBGP peer to ISP1, as shown here:

```
SanJose1(config)#ip route 172.16.0.0 255.255.0.0 null0
SanJose1(config)#router bgp 64512
SanJose1(config-router)#neighbor 192.168.1.5 remote-as 200
SanJose1(config-router)#network 172.16.0.0
```

Use the **show ip bgp neighbors** command to verify that SanJose1 and ISP1 have reached the Established state. Troubleshoot if necessary.

Step 7

Configure SanJose2 as an EBGP peer to ISP1:

```
SanJose2(config)#ip route 172.16.0.0 255.255.0.0 null0
SanJose2(config)#router bgp 64512
SanJose2(config-router)#neighbor 192.168.1.1 remote-as 200
SanJose2(config-router)#network 172.16.0.0
```

In Step 6, you used the **show ip bgp neighbors** command to verify that SanJose1 and ISP1 had reached the Established state. You can also use the **show ip bgp summary** command. Output should be similar to the sample output displayed here:

```
SanJose2#show ip bgp summary

BGP router identifier 172.16.32.1, local AS number 64512
BGP table version is 2, main routing table version 2
1 network entries and 1 paths using 137 bytes of memory
1 BGP path attribute entries using 60 bytes of memory
0 BGP route-map cache entries using 0 bytes of memory
0 BGP filter-list cache entries using 0 bytes of memory
BGP activity 2/1 prefixes, 2/1 paths, scan interval 15 secs

Neighbor        V    AS MsgRcvd MsgSent   TblVer  InQ OutQ Up/Down  State/PfxRcd
172.16.64.1     4 64512      21      24        2    0    0 00:03:02         0
192.168.1.1     4   200      14      15        2    0    0 00:03:36         0
```

Step 8

Test whether ISP1 can ping the Loopback 0 address of 172.16.64.1 of SanJose1, as well as the serial link between SanJose1 and SanJose2, 172.16.1.1.

Ping from ISP1 to the Loopback 0 address of 172.16.32.1 of SanJose2, as well as the serial link between SanJose1 and SanJose2. This time, try 172.16.1.2.

You should see successful pings to each IP address on the SanJose2 router. Ping attempts to the 172.16.64.1 and 172.16.1.1 should fail.

1.   Why is this the case?

___

Issue the **show ip bgp** command on ISP1 to verify BGP routes and metrics:

```
ISP1#show ip bgp

BGP table version is 3, local router ID is 192.168.100.1
Status codes: s suppressed, d damped, h history, * valid, > best, i - internal
Origin codes: i - IGP, e - EGP, ? - incomplete

     Network          Next Hop        Metric LocPrf Weight Path
*    172.16.0.0       192.168.1.6                        0 64512 i
*>                    192.168.1.2          0             0 64512 i
*> 192.168.100.0      0.0.0.0              0         32768 i
```

Notice that ISP1 has two valid routes to the 172.16.0.0 network, indicated by the *. However, the link to SanJose2, the metered T1, has been selected as the best path. Although that might be better for the ISP, you will pay a premium for each megabyte transferred across this link.

2.   Was this a malicious attempt by the ISP to get more money? Why did the ISP prefer the link to SanJose2 over SanJose1?

___

3.   Would changing the bandwidth metric on each link help to correct this issue?

___

BGP operates differently from all other protocols. Unlike other routing protocols, which might use complex algorithms involving factors such as bandwidth, delay, reliability, and load to formulate a metric, BGP is based on policy. BGP will determine the best path based on variables such as AS_Path, Weight, Local Preference, MED, and so on. All things being equal, as in this case, BGP will prefer the route leading to the BGP speaker with the lowest IP address. This was not a malicious attempt by the ISP to obtain additional funds. In fact, this ISP1 router was configured from the beginning. The SanJose2 router with address 192.168.1.2 was preferred to the higher IP address of the SanJose1 router, 192.168.1.6.

At this point, the ISP1 router should be able to get to each network connected to SanJose1 and SanJose2 from the FastEthernet address 192.168.100.1:

```
ISP1#ping
Protocol [ip]:
Target IP address: 172.16.64.1
Repeat count [5]:
Datagram size [100]:
Timeout in seconds [2]:
Extended commands [n]: y
Source address or interface: 192.168.100.1
Type of service [0]:
```

```
Set DF bit in IP header? [no]:
Validate reply data? [no]:
Data pattern [0xABCD]:
Loose, Strict, Record, Timestamp, Verbose[none]:
Sweep range of sizes [n]:
Type escape sequence to abort.
Sending 5, 100-byte ICMP Echos to 172.16.64.1, timeout is 2 seconds:
!!!!!
Success rate is 100 percent (5/5), round-trip min/avg/max = 48/48/52 ms
ISP1#ping
Protocol [ip]:
Target IP address: 172.16.1.1
Repeat count [5]:
Datagram size [100]:
Timeout in seconds [2]:
Extended commands [n]: y
Source address or interface: 192.168.100.1
Type of service [0]:
Set DF bit in IP header? [no]:
Validate reply data? [no]:
Data pattern [0xABCD]:
Loose, Strict, Record, Timestamp, Verbose[none]:
Sweep range of sizes [n]:
Type escape sequence to abort.
Sending 5, 100-byte ICMP Echos to 172.16.1.1, timeout is 2 seconds:
!!!!!
Success rate is 100 percent (5/5), round-trip min/avg/max = 48/48/48 ms
ISP1#ping
Protocol [ip]:
Target IP address: 172.16.32.1
Repeat count [5]:
Datagram size [100]:
Timeout in seconds [2]:
Extended commands [n]: y
Source address or interface: 192.168.100.1
Type of service [0]:
Set DF bit in IP header? [no]:
Validate reply data? [no]:
Data pattern [0xABCD]:
Loose, Strict, Record, Timestamp, Verbose[none]:
Sweep range of sizes [n]:
Type escape sequence to abort.
Sending 5, 100-byte ICMP Echos to 172.16.32.1, timeout is 2 seconds:
!!!!!
Success rate is 100 percent (5/5), round-trip min/avg/max = 32/33/36 ms
ISP1#ping
Protocol [ip]:
Target IP address: 172.16.1.2
Repeat count [5]:
Datagram size [100]:
Timeout in seconds [2]:
Extended commands [n]: y
Source address or interface: 192.168.100.1
Type of service [0]:
Set DF bit in IP header? [no]:
Validate reply data? [no]:
Data pattern [0xABCD]:
Loose, Strict, Record, Timestamp, Verbose[none]:
Sweep range of sizes [n]:
Type escape sequence to abort.
Sending 5, 100-byte ICMP Echos to 172.16.1.2, timeout is 2 seconds:
!!!!!
Success rate is 100 percent (5/5), round-trip min/avg/max = 32/36/56 ms
```

Complete reachability was proven between the ISP1 router and both SanJose1 and SanJose2.

4.   Why do the following ping requests fail?

```
ISP1#ping 172.16.1.1

Type escape sequence to abort.
Sending 5, 100-byte ICMP Echos to 172.16.1.1, timeout is 2 seconds:
.....
Success rate is 0 percent (0/5)
ISP1#ping 172.16.64.1

Type escape sequence to abort.
Sending 5, 100-byte ICMP Echos to 172.16.64.1, timeout is 2 seconds:
.....
Success rate is 0 percent (0/5)
```

Step 9

Before the ISP can successfully ping the internal serial interfaces of AS 64512, it must resolve two issues. First, SanJose1 does not know about the link between the ISP and SanJose2. Second, SanJose2 is unaware of the link between the ISP and SanJose1. This can be resolved by an advertisement of these serial links by way of BGP on the ISP router. This can also be resolved by way of EIGRP on each of the SanJose routers. The preferred method is for the ISP to advertise these links. If these links are advertised and a BGP link is activated later to another ISP in addition to ISP1 at AS 200, there is a risk of becoming a transit AS.

Issue the following commands on the ISP1 router:

```
ISP1(config)#router bgp 200
ISP1(config-router)#network 192.168.1.0 mask 255.255.255.252
ISP1(config-router)#network 192.168.1.4 mask 255.255.255.252
```

Clear the IP BGP conversation with the **clear ip bgp *** command on ISP1. Wait for the conversations to re-establish with each SanJose router. Issue the **show ip bgp** command as follows to verify that the ISP1 router can see its own WAN links through BGP:

```
ISP1#show ip bgp
BGP table version is 5, local router ID is 192.168.100.1
Status codes: s suppressed, d damped, h history, * valid, > best, i - internal Origin
  codes: i - IGP, e - EGP, ? - incomplete

  Network          Next Hop        Metric LocPrf Weight Path
*  172.16.0.0      192.168.1.6                        0 64512 i
*>                 192.168.1.2          0             0 64512 i
*> 192.168.1.0/30  0.0.0.0              0         32768 i
*> 192.168.1.4/30  0.0.0.0              0         32768 i
*> 192.168.100.0   0.0.0.0              0         32768 i
```

Verify on SanJose1 and SanJose2 that the opposite WAN link is included in the routing table. The output from SanJose2 is shown here:

```
Gateway of last resort is not set

     172.16.0.0/24 is subnetted, 3 subnets
C       172.16.32.0 is directly connected, Loopback0
C       172.16.1.0 is directly connected, Serial0/0
D       172.16.64.0 [90/20640000] via 172.16.1.1, 00:57:10, Serial0/0
     192.168.1.0/30 is subnetted, 2 subnets
C       192.168.1.0 is directly connected, Serial0/1
B       192.168.1.4 [20/0] via 192.168.1.1, 00:04:23
B    192.168.100.0/24 [20/0] via 192.168.1.1, 00:04:23
```

The next issue to consider is BGP policy routing between AS systems. BGP routers do not increment the next hop address to their IBGP peers. The SanJose2 router is passing a policy to SanJose1 and vice versa. The policy for routing from AS 64512 to AS 200 is to forward packets to the 192.168.1.1 interface. SanJose1 has a similar yet opposite policy, forwarding requests to the 192.168.1.5 interface. If either WAN link fails, the opposite router must become a valid gateway. This is only achieved if the **next-hop-self** command is configured on SanJose1 and SanJose2.

The following is output from before the **next-hop-self** command was issued:

```
SanJose2#show ip bgp
BGP table version is 11, local router ID is 172.16.32.1
Status codes: s suppressed, d damped, h history, * valid, > best, i - internal  Origin
  codes: i - IGP, e - EGP, ? - incomplete

   Network          Next Hop          Metric LocPrf Weight Path
*> 172.16.0.0       0.0.0.0                0          32768 i
*  i192.168.1.0/30  192.168.1.5            0     100      0 200 i
*>                  192.168.1.1            0              0 200 i
*  i192.168.1.4/30  192.168.1.5            0     100      0 200 i
*>                  192.168.1.1            0              0 200 i
*  i192.168.100.0   192.168.1.5            0     100      0 200 i
*>                  192.168.1.1            0              0 200 i

SanJose1(config)#router bgp 64512
SanJose1(config-router)#neighbor 172.16.32.1 next-hop-self

SanJose2(config)#router bgp 64512
SanJose2(config-router)#neighbor 172.16.64.1 next-hop-self
```

After you issue these commands, reset BGP operation on either router by entering the command **clear ip bgp ***.

After the routers have returned to established BGP speakers, issue the **show ip bgp** command to validate that the next hop has been corrected as well:

```
SanJose2#show ip bgp
BGP table version is 11, local router ID is 172.16.32.1
Status codes: s suppressed, d damped, h history, * valid, > best, i - internal
Origin codes: i - IGP, e - EGP, ? - incomplete

   Network          Next Hop          Metric LocPrf Weight Path
*> 172.16.0.0       0.0.0.0                0          32768 i
*  i192.168.1.0/30  172.16.64.1            0     100      0 200 i
*>                  192.168.1.1            0              0 200 i
*  i192.168.1.4/30  172.16.64.1            0     100      0 200 i
*>                  192.168.1.1            0              0 200 i
*  i192.168.100.0   172.16.64.1            0     100      0 200 i
*>                  192.168.1.1            0              0 200 i
```

Step 10

At this point, everything looks good with the exception of default routes, the outbound flow of data, and inbound packet flow.

Because the local preference value is shared between IBGP neighbors, configure a simple route map that references a local preference value on SanJose1 and SanJose2. This policy adjusts outbound traffic to prefer the link off the SanJose1 router instead of the metered T1 off SanJose2.

Issue the following commands on SanJose1 and SanJose2, respectively:

```
SanJose1(config)#route-map PRIMARY_T1_IN permit 10
SanJose1(config-route-map)#set local-preference 150
SanJose1(config-route-map)#exit
SanJose1(config)#router bgp 64512
SanJose1(config-router)#neighbor 192.168.1.5 route-map PRIMARY_T1_IN in

SanJose2(config)#route-map SECONDARY_T1_IN permit 10
SanJose2(config-route-map)#set local-preference 125
SanJose2(config-route-map)#router bgp 64512
SanJose2(config-router)#neighbor 192.168.1.1 route-map SECONDARY_T1_IN in
```

Do not forget to use the command **clear ip bgp** * after you configure this new policy. After the conversations have been re-established, issue the **show ip bgp** command on SanJose1 and SanJose2, as follows:

```
SanJose1#show ip bgp

BGP table version is 8, local router ID is 172.16.64.1
Status codes: s suppressed, d damped, h history, * valid, > best, i - internal
Origin codes: i - IGP, e - EGP, ? - incomplete

   Network          Next Hop         Metric LocPrf Weight Path
*>i172.16.0.0       172.16.32.1           0    100      0 i
*>  192.168.1.0/30  192.168.1.5           0    150      0 200 i
*>  192.168.1.4/30  192.168.1.5           0    150      0 200 i
*>  192.168.100.0   192.168.1.5           0    150      0 200 i

SanJose2#show ip bgp

BGP table version is 11, local router ID is 172.16.32.1
Status codes: s suppressed, d damped, h history, * valid, > best, i - internal
Origin codes: i - IGP, e - EGP, ? - incomplete

   Network          Next Hop         Metric LocPrf Weight Path
*>  172.16.0.0       0.0.0.0              0         32768 i
*>i192.168.1.0/30   172.16.64.1           0    150      0 200 i
*                   192.168.1.1           0    125      0 200 i
*>i192.168.1.4/30   172.16.64.1           0    150      0 200 i
*                   192.168.1.1           0    125      0 200 i
*>i192.168.100.0    172.16.64.1           0    150      0 200 i
*                   192.168.1.1           0    125      0 200 i
```

The **show** output now indicates that routing to the FastEthernet segment for ISP1, 192.168.100.0 /24, will be reached only through the link common to SanJose1 and ISP1.

Step 11

1. How will traffic return from network 192.168.100.0 /24? Will it be routed through SanJose1 or SanJose2?

2. The simplest solution would be to issue **show ip bgp** on the ISP1 router. What if access was not given to the ISP router? Would there be a simple way to verify before receiving the monthly bill? You should not pass traffic returning from the Internet across the metered T1. How can you check it instantly?

Use an extended ping in this situation. Issue the following command and compare the output to that provided in the following:

```
SanJose2#ping
Protocol [ip]:
Target IP address: 192.168.100.1
Repeat count [5]: 2
Datagram size [100]:
Timeout in seconds [2]:
Extended commands [n]: y
Source address or interface: 172.16.32.1
Type of service [0]:
Set DF bit in IP header? [no]:
Validate reply data? [no]:
Data pattern [0xABCD]:
Loose, Strict, Record, Timestamp, Verbose[none]: record
Number of hops [ 9 ]:
Loose, Strict, Record, Timestamp, Verbose[RV]:
```

```
Sweep range of sizes [n]:
Type escape sequence to abort.
Sending 5, 100-byte ICMP Echos to 192.168.100.1, timeout is 2 seconds:
Packet has IP options:  Total option bytes= 39, padded length=40
 Record route: <*>
    (0.0.0.0)
    (0.0.0.0)
    (0.0.0.0)
    (0.0.0.0)
    (0.0.0.0)
    (0.0.0.0)
    (0.0.0.0)
    (0.0.0.0)
    (0.0.0.0)

Reply to request 0 (48 ms).  Received packet has options
 Total option bytes= 40, padded length=40
 Record route:
    (172.16.1.2)
    (192.168.1.6)
    (192.168.100.1)
    (192.168.1.1)
    (172.16.32.1) <*>
    (0.0.0.0)
    (0.0.0.0)
    (0.0.0.0)
    (0.0.0.0)
 End of list

Reply to request 1 (48 ms).  Received packet has options
 Total option bytes= 40, padded length=40
 Record route:
    (172.16.1.2)
    (192.168.1.6)
    (192.168.100.1)
    (192.168.1.1)
    (172.16.32.1) <*>
    (0.0.0.0)
    (0.0.0.0)
    (0.0.0.0)
    (0.0.0.0)
 End of list
```

If you have not used the record option prior to this, note that each of the IP addresses in brackets is an outgoing interface. You can interpret the output as follows:

1.   A ping that is sourced from 172.16.32.1 exits SanJose2 through s0/0, 172.16.1.2. It then arrives at the S0/1 interface for SanJose1.

2.   SanJose1 S0/0, 192.168.1.6, routes the packet out to arrive at the S0/0 interface of ISP1.

3.   The target of 192.168.100.1 is reached.

4.   The packet is forwarded out the S0/1, 192.168.1.1, interface for ISP1 and arrives at the S0/1 interface for SanJose2.

5.   SanJose2 forwards the packet out the last interface, Loopback 0, 172.16.32.1.

Although the unlimited use of the T1 from SanJose1 is preferred here, the ISP prefers the link from SanJose2 for all return traffic.

The next step is to create a new policy to force the ISP to return all traffic via SanJose1. Create a second route map utilizing the MED (metric) that is shared between EBGP neighbors:

```
SanJose1(config)#route-map PRIMARY_T1_MED_OUT permit 10
SanJose1(config-route-map)#set Metric 50
SanJose1(config-route-map)#exit
```

```
SanJose1(config)#router bgp 64512
SanJose1(config-router)#neighbor 192.168.1.5 route-map PRIMARY_T1_MED_OUT out

SanJose2(config)#route-map SECONDARY_T1_MED_OUT permit 10
SanJose2(config-route-map)#set Metric 75
SanJose2(config-route-map)#exit
SanJose2(config)#router bgp 64512
SanJose2(config-router)#neighbor 192.168.1.1 route-map SECONDARY_T1_MED_OUT out
```

As before, do not forget to use **clear ip bgp *** after issuing this new policy. Issuing the **show ip bgp** command as follows on SanJose1 or SanJose2 will not indicate anything about this newly defined policy:

```
SanJose1#show ip bgp
BGP table version is 10, local router ID is 172.16.64.1
Status codes: s suppressed, d damped, h history, * valid, > best, i - internal  Origin
   codes: i - IGP, e - EGP, ? - incomplete

   Network          Next Hop          Metric LocPrf Weight Path
*>i172.16.0.0       172.16.32.1            0    100      0 i
*>  192.168.1.0/30  192.168.1.5           0    150      0 200 i
*>  192.168.1.4/30  192.168.1.5           0    150      0 200 i
*>  192.168.100.0   192.168.1.5           0    150      0 200 i
```

Now, reissue an extended **ping** with a **record** command, as follows:

```
SanJose2#ping
Protocol [ip]:
Target IP address: 192.168.100.1
Repeat count [5]: 2
Datagram size [100]:
Timeout in seconds [2]:
Extended commands [n]: y
Source address or interface: 172.16.32.1
Type of service [0]:
Set DF bit in IP header? [no]:
Validate reply data? [no]:
Data pattern [0xABCD]:
Loose, Strict, Record, Timestamp, Verbose[none]: record
Number of hops [ 9 ]:
Loose, Strict, Record, Timestamp, Verbose[RV]:
Sweep range of sizes [n]:
Type escape sequence to abort.
Sending 5, 100-byte ICMP Echos to 192.168.100.1, timeout is 2 seconds:
Packet has IP options:  Total option bytes= 39, padded length=40
 Record route: <*>
    (0.0.0.0)
    (0.0.0.0)
    (0.0.0.0)
    (0.0.0.0)
    (0.0.0.0)
    (0.0.0.0)
    (0.0.0.0)
    (0.0.0.0)
    (0.0.0.0)
Reply to request 0 (64 ms).  Received packet has options
 Total option bytes= 40, padded length=40
 Record route:
    (172.16.1.2)
    (192.168.1.6)
    (192.168.100.1)
    (192.168.1.5)
    (172.16.1.1)
    (172.16.32.1) <*>
    (0.0.0.0)
    (0.0.0.0)
    (0.0.0.0)
 End of list
Reply to request 1 (64 ms).  Received packet has options
 Total option bytes= 40, padded length=40
```

```
Record route:
   (172.16.1.2)
   (192.168.1.6)
   (192.168.100.1)
   (192.168.1.5)
   (172.16.1.1)
   (172.16.32.1) <*>
   (0.0.0.0)
   (0.0.0.0)
   (0.0.0.0)
End of list
```

Does the output look correct? Does the 192.168.1.5 mean that the ISP1 now prefers SanJose1 for return traffic?

There might not be a chance to Telnet to the ISP router and to issue the **show ip bgp** command. However, the extended ping results after the policy MED has been configured clearly show that the lower value is considered best. The ISP now prefers the route with the lower MED value to AS 64512. This is opposite from the local-preference knob configured earlier:

```
BGP table version is 12, local router ID is 192.168.100.1
Status codes: s suppressed, d damped, h history, * valid, > best, i - internal
Origin codes: i - IGP, e - EGP, ? - incomplete
   Network          Next Hop          Metric LocPrf Weight Path
*  172.16.0.0       192.168.1.2          75               0 64512 i
*>                  192.168.1.6          50               0 64512 i
*> 192.168.1.0/30   0.0.0.0               0          32768 i
*> 192.168.1.4/30   0.0.0.0               0          32768 i
*> 192.168.100.0    0.0.0.0               0          32768 i
```

Step 12

The final step is to establish a default route that uses a policy statement that adjusts to changes in the network. Configure both SanJose1 and SanJose2 to use the 192.168.100.0 /24 network as the default network. The output that follows includes the routing table prior to the **default-network** statement being issued, the actual command syntax, and then the routing table after the command was issued. Complete the same task on the SanJose2 router:

```
SanJose1#show ip route
Gateway of last resort is not set
     172.16.0.0/16 is variably subnetted, 4 subnets, 2 masks
D       172.16.32.0/24 [90/20640000] via 172.16.1.2, 02:43:46, Serial0/1
B       172.16.0.0/16 [200/0] via 172.16.32.1, 00:12:32
C       172.16.1.0/24 is directly connected, Serial0/1
C       172.16.64.0/24 is directly connected, Loopback0
     192.168.1.0/30 is subnetted, 2 subnets
B       192.168.1.0 [20/0] via 192.168.1.5, 00:14:05
C       192.168.1.4 is directly connected, Serial0/0
B    192.168.100.0/24 [20/0] via 192.168.1.5, 00:14:05

SanJose1(config)#ip default-network 192.168.100.0

SanJose1#show ip route
Gateway of last resort is 192.168.1.5 to network 192.168.100.0
     172.16.0.0/16 is variably subnetted, 4 subnets, 2 masks
D       172.16.32.0/24 [90/20640000] via 172.16.1.2, 02:44:09, Serial0/1
B       172.16.0.0/16 [200/0] via 172.16.32.1, 00:12:55
C       172.16.1.0/24 is directly connected, Serial0/1
C       172.16.64.0/24 is directly connected, Loopback0
     192.168.1.0/30 is subnetted, 2 subnets
B       192.168.1.0 [20/0] via 192.168.1.5, 00:14:28
C       192.168.1.4 is directly connected, Serial0/0
B*   192.168.100.0/24 [20/0] via 192.168.1.5, 00:14:29
```

What would be required to add a future T3 link on SanJose2 and for this future link to have preference for incoming and outgoing traffic?

_____

_____

A newly added route would be as easy as adding another route map for local preference with a value of 175 and a route map referencing a MED (metric) value of 35. Issue the **clear ip bgp *** command to complete this lab.

Lab 9.11.4b: BGP Route Reflectors and Route Filters

Estimated Time: 30 Minutes

Objective

In this lab, you configure IBGP routers to use a route reflector (RR) and a simple route filter, as shown in Figure 9-5.

Figure 9-5   Sample Topology for Lab 9.11.4b

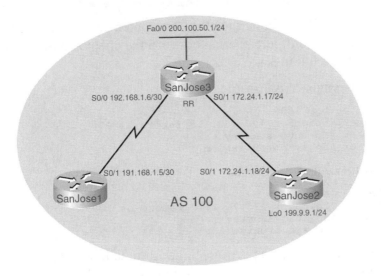

Equipment Requirements

You need the following equipment for this exercise:

- Three Cisco 2600 series routers

- Two serial cables

Scenario

The International Travel Agency had previously maintained a full-mesh IBGP network, but it has quickly scaled beyond 100 routers, thus making full mesh impractical. The company wants to implement route reflectors to work around the full-mesh IBGP requirement. Configure a small cluster and observe how BGP operates in this configuration. Use IP prefix filters to control the updates between IBGP peers.

Step 1

Build and configure the network according to the diagram, and use RIP as the IGP. Do not configure the 199.9.9.0 network. Make sure to either erase any configurations on the routers or configure the appropriate IP addresses and subnet masks on the interfaces indicated in Figure 9-5. Use **ping** to test connectivity among all interfaces. Each router should have a complete routing table.

Step 2

Configure the IBGP peers for BGP. SanJose3 will later be configured as the route reflector. However, first configure it to peer with both of the other routers, as shown here:

```
SanJose3(config)#router bgp 100
SanJose3(config-router)#neighbor 192.168.1.5 remote-as 100
SanJose3(config-router)#neighbor 172.24.1.18 remote-as 100
SanJose3(config-router)#no auto-summary
SanJose3(config-router)#no synchronization
SanJose3(config-router)#network 200.100.50.0
SanJose3(config-router)#network 172.24.1.0 mask 255.255.255.0
SanJose3(config-router)#network 192.168.1.4 mask 255.255.255.252
```

After you configure SanJose3, configure the other two routers as route reflector clients. Remember that to set up clients, you configure peering between the client and the server. You do not need to configure IBGP to a full mesh.

Issue the following commands on SanJose1:

```
SanJose1(config)#router bgp 100
SanJose1(config-router)#neighbor 192.168.1.6 remote-as 100
SanJose1(config-router)#no auto-summary
SanJose1(config-router)#no synchronization
```

Issue the following commands on SanJose2:

```
SanJose2(config)#router bgp 100
SanJose2(config-router)#neighbor 172.24.1.17 remote-as 100
SanJose2(config-router)#no auto-summary
SanJose2(config-router)#no synchronization
```

Verify that SanJose3 has established a peering relationship with both SanJose1 and SanJose2. Troubleshoot as necessary.

1.   SanJose1 and SanJose2 should not have established a connection. Why?

_____

_____

SanJose2 was not configured with the appropriate BGP **neighbor** command. As a route reflector client, SanJose1 does not need to reach an Established state with SanJose2.

Step 3

To observe the full effect of using a route reflector, configure SanJose2 to inject external routing information into BGP, as follows:

```
SanJose2(config)#int lo0
SanJose2(config-if)#ip address 199.9.9.1 255.255.255.0
SanJose2(config)#router bgp 100
SanJose2(config-router)#network 199.9.9.0
```

This configuration forces SanJose2 to inject the external route 199.9.9.0 into BGP. Use the **show ip route** command to check whether SanJose3 has picked up this route through BGP. SanJose3 should have a route to 199.9.9.0.

1.   Is the next hop for this route 172.24.1.18?

_____

199.9.9.1 should ping from SanJose3. If not, troubleshoot.

Now, check the routing table of SanJose1.

2.   There should be no route to 199.9.9.0. Why?

_____

_____

Remember that SanJose1 is not configured to peer with SanJose2. To eliminate the need for a full IBGP mesh, you must configure SanJose3 as a route reflector server. Issue the following commands on SanJose3:

```
SanJose3(config)#router bgp 100
SanJose3(config-router)#neighbor 192.168.1.5 route-reflector-client
SanJose3(config-router)#neighbor 172.24.1.18 route-reflector-client
```

Verify that an IBGP cluster was created successfully by issuing the **show ip protocols** command on SanJose3. The output of this command should indicate that SanJose3 is a route reflector.

3.   How many clients does SanJose3 have?

_____

Issue the **show ip protocols** command on SanJose1. The output of this command does not include information about route reflectors. Remember that SanJose1 is a client and not a route reflector server, so it is unaware of route reflection.

Finally, verify that route reflection is working by checking the routing table on SanJose1. SanJose1 should have a route to 199.9.9.0, at least.

4.   Is 172.24.1.18 the IP address of the next hop of this route on the SanJose1 table?

_____

5.   Notice that SanJose1 is not connected directly to the IP network for the next hop. Why?
      (Hint: From which router did SanJose1 learn the route?)

_____

_____

Ping 199.9.9.1 from SanJose1. This ping should be successful.

Notice that SanJose1 pings 199.9.9.1 even though the next-hop address is not on a directly connected network. For example, the next-hop address could be 172.24.1.18.

Step 4

For the purposes of this lab, configure SanJose2 to inject a summary address into BGP, as shown here:

```
SanJose2(config)#router bgp 100
SanJose2(config-router)#aggregate-address 199.0.0.0 255.0.0.0
```

BGP should now send the supernet route, 199.0.0.0/8, to SanJose3 with the ATOMIC_AGGREGATE attribute set.

On SanJose3, issue the following command:

```
SanJose3#show ip bgp 199.0.0.0
BGP routing table entry for 199.0.0.0/8, version 6
Paths: (1 available, best #1)
```

```
Bestpath transition flag: 0x208
               Advertised to non peer-group peers:
               192.168.1.5
  Local, (aggregated by 100 172.24.1.18), (Received from a RR-client)
     172.24.1.18 from 172.24.1.18 (172.24.1.18)
        Origin IGP, localpref 100, valid, internal, atomic-aggregate, best,
ref 2
```

1.   According to the output of this command, what address aggregated this route?

_____

2.   What indicates that route reflection is involved in this process?

_____

3.   Is there an indication that the ATOMIC_AGGREGATE attribute has been set?

_____

SanJose3 should, in turn, reflect this route to SanJose1. Check both the routing table and BGP table on SanJose1 to be sure. Both the route to 199.9.9.0 and the supernet route, 199.0.0.0, should be installed in the SanJose1 routing table and the BGP table.

The International Travel Agency has decided to filter specific routes to the 199.0.0.0/8 address space. Configure a route filter to prevent SanJose3 from sending the 199.9.9.0/24 route to its other clients—in this case, to SanJose1.

Issue the following commands on SanJose3:

```
SanJose3(config)#ip prefix-list supernetonly permit 199.0.0.0/8
SanJose3(config)#ip prefix-list supernetonly permit 172.24.1.0/24
SanJose3(config)#ip prefix-list supernetonly permit 200.100.50.0/24
SanJose3(config)#router bgp 100
SanJose3(config-router)#neighbor 192.168.1.5 prefix-list supernetonly out
```

Return to SanJose1, issue the **clear ip bgp *** command, and verify that the prefix list has done its job by issuing a **show ip bgp** command. Troubleshoot as necessary.

Unlike before, where routes to 199.9.9.0 and 199.0.0.0 were present, you should see only one route to 199.0.0.0 in the routing and BGP tables. Troubleshoot as necessary.

Lab 9.11.4c: The BGP COMMUNITIES Attribute

Estimated Time: 20 Minutes

Objective

In this lab, you use the COMMUNITIES attribute to enforce routing policy for the topology shown in Figure 9-6.

Figure 9-6   Sample Topology for Lab 9.11.4c

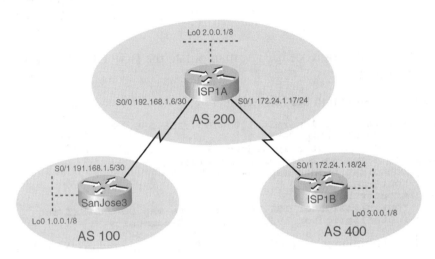

Equipment Requirements

You need the following equipment for this exercise:

*   Three Cisco 2600 series routers

*   Two serial cables

Scenario

The International Travel Agency peers with ISP ISP1A and exchanges complete routing information with its AS 200. However, as a matter of policy, the International Travel Agency does not want AS 400 to learn about specific routes within the International Travel Agency's AS 100. Configure BGP on SanJose3 so that ISP1A will not forward certain routes to ISP1B in AS 400.

Step 1

Build and configure the network according to the diagram, but do not configure a routing protocol yet. Configure a loopback interface with an IP address for each router, as shown in Figure 9-6. Make sure to either erase any configurations on the routers or configure the appropriate IP addresses and subnet masks on the interfaces indicated in Figure 9-6. These loopbacks will simulate networks that reside within each AS.

Use **ping** to test connectivity between all directly connected interfaces.

Step 2

Configure the three routers as EBGP peers. The following is an example of the SanJose3 configuration:

```
SanJose3(config)#router bgp 100
SanJose3(config-router)#neighbor 192.168.1.6 remote-as 200
SanJose3(config-router)#network 1.0.0.0
```

When BGP is configured on all three routers, use the **show ip route** and **show ip bgp** commands. This verifies that ISP1B has learned about the network, 1.0.0.0/8, which belongs to AS 100.

Step 3

To influence the routing decisions of ISP1A, manipulate the BGP COMMUNITIES attribute of the route being advertised.

Configure SanJose3, as shown in the following:

```
SanJose3(config)#access-list 1 permit 1.0.0.0 0.255.255.255
SanJose3(config)#route-map NO-ONE-NET 10
SanJose3(config-route-map)#match ip address 1
SanJose3(config-route-map)#set community no-export
SanJose3(config-route-map)#route-map NO-ONE-NET 20
SanJose3(config-route-map)#exit
SanJose3(config)#router bgp 100
SanJose3(config-router)#neighbor 192.168.1.6 route-map NO-ONE-NET out
SanJose3(config-router)#neighbor 192.168.1.6 send-community
```

After you enter these commands, issue the **clear ip bgp *** command on ISP1A. Wait a few seconds, and then verify the configuration on ISP1A by entering the following command:

```
ISP1A#show ip bgp 1.0.0.0
```

1.   According to this command's output, what is the community value of this route set to?

_____

Now, check the routing table on ISP1B to see if this has prevented ISP1A from updating ISP1B. The route to 1.0.0.0/8 should be missing from the routing table of ISP1B. Troubleshoot as necessary.

Lab 9.11.4d: BGP Peer Groups

Estimated Time: 20 Minutes

Objective

In this lab, you use BGP peer groups to simplify the configuration tasks, as shown in Figure 9-7.

Figure 9-7   Sample Topology for Lab 9.11.4.d

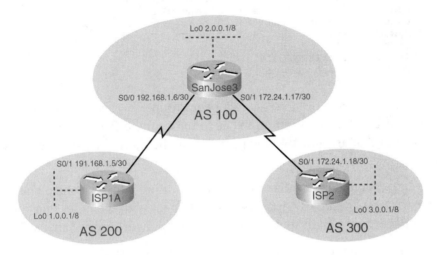

Equipment Requirements

You need the following equipment for this exercise:

*   Three Cisco 2600 series routers
*   Two serial cables

Scenario

The International Travel Agency peers with ISP1A in AS 200 and ISP2 in AS 300. The company applies similar policies to both neighbors. Rather than configuring policies separately for each neighbor, configure a BGP peer group.

Step 1

Build and configure the network according to the diagram, but do not configure a routing protocol yet. Configure a loopback interface with an IP address for each ISP router, as shown. These loopbacks simulate networks that reside within each AS.

Use **ping** to test connectivity between all directly connected interfaces.

Step 2

Configure ISP1A and ISP2 for EBGP. The following is an example of the ISP1A configuration:

```
ISP1A(config)#router bgp 200
ISP1A(config-router)#neighbor 192.168.1.6 remote-as 100
ISP1A(config-router)#network 1.0.0.0
```

Step 3

Use a peer group to configure SanJose3 so that it applies policies jointly to both ISP1A and ISP2, as follows:

```
SanJose3(config)#router bgp 100
SanJose3(config-router)#network 2.0.0.0
SanJose3(config-router)#neighbor EBGP-PEERS peer-group
SanJose3(config-router)#neighbor EBGP-PEERS send-community
SanJose3(config-router)#neighbor EBGP-PEERS route-map EXTERNAL out
SanJose3(config-router)#neighbor 192.168.1.5 remote-as 200
SanJose3(config-router)#neighbor 172.24.1.18 remote-as 300
SanJose3(config-router)#neighbor 192.168.1.5 peer-group EBGP-PEERS
SanJose3(config-router)#neighbor 172.24.1.18 peer-group EBGP-PEERS
SanJose3(config-router)#exit
SanJose3(config)#route-map EXTERNAL 10
SanJose3(config-route-map)#set community 40
SanJose3(config-route-map)#exit
```

The neighbors of SanJose3 have been assigned a peer group—in this case, a group called EBGP-PEERS. Because of this, configurations need to be applied only once—to the group itself. The more routers that are added to the peer group, the more time will be saved entering configurations.

Issue the **clear ip bgp *** command on SanJose3. After waiting a few seconds, check the routing tables of the three routers. Eventually, SanJose3 should peer with the other two routers. Both ISP1A and ISP2 will receive a BGP route to the 2.0.0.0/8 network from SanJose3.

When ISP1A and ISP2 have the route to 2.0.0.0, verify that SanJose3 is actually applying the same policies to both neighbors. Issue the following command on ISP1A and ISP2:

```
ISP1A#show ip bgp 2.0.0.0
```

1. According to the output of this command, what is the community value for this route on ISP1A?

_____

2. What is the community value on ISP2?

_____

On SanJose3, issue the command **show ip bgp neighbors**.

Check that both neighbors have a member of peer group EBGP-PEERS listed as a session parameter. If not, troubleshoot.

Lab 9.12.1: BGP Challenge Lab

Estimated Time: 90 Minutes

Objective

In this lab, you configure EBGP between the company's core routers and the two ISP routers, as shown in Figure 9-8. Configure IBGP with peers to create a network that provides the International Travel Agency with a fully meshed, reliable, and efficient core network.

Figure 9-8   Sample Topology for Lab 9.12.1

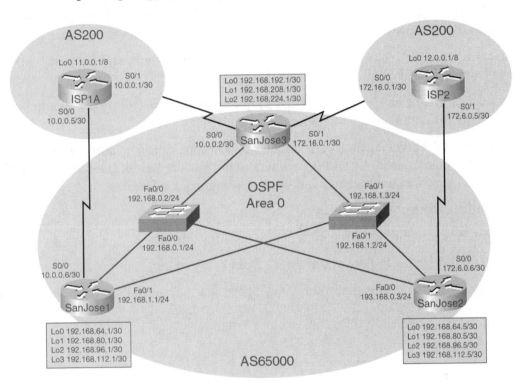

Equipment Requirements

You need the following equipment for this exercise:

- Five Cisco 2600 series routers
- Two Cisco Catalyst switches
- Six Ethernet cables
- Four serial cables

Scenario

The International Travel Agency relies heavily on the Internet for advertisement, sales, and communication within the company and with its customers throughout the world. Therefore, it has decided to contract with two ISPs. The ISPs are connected as shown in the figure. The company requires its network to be readily available and reliable at all times. The loopback addresses on the ISP1A and ISP2 routers represent other customers. The loopback addresses on the San Jose routers represent networks to regional headquarters and local branch offices.

Implementation Requirements

The following are the implementation requirements for this lab:

- Configure EBGP between the International Travel Agency core routers and ISP1A and ISP2.

- Configure IBGP between the International Travel Agency core routers.

- Only advertise the internal 192.168.0.0 network to ISP1A and ISP2 distributed access lists.

- SanJose1 should be able to communicate with ISP2 through SanJose3. SanJose2 should be able to communicate with ISP1A through SanJose3 using next-hop-self.

- SanJose1 will use ISP1A as its primary ISP through its direct link, and SanJose2 will use ISP2 as its primary ISP.

- If either direct link of SanJose1 or SanJose2 fails for any reason, all traffic should be routed automatically through SanJose3 to either ISP1A or ISP2.

- The International Travel Agency's AS number 65000 should be prevented from being advertised beyond the ISP1A and ISP2 routers to the outside world. It also should not be advertised to its other customer networks, such as loopback addresses.

Implementation Completion Tests

The following are the implementation completion tests for this lab:

- A successful ping to every network interface from every router.

- The **show** command verifies that routing tables contain the routes that the requirements specify.

Notes

Notes

Notes

Notes

Notes

Notes

Notes

Notes